WHEN PIGS MOVE IN

DON DICKERMAN

Charisma
HOUSE
A STRANG COMPANY

Most STRANG COMMUNICATIONS BOOK GROUP products are available at special quantity discounts for bulk purchase for sales promotions, premiums, fund-raising, and educational needs. For details, write Strang Communications Book Group, 600 Rinehart Road, Lake Mary, Florida 32746, or telephone (407) 333-0600.

WHEN PIGS MOVE IN by Don Dickerman
Published by Charisma House
A Strang Company
600 Rinehart Road
Lake Mary, Florida 32746
www.strangbookgroup.com

Unless otherwise noted, all Scripture quotations are from the King James Version of the Bible.

Scripture quotations marked NKJV are from the New King James Version of the Bible. Copyright © 1979, 1980, 1982 by Thomas Nelson, Inc., publishers. Used by permission.

Scripture quotations marked NIV are from the Holy Bible, New International Version. Copyright © 1973, 1978, 1984, International Bible Society. Used by permission.

Some people and incidents in this book are composites created by the author from his experience as a minister. Names and details have been changed, and any similarity between the names and stories of individuals described in this book known to readers is purely coincidental.

Design Director: Bill Johnson
Cover design by Justin Evans

Library of Congress Cataloging-in-Publication Data:

Dickerman, Don.
  When pigs move in / Don Dickerman. -- 1st ed.
       p. cm.
  Includes bibliographical references.
  ISBN 978-1-59979-461-7
  1. Exorcism. 2. Demoniac possession. 3. Spirit possession. 4. Spiritual
warfare. I. Title.
  BV873.E8D53 2009
  235'.4--dc22
                        2008047955

Portions of this book were previously published as *Turmoil in the Temple*
by Don Dickerman, copyright © 2002 by Impact Christian Books, Inc.,
0-89228-172-3; and *Serpents in the Sanctuary* by Don Dickerman, copyright
© 2002 by Impact Christian Books, Inc., 0-89228-147-2.

09 10 11 12 13 — 9 8 7 6 5 4 3 2
Printed in Canada

CONTENTS

ↄ

FOREWORD

ح

WHEN THE VALIDITY OF JESUS'S DELIVERANCE MINISTRY WAS challenged and He was accused of casting out demons by the power of Beelzebub, He responded by saying, "Either make the tree good and its fruit good, or else make the tree bad and its fruit bad, for a tree is known by its fruit" (Matt. 12:33, NKJV). Likewise, the author of this book demonstrates the validly of his deliverance ministry by the fruit it bears. There is much fruit—good fruit and fruit that remains.

Don Dickerman's extensive involvement in prison ministry makes this book unique. Many of the cases he cites are those of incarcerated men and women; persons who are readily recognizable as candidates for salvation and deliverance from demonic oppression.

Dickerman also gives a strong and straightforward challenge to local churches to get involved in this scriptural and vital ministry. Scriptural principles of deliverance are clearly set forth. It is obvious that Don Dickerman is part of a powerful and fresh spiritual army that God is raising up today, for which I am very thankful. The body of Christ is blessed to have Don's experiences and insights put into writing. This is a book that I found impossible to lay aside until I had read it in its entirety. I am persuaded that others will find this true as well.

—FRANK D. HAMMOND
AUTHOR, *PIGS IN THE PARLOR*

Author's note: Rev. Hammond was a graduate of Baylor University in Waco and Southwestern Theological Seminary in Ft. Worth. Frank Hammond, whom I considered a friend and mentor, died in March of 2006.

PART I

TESTIMONIES OF DELIVERANCE

CHAPTER 1

ANOINTING MAKES THE DIFFERENCE

I BELIEVE THAT PREACHING WITHOUT ANOINTING IS JUST GOOD information. The presence and power of the Holy Spirit should be the desire of every preacher and every believer. I want to share with you why I believe that to be so important and why I believe that anything short of that cannot produce what God desires for His people. I see a change coming in the body of Christ. We are in the midst of it now. We are facing more demonic opposition, and at the same time, the Holy Spirit is saturating the body of Christ as never before. I experienced something glorious in my life, and since that day, I have seen God's people healed and delivered of demonic oppression.

I had preached in more than seven hundred different prisons and had been preaching in prisons for more than twenty years when the most amazing thing happened. I had seen thousands receive Jesus Christ as Savior, but I had never experienced anything beyond salvation. That is, I had never seen anyone delivered of demons or anyone receive genuine healing.

STILL IN BONDAGE AND UNABLE TO FUNCTION IN SOCIETY

I had always longed for more, but I don't think my education and spiritual training had allowed me to receive it. I'm really not sure why I was in this "box" of Holy Spirit restriction, but I was. I was hungry to see the people to whom I ministered receive complete freedom. I was not able to take them beyond the salvation experience and get them started in Bible study and prayer. I was always excited when I would see men and women come to Christ, but it was so frustrating to see them still in bondage and unable to function in society.

I do recall an instance that I believe was significant to what I am about to share. I was preaching about one hundred fifty times a year in prisons throughout the United States and in some other countries, though most of my ministering was in Texas prisons. I recall after a long weekend in Texas prisons that I drove to Galveston for a day or two of fishing. I just needed some relaxation and a break from the rigors of prison ministry. I was hurting so badly for inmates that I felt my heart would burst. They are in such spiritual bondage, and it seems they just keep coming back to prison.

I wanted to make a difference but seemed to be having little success. I remember, like it was yesterday, climbing up in the middle of the motel bed on my hands and knees and just weeping. I just sobbed with my face in my hands. I remember crying out to God, "Lord, let me be a deliverer. Let me, like Moses, lead people out of bondage." I prayed a prayer very similar to this, and it was from deep in my heart. I wanted to be God's instrument of freedom. I mostly remember just weeping with that desire being deep within me. Nothing happened—not then!

GOD ANSWERED THAT PRAYER

God answered that prayer, but like so many times, it was not how I expected the answer to come. It was several years later, in October of 1995. I was preaching at the Federal Correctional Institution in Three Rivers, Texas. The medium-security prison is located about halfway between San Antonio and Corpus Christi, just off Interstate 37. This is a complex of about 1,400 inmates. My friend David Pequeno served as the chaplain there. There was something very unusual in the chapel service that evening. A uniformed correctional officer was seated among the inmates, worshiping with them. That just never happens. If there is an officer present, it is because he has been assigned to the chapel.

It is very unusual for an officer to mingle with the inmates. I found out later that he was off duty and studying to become a federal prison chaplain. His name is Warren Rabb. After the service, he told the officer on duty that he would escort me to my car, that he wanted to talk with me.

MY LIFE AND MINISTRY WERE ABOUT TO BE CHANGED

When the service was over, this officer came up to me and shook my hand. I recall that as we walked across the prison grounds, the evening was brisk and the sky was so clear and crisp. It was one of those perfect evenings. Officer Rabb told me of his call to the ministry and of his desire to become a federal prison chaplain. We visited awhile longer after reaching the prison parking lot, and after we prayed together, I headed south to Corpus Christi. Officer Rabb headed east toward his home in Beeville. I stopped at a convenience store for a soft drink and a snack before getting on Interstate 37 to drive back to Corpus Christi, where I was staying.

As I pulled up at the convenience store service station, unbeknownst to me, Officer Rabb pulled in right behind me. Before I could get out of my car, he came running over and told me, with great excitement, that God had given him a vision about me and he "had" to share it with me. He said, "I would have followed you all the way to Corpus to tell you about the vision." He was so excited. I could feel and sense that God had spoken to him. This is what he told me:

> I saw you standing in this big black pot, and there was oil bubbling all around you—not boiling, just bubbling. All around the pot there was a sea of people as far as you could see, and they were all sick. The stench of their sickness was nauseating as it went up to the heavens. Then the oil began to bubble up and cover you, and as it ran from your head and down your arms and touched the people, they were healed! Get ready, brother; God's fixin' to pour it out on you!

I cannot adequately describe what I felt. It was like I was just bathed in God's glory. While he was sharing the words with me, I sensed the presence of God's Spirit stirring in me. I knew these words were from God, but I didn't know what to do with the words from the vision. As I drove back to Corpus Christi, tears continually moistened my eyes. There was subdued excitement in my spirit. I thanked God many times and gladly received the anointing. I honestly didn't know how to process all of it. My seminary training had not covered this. I knew how to preach; I had seen thousands receive Christ as Savior, perhaps one hundred thousand or more; but I had never seen anyone healed or delivered from demons.

I Had Been Taught That Spiritual Gifts Had Died Out

Actually, what I had been taught was contrary to the word given to me by Officer Rabb. I had been taught that the gifts of the Spirit had died out with the apostles. I had been taught that the gifts would cease "when that which is perfect had come" (1 Cor. 13:10) and that this meant God's Word. Since we have God's Word, then there is no need for the gifts of the Spirit to operate. That's what I had been taught. I am ashamed today that I was so blinded to scriptural truth and that I was so heavily influenced by religious tradition that I had missed some of the greatest truths! I didn't know how to make this happen. I didn't know how to give altar calls except for salvation. I would find out I didn't need to know.

As You Extend Your Hand, so Will I Extend Mine

Not long after this incredible experience, I was back in that same area of the state, preaching at a state prison in Beeville. The unit of the Texas Department of Criminal Justice is named the Garza West facility. About five hundred inmates were in the gym that night, and perhaps as many as two-thirds of the men had answered the altar call. When the service was over, the men returned to their seats and were called back to their housing area by dorm location. As they filed out in single file, one of the men stepped from the line and approached the chaplain.

I had noticed this young man during the service. He sat on the front row, and he stared at me as though he "saw something." There was a look of wonderment on his face as I ministered. The chaplain brought him over to me and said, "This inmate has a word for you from the Lord, something the Lord showed him as you preached."

He still had this look on his face. He said, "Sir, while you were preaching, I saw something, and God told me something to tell you." He moved beside me and asked me to stretch my arm forward, straight out toward the now empty seats. He placed his arm on top of mine and said, "God told me to tell you that as you extend your hand, so will He extend His." He seemed puzzled, like he was just passing a message. "Do you know what that means, sir?" "Yes," I told him. "Yes, I do. Thanks for sharing that with me." When I left the prison that night, again, the Holy Spirit of God just seemed to cover me. It is so holy that it is very difficult to share. Tears again filled my eyes simply from the glory of His presence. I knew God had spoken to me again, and I am just unable to describe how humbling this was and is to me.

IT STARTED HAPPENING

I still didn't know "how" to minister in this area. I didn't need to know. It just started happening! People would be healed while I was preaching. I didn't even know how to pray for their healing. It happened anyway. I remember the first healing that took place was at a correctional facility in Texas. I didn't know that it happened until several weeks afterward.

I received a letter from an inmate named Gary Jenkins. His letter said that while I was preaching, he felt heat come all over him. He continued to tell me about a pain that he had in his leg and how he could hardly move it. He said that the pain left him immediately, and he has had complete mobility in his leg ever since.

I have seen Gary many times since that meeting, and every time I see him, he reminds me that he is healed! I started getting many letters like that. All of them said basically the same thing: "I used to have this problem, but I don't have it anymore, not since the Holy Spirit touched me while you were preaching."

I could hardly contain the excitement of people being healed in my services, yet I didn't even know it was happening. I began to experience boldness in this area. While there was increased boldness, there was also incredible humility that accompanied this. I still often have to pull over to the side of the road after a service and just weep with thanksgiving. What a humbling experience it is to see people genuinely healed. There is always a deep consciousness that I have absolutely nothing to do with this, but it is the sovereign work of God! I was experiencing miracles. God was allowing me to participate in something He was doing. Think about it!

What happened in my life? I'm not sure. I don't think I can explain it. Was it the so-called Pentecostal "second blessing"? Was it the baptism of the Holy Spirit? No, it was an encounter with God's Holy Spirit. I don't believe it is important to have a definition of it. It certainly was a deep emotional experience with God's Holy Spirit. It was not a one-time thing; I can say it was a spiritual marker in an ongoing anointing.

I get so frustrated with denominational "stuff" when I see the division and the disagreement it causes in the body of Christ. I'll let you decide what to call what I experienced. All I know is that it was an anointing that changed me and changed the ministry God had given to me. I began to experience spiritual gifts and operate in them. This was all new to me. It was also thoroughly exciting. I was refreshed in the Spirit. It was fresh and new, and it is wonderful.

Along with this anointing came a fresh insight to Scripture. I was able to see things in Scripture that I had not seen before. I understood who I was in Christ. I understood who Christ is and who Satan is. Having a good understanding of this gave me great boldness in the realm of spiritual warfare. I believe if we can grasp these three things, our lives will be changed:

1. Who is Christ?
2. Who am I in Christ?
3. Who is Satan?

CHAPTER 2

I MET CHRISTIANS WHO WERE DEMONIZED

S upernaturally, God began to place people in my life. Inmates would seek me out, tell me they had demons, and ask me to help them. These were always believers, and I had always been taught that Christians could not have demons. I now believe this is the biggest lie that Satan has perpetrated on the body of Christ. The deception is so great that most believers will not even consider that they may be demonically oppressed. Christians can, and often do, have demons in their souls and flesh working great oppression in their lives. We are possessed by the Holy Spirit who lives in our spirit. *Possession* implies ownership. We are owned, purchased, and bought with a price by the Lord Jesus. It is correct, possibly, to say that a demon may possess an area of a Christian's life, but never can they own us. A well-known pastor in Atlanta, Georgia, refers to this as "demonic control" in particular areas of a believer's life where legal rights have been surrendered.

You Can't Talk Me Out of This

What someone is taught must always be subject to what they have experienced. You can teach me that the "gift of healing" is no longer available to the church, but you can no longer convince me! I know by experience. Jehovah-Jireh is still in business! God is still the Lord God who heals. The stripes on the back of Jesus Christ were purposeful. The blood from those stripes paid for our healing. You cannot talk me out of this. You can tell me that believers cannot have demon powers in them, but you will never convince me. I have seen more than twenty-five thousand people set free! I now *know*! Knowing is better than believing. You can believe it doesn't happen, but I *know* that it does! I used to believe that "[Jesus] went about

7

doing good, and healing all that were oppressed of the devil" (Acts 10:38). Now I *know* it.

Experience is the best teacher! Man's theological "ideas" must take a back seat to life experience that is based upon scriptural truth. I implore you to read what I have to share with you with an open and honest heart. I have no agenda in writing this book except to lift up Jesus Christ and expose Satan and his kingdom of darkness. I believe pastors must get ready. There will be an onslaught of believers asking for deliverance. I can tell you personally that day is rapidly approaching, and I am touching the tip of it. I really would like all believers to experience the freedom that is available in Christ and not be limited to what a denomination imposes. Find the truth by experiencing it, do not be ashamed to seek full freedom in Christ. If you are sincere in seeking, you will find the Holy Spirit; God will not give you a serpent. That is a scriptural promise from the lips of Jesus.

> If you then, being evil, know how to give good gifts unto your children; how much more shall your heavenly Father give the Holy Spirit to them that ask him?
>
> —Luke 11:13

I'd Never Experienced Anything Like This

I was in a prison service at the Wynne Unit, a Texas Department of Criminal Justice facility in Huntsville. If you have ever driven through Huntsville on Interstate 45, you may have seen this prison. It is located on the north side of Huntsville and the east side of I-45. The old red brick building is visible from the interstate. It is one of the oldest facilities in the state system.

The praise and worship team had opened the service, and a crowd of about three hundred men were in attendance. I was seated on the side of the platform, waiting to be introduced as the minister for the evening. (I had been ministering at that prison on the third Saturday of the month since about 1988.) This night was quite typical until about five minutes before I got up to speak.

I saw something in my spirit, that is, a mental picture. It was that of an ugly rat with jagged teeth chewing on someone's colon. It was like I was seeing inside someone's midsection. I had never experienced anything like this before. I said, "God, what is this? Are You revealing to me that someone is in pain with their colon? I don't know what to do? Do You want me to speak that and then pray for the individual?" The answer seemed to be an obvious yes, almost a stern "of course."

Well, I did. When I got to the pulpit, I shared what I had seen. I said, "I don't know if this is a word of knowledge, a vision, or what. I'm just telling you that if you are having pain like this, God is going to heal it tonight." A man stood to his feet and said, "Sir, that is me." I asked him to come forward, and I prayed for him. He testified that the pain left immediately.

"THE PAIN IS INTENSE"

When the service was over and all but about ten men had filed out of the chapel, an inmate came to me and put a note in my pocket as I talked with the few remaining men. Then, after a minute or two, he came back to me and said, "Sir, can you read that note now?"

I took the note from my pocket and read it. It said, "I am the man you described in your vision. I was embarrassed to come forward. I just came back from John Sealy hospital and was diagnosed with colon cancer. The pain is intense, but since I am going home in a few months, the department said it could wait until I get back out. The pain is exactly as you described—sharp pain as if a rat is gnawing on it." He lifted his shirt and showed me a lump that protruded just below his belt line. It was shaped like a toy football.

I said, "Let's pray right now." I laid my hand on the lump and commanded spirits of cancer to leave him. I called on the healing mercies of the Lord Jesus and commanded evil spirits to put everything back in order. He began to double over in pain and heave from deep in his midsection. He coughed up blood and phlegm—lots of it. One of the remaining inmates got a towel and cleaned up the mess. When he straightened up, he said, "The pain is gone; it is gone!"

I left the prison excited, but the truth is, I didn't know what happened. I didn't *know* that he was healed. I just knew, by his testimony, that the pain was gone. The next month when I went back to that prison, he met me at the chapel door with a big smile on his face. He lifted up his shirt and said, "It's gone, Brother Don. It's gone, and I have had no pain since that night. He told me that he did not even remember coughing up the blood and mucus. Other inmates had told him what had taken place. You can't talk me out of this. I could share stories like this over and over and make this a very long book.

After experiencing many such incidents, I remember having some concern about being genuine. I had seen so much "religious stuff" like this that was not real that I became a little intimidated by it. I was preaching in Gatesville at the Hilltop Unit and also at the Trusty Camp, a prison for female inmates. Between services, I went into town to get a hamburger and was eating in my vehicle when I decided to put out a fleece and ask the Lord to show me clearly. I wanted another clear indication that it was indeed God's Holy Spirit revealing to me that people would be healed of specific diseases, pains, and discomforts. Not only did I not want to be deceived, but also I surely did not want to deceive others. I just wanted to be real and to give no place to Satan.

I Just Wanted to Be Real

I recall praying, "God, I can't be like so many I have seen. I don't want to operate in the flesh. I can't deceive someone in Your name. I need to know that these 'visions,' these words that I am receiving, are from You and that You expect me to act upon them. [I had not had one that was not exactly as He spoke, and healing had always come.] I am asking You to show me one more time, and if You do, I will never question this again. I just want so much to be real that I must have a confirmation."

That was my prayer as I finished my hamburger. As I headed back to Trusty Camp, I got a very strong word that someone was suffering pain on the right side of their body below the rib cage. I went on in, and the service began with the ladies singing a few songs. When I got up to preach, I said, "There is someone here who has pain on your right side just below your rib cage, and God is going to heal that today." Nothing happened. No one stood up or said anything, and I proceeded with the service.

After extending the altar call and praying with many ladies to receive Christ, I asked if anyone there was suffering from the pain I had described earlier. A lady on the back row stood up and walked to the front. She calmly took the microphone from my hand. Tears began to run down her cheeks as she said, "I almost didn't come to church today because I was in such pain. The pain was exactly where Brother Don described it, and it left the moment he spoke that God was going to heal it. All my pain is gone!" Wow, what a confirmation! I've never looked back, and I have never doubted this gift of the Spirit. I have seen this inmate many times since that event, and each time I see her, she says, "I've never had that pain since."

Now, with this anointing for healing there came a boldness to come against Satan, and I could clearly see that the kingdom of darkness was the source of sickness and disease. I did not know that I would soon be casting out demons. I was about to embark on an exciting journey.

DEMON POWERS CAN ACTUALLY LIVE IN CHRISTIANS

I was preaching at a prison when I was first introduced to the reality of demon powers living in Christians. I had always believed that was not possible. I had been taught that it was not possible. I was really not open to discussion that evil spirits could actually dwell within a believer. Never in any of my years of seminary training did I hear that this was a possibility. I had attended nondenominational seminaries and two Baptist seminaries. I was born in a Baptist home, saved in a Baptist church, ordained as a deacon, licensed and ordained as a Baptist minister, and graduated from a Baptist seminary.

I don't recall ever hearing any discussion about demons or spiritual warfare taking place within believers. It was a foreign concept to me. I only recall one professor ever even mentioning demon powers. I do remember that he talked of demon powers he had encountered in people who were *possessed*. He told of opposition from a particular woman who was so possessed with evil that he backed away from the confrontation.

I HAD NEVER ENCOUNTERED ANYTHING LIKE THIS

This Scottish seminary professor told of being asked by church members in the city to go to this woman's house and drive out the evil spirits. They told him of all the evil and how she opposed the body of Christ there. Boldly, he agreed to go, but he said, "I had never encountered anything like this and didn't know what to expect."

He said that when he got to the woman's house, before he even knocked on the door, he heard a cackling, mocking voice call him by name and say, "Come in. I've been expecting you!" As he opened the door, the woman was laughing at him, his legs were heavy, and he was weakened by fear. She said, "Tell me about your Jesus. Tell me about your Jesus...ha, ha, ha." She mocked him as he stood silent and could not speak.

He said that he had to leave that house ashamed that he was so unprepared to deal with the demonic powers. His point simply was that demons did exist.

I have had similar encounters with people *possessed* by demons that I will tell about later. However, while at this prison, I was about to encounter a *believer* who had demons! This happened at the prison for women. I was accompanied by my wife, Peggy, and a few others from our Texas-based ministry. My host was the director of prison fellowship. By this time, I had been preaching in prisons for many years, and I had encountered many inmates who had told me about demons in their lives, but this experience was different.

I preached to a group of about thirty-five women in a very small chapel area. After the service, a young woman came up to me and said, "I don't know why I am telling you this. I just feel drawn to you. I feel like you will understand, and I feel like you will help me."

"I Am Tormented by Demons!"

What she told me would forever change my life and ministry. "Brother Don," she said, "I know I am saved, and I know Jesus lives in my heart, but I am tormented by demons! Will you help me?" Remember, I had always been taught this was not possible. However, I was looking into the eyes of a young lady who was desperate for deliverance. She began to tell me things I never thought I would hear. She told me with pleading eyes, "My parents were Satan worshipers, and I was dedicated to Satan as a baby. I was raised to become the bride of Lucifer." She began to tell me of ritualistic abuse from the time she was born, some of which I cannot even repeat. She explained that she was being groomed to become the highest-ranking female in this satanic group.

She told me of her parents and others urging demon spirits to come into her. This was all part of a plan to fill her with demons so that she could one day become Lucifer's bride.

I listened, and even as I was listening, I wondered how I could help her. She told me many times, "I know I'm saved. I know Jesus lives in my heart, but I am tormented by demons." Again, man's theology must come into agreement with genuine experience. I was looking into the eyes of a desperate, born-again child of God. My mind raced through Scripture and accounts of Jesus commanding evil spirits to leave, but I didn't know how to do it. I didn't know I *could* do it!

SUDDENLY, I HAD A PLAN

God had been preparing me for several years, but I did not know it. Now I began to see some of His preparation. Stories from other inmates began to fill my mind. There was one deliverance session I had on videotape. The person on this tape experienced incredible freedom from demons. She received deliverance in a county jail. I had met and had great respect for the minister who had walked this woman through deliverance. Suddenly, I had a plan.

I told the woman who I was presently ministering to that I knew a man who had a ministry of setting captives free, and I told her I would contact him and make arrangements with the prison to come here and minister to her. "You will be free!" I told her. When I left the prison, my mind began to reflect on all the scriptures I had studied on demonic oppression. I knew that unforgiveness was permission for demons to torment believers. Look what Jesus says about it:

> Then came Peter to him, and said, Lord, how oft shall my brother sin against me, and I forgive him? Til seven times? Jesus saith unto him, I say not unto thee, Until seven times: but, Until seventy times seven. Therefore is the kingdom of heaven likened unto a certain king, which would take account of his servants. And when he had begun to reckon, one was brought unto him, which owed him ten thousand talents.
>
> But forasmuch as he had not to pay, his lord commanded him to be sold, and his wife, and children, and all that he had, and payment to be made. The servant therefore fell down, and worshiped him, saying, Lord, have patience with me, and I will pay thee all.

Then the lord of that servant was moved with compassion, and loosed him and forgave him the debt. The same servant went out and found one of his fellowservants, which owed him an hundred pence: and he laid hands on him, and took him by the throat, saying, Pay me that thou owest.

And his fellowservant fell down at his feet, and besought him, saying, Have patience with me, and I will pay thee all. And he would not: but went and cast him into prison, till he should pay the debt. So when his fellowservants saw what was done, they were very sorry, and came and told unto their lord all that was done.

Then his lord, after that he had called him, said unto him, O thou wicked servant, I forgave thee all that debt, because thou desiredst me: Shouldest not thou also have had compassion on thy fellowservant, even as I had pity on thee?

And his lord was wroth, and delivered him to the tormentors, till he should pay all that was due unto him. So likewise shall my heavenly Father do also unto you, if ye from your hearts forgive not every one his brother their trespasses.

—Matthew 18:21–35

What alarming truth this passage reveals! This is God-given permission for demons to torment believers. I will say more about this later.

Over the next several months, I corresponded with this woman inmate. I learned more about the strongholds and the torment that she was experiencing. I was able to lead her to forgive her parents through our many letters. She would eventually forgive all those who had deceived her and taken advantage of her.

As you might imagine, it's not easy to make arrangements with a prison for something like this, but the prison officials were very cooperative, and arrangements were made. Actually, in retrospect, it was probably easier than making such arrangements in a church.

We were given a private conference room, and there would be no officers present. The only people present would be the woman inmate, the pastor, who would minister deliverance, and myself. I was going to be the one who prayed as the pastor commanded evil spirits to leave.

GOD SET ME UP!

There was just one hitch in the plan: the pastor did not show up! Something had come up. I thought, "Are you kidding me? This woman is expecting deliverance, and I'm the only one here. God set me up!" I'm glad He did. It was clear to me then but even more plain now as I look back over the years. God put me in a situation where I had to act; I had to use the faith that He has given to me.

I don't recall why the pastor was not there, but it was in God's plan for me to face this battle totally dependent on the Word of God and the Holy Spirit.

God has done this through the ages. He has prepared His children for battle through circumstances that they did not understand at the time. Moses had been in preparation to be a deliverer, but I'm certain it was without his understanding. When he turned aside to see the burning bush, he was clueless that God had been working out a plan in his life. He was to be a deliverer who would look Pharaoh in the eye and say, "Let my people go!" I now know that God was preparing me to do the same…to look the enemy straight in the eye and speak the same words over His people today: "Let my people go!" Believers are God's people. With great power and authority in the name of Jesus, we are to speak freedom. But little did I know this at the time.

I will never forget that first deliverance experience. It was, by far, the most dramatic of the thousands I have had since then. I walked up the stairs of this stately government building and presented my papers for clearance to the officer at the front gate. I remember her looking at me with some curiosity in her eyes. She knew why I was there, but I'm sure she didn't understand it. I felt like she must have thought I didn't fit the part of an "exorcist." I wasn't dressed in black. I didn't have a big wooden cross, and I was not a priest. As a matter of fact, I was in my blue jeans, tennis shoes, and golf shirt. Funny how being set free has taken such a dark, negative connotation. *Exorcism* is not the word I would choose anyway. I like "oppression relief" or "oppression healing." Jesus went about doing good and healing all those oppressed of the devil. It is oppression healing! Hollywood has done a lot of damage to the concept of freedom from demon powers.

I Made a Decision to Take a Step of Faith

A correctional officer escorted me up the inside stairs to the third floor of the prison and to a private conference room. I figured this was where prison staff meetings took place. Inside the room was a long table with three chairs on each side and a chair at each end. I had been praying with such intensity since I had arrived the day before and realized the pastor was not going to be there. I had made a decision to take a step of faith. I took my seat with my back to the windows on the west wall and waited in prayer for the inmate to come in through a door to my right.

She arrived and greeted me with a hug, and she sat directly across from me. The officer who escorted her in left, and we talked for several minutes before we prayed.

I thought, "What am I doing? I am going to cast out demons? I am going to take on evil spirits, fallen angels that live in another human being? How did I get here? Was I crazy? Did I think I had authority over the kingdom of darkness?" I was bombarded with all kinds of doubts but kept rebuking those thoughts with Scripture that the Holy Spirit would bring to my mind.

One particular scripture that kept resounding in my spirit was Luke 10:19: "Behold, I give unto you power to tread on serpents and scorpions, and over all the power of the enemy: and nothing shall by any means hurt you." I must have rehearsed that verse five or six times in reassurance and with different emphasis each time. Who gave me power and authority? JESUS! A lot of people will say this authority was given only to the apostles. They refer to this as apostolic doctrine.

However, Jesus spoke this not only to the Twelve but also to the seventy disciples that obviously represent the church, and He said, "Behold, *I* give unto you power..." (emphasis added). Wow, I liked that.

Given Power of Attorney to Act in Jesus's Name

I would then pass the verse through my spirit with different truth stressed. "Behold I give unto *you*..." I know many scoff at this, but that is why they remain powerless in their Christianity. The Holy Spirit was telling me, reassuring me, that Jesus had given power to me to triumph over darkness. Then it would be, "Behold, I give unto you *power*..." The Lord was energizing me with holy boldness for this encounter. I was becoming keenly aware that I had been given *power of attorney*, legal authority, to act in Jesus's name! I understood it. I could see it. The authority was His name, and He commissioned you and me to act in the authority of His name.

The verse continued to run through my mind even though we were having a conversation. "...power to *tread* upon serpents and scorpions and over all the power of the enemy." To trample under the feet of Jesus! I had been given that authority, and I knew demons understood that. They know they are defeated! "*Serpents and scorpions* and over all the power of the enemy!" What an awesome verse of Scripture. And then I have the promise that *nothing by any means shall hurt me.*

I was ready—ready as I could be. My plans, remember, were to sit in and pray as the deliverance took place. Now I am the guy! I am acting in the name of the Lord Jesus. As a blood-washed child of God, I was about to take authority over evil spirits and command them to go. Me! I can't really describe what I was feeling.

This will become more real to you if you put yourself in my place. I was about to make a move in the name of Jesus Christ. I had no teacher. No one had ever given me instruction on this, though I had been exposed to it in many ways and various situations. I didn't attend "Dispelling Demons 101." Had it been offered, I probably would have. I was not a "demon doctor" and still am not. I had no instructor, yet I had the best Teacher. I was forced to trust the Holy Spirit.

I recalled accounts of Jesus dealing with demons. He spoke to them; they spoke to Him. He commanded them, and they obeyed. (I will talk more of this later.) When Jesus encountered the man "possessed" of demons in Mark 5, the demons responded to Jesus's command to come out of the man by saying, "What have I to do with thee, Jesus, thou Son of the most high God? I adjure thee by God, that thou torment me not." Jesus responded by asking, "What is thy name?" The demons then said, "My name is Legion: for we are many."

When Jesus commanded these spirits to go, there was further discussion. The demons requested permission to go to the pigs and were eventually allowed to go there and then to the abyss. I knew that Jesus told us to "First bind the strong man..." (Matt. 12:29), as we entered into spiritual encounters.

I refreshed myself in the Spirit as I was about to begin. I didn't know much more than to (1) bind them in the name of Jesus, (2) find out their identity, (3) determine if they have consent to stay there, and (4) command them to go to the abyss. (I will go into more detail later.)

We had a word of prayer earlier to open the session, but the time had come, and I told the woman what I was going to do. As I looked across the table, she had lowered her head, and her eyes peered up at me almost covered by her eyelids. Never had I seen nor sensed so much evil. Chills went through me. I trembled and felt fear try to overcome me, but I knew fear was a spirit and that God had not given me a spirit of fear but of love, power, and a sound mind! I rebuked fear in the name of Jesus and immediately it stopped.

IT WAS VERY DIFFICULT FOR HER

I asked her to pray a prayer after me, acknowledging Jesus Christ as her Savior and Lord. She confessed and repented of unforgiveness, hatred, bitterness, and anger and renounced all of her involvement in Satanism. It was very difficult for her to get the words out of her mouth. The demons did all they could to prevent her from speaking words that would break their power. She struggled though the prayer as she began to tremble, and her arms jerked. Her head dropped with her chin on her chest. I could not see her facial expression clearly, but her face began to contort and a "growlish" sound came from her lips, low and muffled.

I knew there was likely a demonic kingdom there, and if so, then some demon power would be in charge of the kingdom. I knew they were principalities and powers. After binding them with specific instructions, I commanded the "prince" demon or the demon power that claimed to be in charge to identify himself. I didn't know what to expect. Her voice changed; it became gruff and monotone, and the demons were speaking through her, just as they did through the man Jesus encountered in Gadera.

"Identify yourself," I commanded. The demon immediately gave his name. With each response, I commanded the demon to reveal if the answer would stand as truth before Jehovah God. The pastor, who was supposed to be ministering to this woman, had told me when I first met him that demons will not lie to Jehovah God. I commanded this demon power to reveal how many demons were present and how many were in his kingdom. After several lies and calling the evil spirit before the throne of God, the evil entity said, "We are too many, we are too powerful for you."

He was right, but he was not dealing with me. He was dealing with my Savior. I reminded this spirit that this was not between us but between my Master and his master and that his master had been soundly defeated. He spat out death threats aimed at my family and me. "No," I told him, "you won't do anything but be obedient to the command in the name of the Lord Jesus," I firmly commanded. God had given me boldness beyond my understanding.

I commanded the spirit to reveal if he had any consent from this woman or from Jehovah God to stay there. There was silence. I repeated the question in the authority of Jesus's name and commanded a response. "No." There was no consent for the unclean spirit to be there. Her salvation, repentance, and renunciation of involvement had broken the power of the enemy.

I commanded the spirit to reveal if any demon power present had any permission to remain. More silence. More commands. Eventually there was a "No." I said, "You know you must leave her, don't you? You and all of your kingdom are going to be cast to the abyss, to the pit!" "No, no, no..." the woman's arms had been jerking the whole time. I had placed my hands on hers, and as I commanded the demons to leave, she jerked her hands away and began to strangle herself. She was gagging and coughing, and fluid was running from her mouth. I got up and tried to pull her hands loose. Her face was turning blue. I could not budge her hands or fingers from her throat. She had reared back in the chair, and her body was rigid!

"I FEEL MUCH LIGHTER AND MUCH BETTER."

I commanded the spirits to release her in the name of the Anointed One, Jesus Christ, and immediately her hands fell to her side and she fell limp into the table, face down. I took her again by the hands and asked how she felt. "I feel so much lighter and much better," she said.

When I told her I thought there were more present, again her arms began to quiver and her head dropped on her chest. "Who are you?" I commanded. Again her voice changed, and a name was given. "Why didn't you leave when you were commanded to go?" I asked. "She's mine!"

Angrily the demon persisted, "She's mine!" I began to command with more boldness, "NO! She's not yours, she belongs to Jesus Christ, and she has been bought with a price, purchased, redeemed, born again! She is an heir of God and a joint-heir with Jesus Christ. You have no right to her life, and you will leave her now in Jesus Christ's mighty name." The woman began to cough. She jerked and trembled and cleared her throat as this vile demon left.

"SHE'S MINE. I WANT HER BODY."

Still, there was another, and this one seemed as violent as the first. This spirit with a threatening growl threatened to kill me. "You'll do nothing but leave as you are commanded in Christ Jesus's name." "She's mine. I want her body! Her body is mine!" As I commanded this spirit to leave, the woman again pulled her hands away and grabbed herself. I stood up, and from behind her chair I placed my hands on her forearms and commanded the spirit to release her immediately and go to the abyss. The release was immediate.

She slumped in her chair, and then looked up at me with the most peaceful look. "They're gone. They're gone!" She stood up and began to praise God; the praise just flowed from her lips. She jumped straight up and down like she was on a pogo stick, still praising God.

"Oh," she said, "they are gone. I really am free."

When I left the prison that day, I paused on the top step of the prison. I held my Bible up into the air and shouted, "Yes! In the name of Jesus, yes!"

CHAPTER 3

EXPOSING THE MYTH

Y OU MAY BE JUST LIKE MANY OTHERS WHO QUESTION DELIVER-
ance. Perhaps you have asked the question, "But I am a Christian. How can I have demons?" I don't want to use the entire
book for this issue, but you must get it settled in your mind and heart.
Believers can and most often do have demon spirits living in them. It
may be helpful to explain this in somewhat simplistic terms. The myth
must be destroyed in order for the body of Christ to be free. The "myth"
(a widely held but false belief), has given the evil spirits an advantage
and has kept the church in bondage. Plain and simple, it is spiritual
ignorance that allows this bondage to continue. *Ignorance* is a strong
word, but the Word of God declares, "Where there is no vision, the
people perish" (Prov. 29:18). "My people are destroyed for lack of knowledge" (Hos. 4:6). Lack of knowledge is ignorance. And, in this case, it
is willing ignorance.

May I say here that the people Jesus ministered to were Jewish
believers, and Scripture says, "And if ye be Christ's, then are ye Abraham's seed, and heirs according to the promise" (Gal. 3:29). Very simply,
the body of Christ is called "Abraham's seed." Jesus ministered deliverance to Abraham's seed.

The presence of the Holy Spirit does not prevent evil spirits from
dwelling in a believer's body or soul! Until a believer can recognize and
understand how demonic bondage occurs, he cannot be free. You can be
Spirit-filled; memorize the Word of God; sing in the choir; teach Sunday
school; and be a deacon, teacher, or preacher and still have demons.
I deal with this almost daily! That believers cannot have demons is a
dangerous, widely held but false belief. It is a myth.

21

In Mark's Gospel a man was casting out demons in the name of Jesus, but he was not one of the followers. John said:

> We forbade him, because he followeth not us. But Jesus said, Forbid him not: for there is no man which shall do a miracle in my name, that can lightly speak evil of me.
>
> —Mark 9:38–39

Jesus calls the casting out of demons a "miracle." He also reminds the disciples that just because he was not part of their group did not mean he did not have a relationship with Jesus. It is important to understand that deliverance is not *the* ministry, but it certainly is part of the ministry!

Exploring the Means

You will recall that before Judas betrayed the Lord Jesus, "Satan entered Judas" (Luke 22:3, nkjv). This is perhaps the most conclusive evidence that demons are fallen angels. Satan is a fallen angel; others followed him in rebellion. Satan entered into a follower of Jesus. Likely, Judas was not a believer. The point here is that demons enter through doorways. Jesus must have a doorway to come into those who believe, for he said, "Behold, I stand at the door, and knock: if any man hear my voice, and open the door, I will come in to him, and will sup with him, and he with me" (Rev. 3:20). I don't know what the open door was for Judas. It could have been most anything. Theft, lies, greed… I would guess that it was unbelief. Demons are allowed access to the life of a believer through similar gateways that I will discuss later. The goal of every demon is to steal, kill, and destroy. After betraying the Lord Jesus, a spirit of suicide took Judas to his death (Matt. 27:5). A "daughter of Abraham" was tormented with a spirit of infirmity for eighteen years (Luke 13:11–16). A little boy was thrown into fire and water by demon powers trying to destroy him (Mark 9:21–22). A Gentile woman came on behalf of her young daughter who was grievously vexed with a devil (Matt. 15:22–28). Demons need a gateway, an entrance point to a life. Jesus spoke to deaf ears and healed them by commanding a "spirit of deafness" to leave. God's Word tells us that *fear* is a spirit and that God has not given us that spirit. (See 2 Timothy 1:7.) If a *believer* has an open door, then he may also very well have a demon.

EXPLAINING THE METHOD

Demon spirits are fallen angels. There are many who speculate that they are something else. One theory suggests that demon spirits are spirits of a deceased creation prior to Adam. There is no scriptural suggestion to support this. Another idea proposes that demon spirits are a product of the "giants" produced in Genesis 6 when the "sons of God" had intercourse with the daughters of men. It is possible the spirits from those beings could be a part of the demonic kingdom. Of course, there are even some who believe that demon spirits are actually spirits of the deceased who die as unbelievers. This is also unscriptural. One last thought is that some believe that fallen angels could not be demons because angels are "heaven-bound" and man is "earthbound," hence, demon spirits could not be fallen angels. This theory is also not supported by Scripture. Satan *is* a fallen angel, and he "entered Judas." He walks to and fro on the earth. He personally challenged the Lord Jesus on the earth. First Peter 5:8 tells us that Satan walks about in the earth, seeking whom he may devour. That seems to be very clear and without question in the scripture.

Demon spirits may enter into believers whenever believers open gates to the unclean spirits. Satan desired Peter (Luke 22:31), and the apostle Paul was buffeted by a messenger of Satan (2 Cor. 12:7). It really is not complicated. Demons are on assignment, and believers are their targets. Don't buy into the denominational lie that because you are saved you cannot have evil spirits. If you believe that lie, then you will remain in bondage.

Let's look briefly at how it works:

> Know ye not that ye are the temple of God, and that the Spirit of God dwelleth in you? If any man defile the temple of God, him shall God destroy; for the temple of God is holy, which temple ye are.
>
> —1 CORINTHIANS 3:16–17

Clearly this says that a believer *is* the temple of God.

DEFINING THE TEMPLE

Defining the temple is necessary in order to understand how the temple is defiled and defended. The temple in which God lives on Earth today is the body of a born-again believer. This is such an overwhelming thought that God actually indwells the believer with His Holy Spirit. This can become confusing to some who ask the question, "If the Holy Spirit of God lives in me, how could evil spirits get into me as well." How can sin and evil thoughts live in the temple of God? Evil spirits can get in the temple just like evil thoughts and sinful actions—by choices we make and gates that we open.

Our body is a trinity; we are three in one. We are a *spirit* that has a *soul* that lives in a *body*. The best comparison I know is to look at our body, or more correctly, our being, as a temple or tabernacle, as Paul calls it in 2 Corinthians 5:1: "For we know that if our earthly house of this tabernacle were dissolved, we have a building of God, an house not made with hands, eternal in the heavens." Do you recall the Old Testament tabernacle? It was three parts: an outer courtyard, the holy place, and the holy of holies. The holy place was twice as large as the holy of holies.

The tabernacle is a picture of our being. The courtyard represents our flesh, the holy place represents our soul, and the holy of holies represents our spirit. The holy of holies is where the Spirit of God dwells. This is important in understanding how the temple is defiled. Where does the Spirit of God dwell in the believer? In our spirit! Not in our soul and flesh; that is the part of us that we can yield to God or to disobedience. Our soul is made up of our mind, will, and emotions. Our flesh is that which can be seen, touched, and felt. It has substance. The spirit has no substance; it is intangible. It is our spirit that is born again, and it is in our spirit that the Holy Spirit of God takes up residence.

Perhaps the spirit is also the "inner man." It is very important to understand that we are a trinity. We are a three-part being. The spirit has been born again, and the soul and the flesh are "being saved" as we yield ourselves and conform to the image of Christ. It is the soul and the flesh that can be inhabited by demon powers. It is the soul where spiritual battle takes place, and often it manifests in the flesh.

The mind is the battlefield. The mind and the brain are separate, but I cannot scientifically prove to you how I know this. The brain is physical; the mind is soulish. The seed of sin is in the mind while the fruit of sin may be manifested in the flesh. Demons do not, cannot, *possess* a believer, but they can and do "oppress" believers, and the oppression takes place in the body and soul.

DEFILING THE TEMPLE

How is the temple of God defiled? Do you recall how angry Jesus became when He entered the temple and saw it "defiled" by those buying and selling and by the money changers.

> And Jesus went into the temple of God, and cast out all them that sold and bought in the temple, and overthrew the tables of the moneychangers, and the seats of them that sold doves, and said unto them, It is written, My house shall be called the house of prayer; but ye have made it a den of thieves. And the blind and the lame came to him in the temple; and he healed them.
>
> —MATTHEW 21:12–14

The things of the world had been brought into the temple. That's how it is defiled today, when *we* invite things of the world into our lives. This also becomes an invitation for demon spirits to inhabit the temple! Like rats are attracted to garbage, when our life has unconfessed sin, unbroken curses, or unforgiveness, the demons come and defile the temple.

They must be "driven" out. They cannot be medicated out or counseled out. Neither can they be removed by you willing them to be gone. All Christian activity is helpful in keeping the demons somewhat "in check," but to be rid of them, they must be "cast out." They must be driven out in the name of Jesus Christ! Jesus said, "In my name...*cast* out devils" (Mark 16:17, emphasis added). Can the temple be defiled? Absolutely! Just as Jesus saw the holy temple of God defiled, He sees ours defiled by things we have permitted in our lives. Now the lie we have believed is that once we have confessed our sin, the demons leave, but that is not necessarily so. Repentance and confession of sin cancel the penalty of sin. We are certainly cleansed of sin, but have the demons been commanded to leave? The "permission" of the demon spirit to be there has been canceled, but I have found they often do not leave until they are commanded to do so. Notice that healing came after the temple was cleansed!

No sin could enter the holy of holies; it meant certain death to come into God's holy presence with sin in the life of the high priest. Just as sin could not enter the holy of holies, neither can demon spirits enter the spirit of a believer. The temple polluters that Jesus chased from the temple were not in the holy of holies but in the outer court. So, you see, possession is not the issue. The Holy Spirit possesses our spirit. He is the owner; we are purchased, redeemed, bought with a price. Defiling the temple involves the soul and the flesh. Our mind, our will, our emotions, and our flesh is where the tormentors do their damage. A defiled temple is a troubled temple! A troubled temple must be cleansed by the Lord Jesus. "Cleansed" in this case is more than being forgiven. It is driving out the source of the defilement.

Defending the Temple

How do we defend the temple? If demon spirits are present, we must determine if they have consent to be there. Consent must be from Jehovah God or from ourselves. Demons could be present by permission of generational sin of the forefathers, and if that is the case, then these spirits have consent to be there. Generational sin, or ancestral sin, is consent given by God according to Exodus 20:5: "...for I the Lord thy God am a jealous God, visiting the iniquity of the fathers upon the children of the third and fourth generation of them that hate me." This is a scriptural principle, or law, if you will. It is legal permission for evil spirits to pass from one generation to another. More will be said about this later.

Remember: it is not *possession*; it is *oppression*, and Jesus went about doing good, healing all those who were oppressed of the devil. Do they have consent to stay? That's the issue. Have you confessed the curse-breaking power of Jesus Christ's name over generational sin? Has anyone commanded the spirits to leave? Have you not only repented of unforgiveness, anger, bitterness, and similar sins, but also have you commanded spirits that may have come by that doorway to leave?

It is important that you know! My experience has been that evil spirits do not leave until they are commanded to leave. Repentance cancels their permission to be there, but they leave when they are commanded to leave. Jesus *drove* out those who defiled the temple with great authority. He has given us authority over all the power of the enemy! Keeping the temple cleansed is keeping doorways closed that allow them entrance. Read this statement carefully: the presence of the Holy Spirit does not keep demon spirits out; keeping doorways closed by the leadership of the Holy Spirit does! Man has a choice to "quench" or to "grieve" the Holy Spirit. The Holy Spirit does not fight our battles. He leads and guides us, but our will is always honored.

CHAPTER 4

HOW DO DEMONS ACCESS BELIEVERS?

T HE BIGGEST OBSTACLE I HAVE ENCOUNTERED IN MINISTERING to believers is dislodging the false teaching they have received from well-meaning pastors and teachers. Many will say, "Yeah, I believe Jesus dealt with demons, but He was talking to people on their level of understanding. Don't you think it was really mental illness?" What an insult to Jesus and to Holy Scripture! This portrays both Jesus and the Word of God as *liars*. I hope you have not bought in to that lie. I have heard well-meaning pastors tell their congregations the same lie.

The truth is, believers are the target for demon powers, and our ignorance about the matter makes it that much easier for them. Jesus relieved the torment of the oppressed, and He also drove out the oppressor! The torment takes place in the soul and flesh, not in the spirit where the Holy Spirit abides!

Demons cannot enter a person by choice. That is, they can't occupy anyone they choose. There must be some permission granted by the person. Legal rights are recognized and understood very well by demon powers. There must be a "gate" or doorway of opportunity. I have heard people who were former Satan worshipers call these entryways "portals." It is important to recognize these entryways, or gates, and to keep them closed and guarded.

Proverbs 25:28 says, "He that hath no rule [self control] over his own spirit is like a city that is broken down, and without walls." Unfortunately, the gateways to our life are often controlled by other people and other circumstances prior to birth and in our early childhood.

Gates are mentioned throughout God's Word, and their importance and significance is seen most often in terms of protection, holding in what is good, or keeping out the enemy. In Isaiah 62:6, God appointed watchmen over the gates. The obvious function of a gate is to keep something out or to allow something in. *Gates, doorways, entry points*, and *portals* are various terms that describe the same function. They are access points for demons to reach believers.

God always honors the will of man. Scripture is the legal rule book or contract that governs what access demon powers have to the lives of believers. The Holy Spirit will not come into a person unless He is invited, but He is quick to accept the invitation. Demon powers also cannot and will not come into an individual's soul or body without legal permission! They cannot. But there are numerous ways for an individual to open one of these entryways, and there could be subcategories for all of the gateways I will mention. I am going to list some common permissions that believers give demons to oppress them.

ANCESTRY

Generational curse

This is permission that could be in virtually *anyone's* life today... anyone! Any human being alive in this world is a candidate for evil spirits to be passed by this scriptural permission found in Exodus 20:5. It is God-given consent for evil spirits to be passed to a child because of the sins of the forefathers. Some argue that this doesn't seem fair. *Fair* is not a word in the demon dictionary. This is a consequence of sin, and *every father and mother bears responsibility for breaking this curse in the family.* It is real, and it is by far the most common entryway that I encounter.

Generational or ancestral curses are often recognized by the impairment of normal physiological functions. It will be helpful to read Deuteronomy 28, and cross-reference the various curses. They can be summarized generally as follows:

1. Mental and emotional breakdown. This is a very common work of demon powers and is evidenced by the numbers in treatment.

2. Barrenness and impotency together with miscarriages and related female complications.

3. Failure—plans and projects that never mature. Many times I have encountered "blocking" spirits and "hindering"

spirits whose purpose and assignment is to prevent blessings from coming.

4. Poverty or perpetual financial insufficiency. This curse is
often the result of robbing from God, and may be also a
sin of the forefathers.

5. Spiritual hindrance in hearing God's voice, sensing God's
presence, understanding the Bible, concentration in prayer,
and being devoid of spiritual gifts.

6. Life traumas—going from one crisis to another. This seems
to be a fairly common curse. Virtually everyone knows
someone who falls in this category.

7. Untimely and unnatural deaths.

8. Breakdown of family relationships, including divorce.

9. Sickness and diseases, especially chronic and hereditary
diseases.

...For I the Lord thy God am a jealous God, visiting the *iniquity
of the fathers upon the children unto the third and fourth generation* of them that hate me.
—EXODUS 20:5, EMPHASIS ADDED

Spiritual blessing is also promised to those who obey the commandments of the Lord. The blessings are counterparts of the above-mentioned
curses.

Deuteronomy 28:1–14 tells of the blessings promised to those who
are "set on high" by God—the promise of being the lender and not the
borrower, the head and not the tail. Is your life characterized by fruitfulness? This is another method of checking to see if you may be under
a curse. If you are not enjoying the blessing, then you are suffering the
curse. Do you prosper—coming and going? Are you free from the harassment of enemies both natural and spiritual? Is your life a success? Is your
relationship with God gratifying? Are you recognizing and fulfilling His
purposes? These are the earmarks of a blessed life. According to these
scriptures, there is no middle ground.

Yet another way to determine if curses are in operation is to look for
the effects of curses. Common effects of curses are poverty, barrenness,

pestilence, chronic sickness, failure, defeat, humiliation, insanity, torment, perpetual traumas, spiritual hindrances, domination by others, and a sense of abandonment by God and others. (See Deuteronomy 28:20–68.) See the appendix for a listing of biblical curses.

Mental disorders

Mental disorders such as depression and bipolar disorders are most commonly a result of generational curses or early childhood abuse. Along with many other disorders of the mind, medical authorities attribute these generational curses to "genetics." Therefore, good information about family history can be very beneficial in the deliverance process.

Alcohol and addiction

If there is evidence of alcoholism or abuse of alcohol in the family history, it is almost certain that you will find an addictive spirit has been passed to the offspring. The addiction may manifest in other ways. It may not be to alcohol; it may be nicotine, drugs, food, or even sex. Addictive behavior in the ancestry will give you a clue to what spirits may be lurking in the temple.

Religious spirits

Religious spirits are often "bondage" spirits that keep a person bound to legalistic ways that dishonor God and cause the person to feel that he can never please God. This is a very common spirit that I see passed by ancestral curse. Indian heritage should also be explored and may be a very good clue to possible occult or religious spirits. Virtually any type of demon spirit may be passed through generational permission. Background history can be very helpful.

Birth trauma

Many other doorways should be considered at birth or during the time a mother is carrying a child. Trauma that takes place while the child is in the womb and shortly after birth, even the birth process should be looked into. I have seen evil spirits attach to a life because of difficulties encountered during the birth process.

Early childhood trauma

Spoken words can become curses, granting permission to evil spirits by words from the mother, father, or doctor. Many times I have encountered spirits of rejection and abandonment from trauma after the child's conception. Remember, John the Baptist leapt in the womb when he heard of Jesus's coming through a conversation between his mother, Elizabeth, and Mary the mother of Jesus.

One powerful spirit of abandonment I encountered had gained access from a baby being in an incubator for six weeks. This 35-year-old curled up in a fetal position and began to weep, "Oh, I'm in a box, I want my mother..." He explained, after this tormenting spirit was commanded to leave, that he could see himself as a tiny baby in the incubator separating him from everyone. This is always a place to explore for possible doorways.

The early life of any individual can be a source of demon entry. Remember that demons don't play fair. Fear of the dark, Mom and Dad arguing, fear of divorce, divorce itself, abuse, death, guilt, shame or embarrassment, nightmares... The list is long for doorways that can come through childhood trauma. Injuries or hospitalization may even be a source.

One of the most common spirits encountered in deliverance ministry is a demon of confusion. Often it has it's doorway as mom and dad arguing, threatening to leave, perhaps even leaving, all the while telling the child how much they are loved and how important they are. The confusion spirit generally brings its friends of doubt, unbelief, skepticism, and disbelief. Many times these spirits function as "blocking" or "hindering" spirits.

It is almost certain that if a child is sexually abused, humiliated, or embarrassed sexually, that child will receive a demonic spirit whose work is sexual perversion. This spirit can come in one of two forms called incubus and succubus. This spirit can also come from sexual trauma later in life. Generally, this spirit will drive the person to sexual extremes—promiscuity in one person and frigidity in another.

Sickness

This is a very common gate for evil spirits. Recently, I found a spirit that identified itself as "Mononucleosis." The person suffered from fatigue and extreme lack of energy. When this spirit manifested, she grabbed her jaws on both sides at the lymph node area. They were hurting her. She had suffered this sickness as a child, but the spirit that caused the sickness stayed and had plagued her with various difficulties for fifteen years. When commanded in the name of Jesus Christ, the spirit left and so did the symptoms she had been experiencing.

I have seen hearing problems healed when spirits that came through mumps, chicken pox, measles, high fever, and the like were identified and commanded to leave. Sickness is always a possible doorway for demon spirits. When Jesus ministered healing to deaf people, He spoke, "Come out of him thou deaf and dumb spirit." (See Mark 9:25.) He called deafness a spirit!

Surgery

This one was a puzzle to me when I first began to encounter it. How could evil spirits gain access to a believer's life through surgery? Did they come in through the incision? No. Was it fear? Remember, fear is a spirit. Maybe ungodly doctors? Perhaps the anesthesia? I still can't give you a positive answer. Maybe it is all of those things. I took a doctor through deliverance in Oklahoma, and he asked me how that could happen. He said, "I pray with all my patients before surgery. What prayer do I pray to keep that from happening?"

We discussed it awhile, and he explained the information in medical terms but basically he said this. When a person is under anesthesia, there is a brief window, a transfer state where they are neither conscious nor unconscious. Briefly they are in what is similar to a hypnotic state as they go from consciousness to unconsciousness and the same thing happens when they come back out. Maybe that's when it happens. I believe it is. I have, however, found that words from doctors can become spoken curses, for example, "You'll never walk again." "You will gradually get worse and may never heal." "There is no hope for you to recover fully." Surgery should always be looked at as a possible gate.

Ridicule/humiliation

I have also found that traumas in the school years can be doorways for demon spirits. One such common doorway is ridicule or being embarrassed by a teacher. You might be surprised to know how many times I have seen this be a source of poor self-image spirits, spirits of rejection, or spirits of condemnation. The same can occur by rejection from peers, not feeling accepted in certain circles, and the like.

Immorality

Periods of immorality in the candidate's life should always be explored as possible doorways or invitations to evil spirits. Many of those who come to me for freedom will tell of a period of sexual promiscuity, some drinking and drugs during their high school and/or college days. Sex outside of marriage cannot only open doors for demons, but it can also create a soul tie that gives them permission to stay until that curse is broken. A soul tie may occur whenever there is an unhealthy relationship. The most common is sexual relations outside of marriage.

Unconfessed sin

Virtually any sin that is unconfessed can be an open door for demons to torment believers. Some sins do, however, appear to be bigger doorways.

Anger

One particular verse that comes to mind is Ephesians 4:26: "Be angry and sin not, let not the sun go down on your wrath, neither give place to the devil." This clearly says that anger that lingers from one day to the next can give place to the devil. Just because there is a gate or entryway does not mean that a demon always comes in. Probably more often than not, they don't come in; however, it is an invitation and we are to keep our lives covered and cleansed by the blood of Jesus.

Pain

Both physical and emotional pain often will invite spirits of pain to take up residence through the pain trauma and remain in the life to torment with pain. I have found "chronic" pain spirits, and I have encountered "nagging" pain spirits. The pain spirit many times will invite an addictive spirit to cover the pain, resulting in more bondage.

Death

It is not just the trauma of someone dying who is close to us, but there is also another consideration. When a person dies, if they had evil spirits oppressing or possessing them, suddenly those spirits are without a home. They will seek another, and my experience is that they tend to stay in the family.

I preached at the funeral of the father of one of my best friends. The father was an alcoholic and barely held his home together through the years. His son (my friend) did not drink. That is, until a few months after his father's death. Now my friend is struggling to hold his home together and is becoming an alcoholic. His mother told him, "You are acting just like your father!" I have seen this play out many times in many different ways.

Pornography

This gate is being attempted in the lives of virtually every healthy male in the world—and females, as well. This gate can lead to a very powerfully addictive spirit that is bent on your destruction. Pastors, teachers, political leaders, men in high office, and the guy who cleans the basement are often victims here and find this demon one of the most difficult to be rid of. Once this gate is opened, it often stays open. The destructive demons slowly go about their work of destroying families, self-image, health, churches, children, and so on. This is a much too common gate for demons today.

Criminal activity

This is most certainly an invitation for demon spirits. After ministering in prisons since 1974, I have seen this to be a very common and consistent doorway for evil spirits. The demons don't miss this opportunity very often. This, probably more than anything else, explains the revolving doors to our nation's penitentiaries. Many men and women accept Christ as Savior while incarcerated but are still not able to function in society because they are free only from the penalty of sin but are still in bondage to the powers of darkness.

Spoken curses

The tongue can speak blessing or curses, and the words we speak or the words spoken to us, or over us, can lend opportunity for demons to enter. The power of life and death is in the tongue. (See Proverbs 18:21.) Words as simple as "We are never going to have anything," can invite a spirit of poverty to help insure that those spoken words come to pass. If you will visualize a big angel on your right and a big demon on your left, each of them acting upon the words that come out of your mouth, then you might have a fairly accurate picture of how this works. Angels react to words of faith that you speak and demons respond to words of doubt and disbelief.

Lust

This includes lust for money and material things or for bodily appetites, such as food and sex. Envy, covetousness, and jealousy are certain doorways for evil spirits. Lust is certainly a doorway that is present in many lives.

The mind

The mind is clearly the battlefield. What we allow in through our eyes and ears can be entryways for demon powers. It can be books we have read; something as simple as fascinations with Greek, Roman, or Egyptian mythology; or movies that are fearful or grossly depict sin along with television programs and even cartoons. I minister to children who have received demons from cartoons. Creatures become their friends, and they fantasize. This can invite demons. The Harry Potter books and movies are among the absolute worst! Parents bear a heavy responsibility, and I see many simply turning their heads.

The occult

Remember, there can be almost as many divisions of doorways as you could imagine depending on the categories and subcategories. Let me just say here that I don't think I can cover all of the possible occult doorways. But I want to list some that may surprise you.

- Freemasonry
- Eastern Star
- DeMolay
- Job's Daughters
- Elk
- Mormon
- Gurus
- Islam
- Spiritism
- Hinduism
- Unity
- Baha'i
- Pokémon cards and characters
- Fortune-tellers
- Oddfellows
- Rainbow Girls
- Shriner
- Daughters of the Nile
- Christian Science
- Jehovah's Witness
- Scientology
- Religious communes
- Buddhism
- Tibetan
- Rosicrucian
- Theosophy
- Harry Potter
- Tarot cards

- Ouija boards
- Mediums
- Astrology
- Levitation
- Horoscope
- Black magic
- Spirit guides
- Crystals
- Native (Indian) curiosity
- Witchcraft
- Satanism

- Séances
- Palmistry
- Color therapy
- Astral travel
- Lucky charms
- Demon worship
- Clairvoyance
- New Age
- Eastern religions
- Voodoo
- Hypnotism

Although this is not a list of every possible doorway, it should, however, give you an idea of what gives permission for demons to enter the soul and flesh of believers. (See symptoms of demonic oppression in the appendix in the back of book.)

CHAPTER 5

WHAT KINDS OF PEOPLE COME FOR DELIVERANCE?

FICTION CHARACTERS LIKE FRANKENSTEIN AND THE WOLF MAN played their part in making it difficult for people to come for deliverance or even see a need for it. The movie *The Exorcist* and other Hollywood productions about demons have also made it hard for the average person to believe that they themselves could have demons. So we have believed another lie, and for the most part, many have made the choice to remain in bondage rather than face the risk of ridicule by seeking help. So the kinds of people that I have seen come for deliverance and the ones to whom I have directly ministered are silent seekers because of the stigma that goes with the thought of deliverance. They indeed come the way Nicodemus came to Jesus. Boy, give the demons credit. They have done a good job of making it really difficult for people to be free.

It has been my experience that the oppressor never voluntarily releases the oppressed! Let me say that sentence again. *The oppressor never voluntarily releases the oppressed.* That is true in the physical realm and in the spiritual. If you want freedom, then you have to make an effort. Often, you must demand it.

Most believers know that they suffer from the oppressing hand of Satan through his demon powers, but they choose to call it something else. "It's just the way I am." "It's just the way life is." "I've been to a counselor and I've been to a doctor, so I just accept that it's something I have to deal with." "Demons don't really live in Christians, do they? I mean, how could they be where the Holy Spirit is?" I don't know how many times I have heard these statements.

Over the years, I have dealt with people from virtually every walk of life. Not bad people, not evil people, but good people, godly people. I only deal with believers. There would be little point in casting demons from a lost person. Others would immediately enter because there is no resistance. It is only believers that I minister to, and it has been to thousands!

What kind of people? Let me share a few situations with you.

A city councilman came for deliverance, and during the session a spirit of self-mutilation introduced himself. The councilman was astounded when the demon revealed his function to him. "I don't cut myself or do any self-harm. What in the world does self-mutilation mean in my life?" Well, as we probed some more and allowed the Holy Spirit to reveal information to us, he remembered that since he was a child, he had a compulsion to pull strands of hair from his head. "I got so many spankings for that," he said. "Sometimes I'd come home from school with bald spots in my head. I still do it." The spirit was a trichotillomania spirit—a compulsion spirit that he could not control. He was freed from that spirit and from other spirits that were in his life by permission of a generational curse.

Trichotillomania is a term coined by a French dermatologist in 1889 to describe the compulsive or irresistible urge he saw in patients to pluck out their hair. The word *trichotillomania* is derived from the Greek words *thrix* meaning "hair"; *tillein*, which means "to pull"; and *mania*, which means "madness" or "frenzy." This name is somewhat of a misnomer in that people with trichotillomania are not "mad," "psychotic," or "crazy" as the name suggests. In psychiatry, trichotillomania is classified as an impulse control disorder as are conditions such as compulsive gambling, klepto-mania (compulsive stealing), and pyromania (compulsive fire setting). I have seen that demons can be responsible for all of these disorders.

Impulse control disorders are characterized by the inability to control or resist the temptation (or impulse) to do something harmful to oneself or someone else. A sufferer sometimes experiences a sense of increasing tension before performing the behavior and can feel a sense of relief or release of tension afterward. Sometimes people even express a degree of pleasure after having performed the act. Features of trichotillomania include the inability to resist urges to pull out one's hair, mounting tension before pulling, and a feeling of relief afterward.

I also saw this spirit in a high school cheerleader who since has testi-fied that she has not had that problem since she left my office several years ago. Just recently, a housewife was also freed from this same spirit. There have been many others—just regular people. My experience is that virtually everything that a doctor calls a "disorder" may be caused by demons. God puts things in order; demons take them out of order!

A surgeon and his wife came for deliverance. The wife had many sickness spirits that had come by permission of anesthesia and various surgeries. The surgeon told me after his wife completed deliverance, "I think I need to schedule a time to see you. While you were ministering to my wife, I felt lots of stirring inside of me."

I met with that doctor about a month later. He had to excuse himself and run to the hospital in the middle of the deliverance. He got an emergency page. "Don't go anywhere," he said, "I'll be right back." Well, he did get back in less than thirty minutes, and we continued the deliverance. This very respected, highly educated surgeon told me when we finished. "I probably won't be able to tell anyone else about this, but I want to tell you that when you commanded that last spirit to leave, I could see and feel it on my back, like a very large bird. Its claws were dug into my shoulders when a large angel came and swatted it from me. I could see this ugly creature rolling and tumbling as it disappeared into darkness." He said, "Man, that is exciting! I feel so free right now."

This doctor had been betrayed by a partner in the years past. He had felt some bitterness and unforgiveness toward the other doctor. That had been a doorway, as well as fraternal oaths and pledges he had made in college. But now he is free. What kind of people? Regular, normal, everyday people just like you.

The list of people I have led through deliverance includes lawyers, many pastors, deacons, housewives, children, athletes, college students, missionaries, financial planners, engineers, Sunday school teachers, professional singers, choir members, bankers, retirees, computer programmers, schoolteachers, counselors, principals, probation officers, correctional officers, chaplains, policemen, inmates, coaches, writers, and on and on. I guess that makes the point. Just people.

CHAPTER 6

MY EARLY EXPOSURE TO DEMONS

I HAD TWO VERY UNUSUAL EXPERIENCES WHEN I WAS ATTENDING the seminary and working in Fort Worth. I had taken a job with the electric company as a meter reader. Reading electric meters meant that over a month's time, you had made the complete rounds of the city and had been in thousands of backyards in dozens of communities. I think I got to know every kind of dog and learned their characteristics and traits. I came to know very quickly which dogs I could trust and which ones I could bluff. I also learned which ones to leave alone.

One of the things meter readers would do was to make notes on the reading cards about any bad experiences with dogs at particular addresses. So most often, you might know in advance if you were about to encounter a "bad dog." Sometimes the note would read: "Vicious...long chain." The length of the chain could be very important. I read meters for two years and was bitten once. A cocker spaniel that did not bark and looked totally innocent just walked up and bit me.

I will never forget the most frightening encounter I had. There was a house with a detached garage in the back that could be entered from the alley. As I read the meter on the back of the house and started to go to the next house directly behind it on the next street, I noticed a chain going into the open garage. There was a large stake in the ground and I assumed there was a large dog on the other end. I saw the chain move but I didn't hear any barking.

I eased my way a safe distance from the garage door to pass on to the next yard. When I looked into the garage, expecting to see this a dog, my heart almost stopped. It was not a dog. It was a human being! A man who may have been eighteen to twenty years old. He was hunched over and bedraggled. He did not speak, but he did move toward me and sort of groaned as he did.

I cannot describe what I felt. To be honest, I was frightened. I never thought I would see anything like that. I wish I had known then what I know now. I did not speak, and I'm not sure I could have. I remember wondering, "What is this all about?"

I asked some of the other workers that afternoon if they had seen this young man. Several of them had. One man said, "That guy's crazy, man! His parents can't control him. That's all they know to do." Could this be true?

Was this guy like the demoniac in Mark chapter 5? I never saw him after that. I returned to that same house in the months that followed, but I did not see the man or the chain that held him. This was probably a case of demon possession. I thought it was then and still do.

GOD'S PREACHERS!

About a year later, I encountered something similar. This was on the south side of the city, near Southwestern Theological Seminary. This was also a corner house, but the setting was much different. The house was run-down, and the yard was unkempt. It even appeared unoccupied. There were hedges all around the backyard, and they too were overgrown and in need of trimming. I worked my way through a slight opening in the hedges and into the backyard. I was surprised to see a woman with her back to me. Her dress was ragged and her hair looked like it may have never been combed. I spoke very softly so as not to frighten her.

The woman turned slowly and started laughing with a "witchlike" cackle. Her countenance was dark, and her eyes were steely. She was ugly, and there was a snarl on her face. She pointed at me and said, "YOU! God's preacher!" with her cackle and mocking tone. My legs became heavy, and I could hardly move. I couldn't speak, but I left the yard as quickly as possible. My energy was gone. I stopped and sat down on the curb across from this house, trying to regain my composure and wondering what I had just experienced.

Her words, laughter, and mockery still linger in my mind. How did she know I was a preacher? What was the drain on my energy and the heaviness in my legs? I believe it was the power of the demons in that woman. After about fifteen minutes of rest and reflection, I started back and about four houses down from this woman I saw a lady in her yard working, and I inquired about the woman in the corner house.

"Do you know this woman?" I asked.

"Oh no, I don't think anyone around here knows her. There is never anyone at that house. Kids won't go near there. I've never even seen anyone go in or out of that house. There's all kinds of stories," she said.

There have been many situations that I could attribute to demonic activity, and I will share a few more.

I Know Who You Are

I was still working for the electric company, but when this event took place I was working as an outside customer representative. This job involved responding to customers' complaints or questions about their service. We worked territories of the city. My territory was in west Fort Worth, and there were five others who worked in my office with the same responsibilities. Customers who called the electric company and did not receive satisfactory answers by phone were told that a representative would contact them personally. The phone operators would send a ticket to our department with the customers account information and the nature of their question.

When I left the office that day, I noticed that I had among my allotted contacts one that was not in my territory. I decided I would go ahead and work this stop myself rather than bringing it back to the proper representative. I found the house and proceeded to the front door. I introduced myself, and the lady invited me inside. She thought her electric bill was too high. I thought that seemed very strange because it was an unusually low amount. I listened to her complaint, explained how the billing process worked, what appliances used the most electricity, and so on, and she seemed to be satisfied. It was a very small house and in a low-income neighborhood. Perhaps she just couldn't afford to pay her bill.

I had the door opened and was about to leave. She said, "You're not going anywhere. Not until you..." She was seated on a couch very near the door as she made some very explicit sexual suggestions. I was stunned. I was glad I was at the door, and it was already open.

"No, ma'am," I said. "I am married, and I am not interested. Besides that, I am a preacher…"

She interrupted me, "I know who you are. I knew when I called that you would be here." She smirked, "I know who you are, servant of Jesus Christ!"

"You see that wall over there?" she asked, pointing to the wall across from the doorway. "There used to be a picture of Jesus Christ on that wall. I smashed it into the floor, stomped on it, and then ripped the picture to pieces. I know who you are!"

I told her I was leaving, and as I began to ease out the door, she yelled, "You'll be back. You'll be back!"

Again I felt my legs getting heavy, and I felt like I could even smell demons as I left. It smelled like someone striking a match, a sulphur-like odor.

When I reached my car, I sat in the front seat and tried to digest what had just happened. I put the key in the ignition and nothing happened. The car engine made no sound. Nothing. Several times I tried it. Nothing. Looking back toward the house, I could see her peering out the window with a smirk on her face. She seemed to be letting me know that she was responsible. I thought about the situation. Maybe the Lord wanted me to go back and witness to her and pray with her. I wasn't sure. I remember praying a prayer that sounds strange now, but it is what I prayed. "Lord, if You want me to go back and talk with this lady I will, but if You don't, I need this car to start." Again, I tried the ignition and the car started.

A "BIG-SHOT" DEMON SHOWS UP IN FLORIDA

Some time ago I was in Florida for several prison services. This was before I had received anointing and insight into the realm of the demonic. Some of our team members were with me. We were in a rented van as we pulled into the prison parking lot.

The service was scheduled to be held in the visiting room. Always before I enter a prison, I pray. When people are with me, we pray just prior to leaving the vehicle. I will always remember this particular prayer time. As one of the ladies was praying, I "saw" something. Let me add that I am a fairly regular guy. I don't see things and had never experienced a vision of any kind to my recollection. But I saw something that evening. With my head bowed and my face toward the floorboard, I saw a vision of a large demon hovered over the front gate of the prison.

The demon appeared to be twelve to fourteen feet tall. It was black with two wings spread that may have spanned ten to twelve feet. The face was black and leatherlike with bird features. It looked as if the demon was declaring, "This is my place!" I stopped the prayer meeting and shared what I had seen. I said, "We must pray differently. We must bind evil spirits so that the service is not hindered. Let's ask God to send holy angels to do warfare on our behalf and for the sake of the gospel. We are entering into an area of spiritual warfare." We changed our prayer.

When we walked through the front gate of that facility, I didn't feel anything, but I knew the Holy Spirit was working. The chaplain met us at the visiting room entrance and said he was setting out some folding chairs for the service. We all helped. "We probably won't need more than forty," he said. He told us that would be a good crowd.

However, when the church service was announced and the men began to filter in the visiting room, the chairs quickly filled up. Men retrieved all of the remaining chairs, and they too were filled. When the visiting room doors were shut, there were more than two hundred men in the room for church! At least two-thirds of that number made public commitments to receive Jesus Christ. Wow! That experience really turned my head toward the validity of our power and authority in spiritual warfare!

My Mother Had Demons

From the time I graduated high school my mother began having problems. It seemed it all started with a hysterectomy, but now I am certain it was generational spirits that tormented her. She was in and out of psychiatric hospitals, and she saw a half dozen or more psychiatrists and psychologists. She was a regular patient with medical doctors and chiropractors. She was tormented, and we didn't know how to help. I prayed. All of us did. She prayed, but still she was tormented.

About three years prior to her death, she attempted suicide nine times in a six-week period. I cannot describe to you what that time was like. My parents lived only a few miles from us. I would get phone calls on a regular basis from my father, who did not know what to do. One night, he called around 2:00 a.m. He was frantic! I rushed over to their home and saw fire trucks and an ambulance. When I got into the house, my mother was sitting in a chair in her gown with both wrists slit and blood all over her. She sat there calmly as paramedics helped and prepared to take her to the hospital.

When a family member is tormented by demons, the entire family suffers. My father had used up virtually all of his retirement fund on doctors and hospitals. Nothing helped. I didn't know what to do but pray. I shared this request with many inmates and with my friend in Christ, David Berkowitz (aka Son of Sam). David is now a believer, but prior to his salvation, he worshiped demons. He called me one evening from his prison in Fallsburg, New York.

"Don, I have been praying for you and for your mother. The Holy Spirit has shown me that she is being attacked by demons of depression and demons of suicide. If you will have praise music in her home, the demons will leave."

Of course, of course! Why couldn't I see that it was demons? Was it because it was my own mother? I knew immediately that was the problem. I went the next morning to an electronics outlet and purchased a continuous play cassette player. I took praise tapes and the player to my mom's house and told her, "Mom, don't ever turn this off. You don't have to listen to it all the time, it doesn't need to be up loud, just let it play softly day and night." She was glad to do that. You see, my mom loved the Lord.

That evening I asked three or four from our ministry to go with me to my mom's house. We just gathered around her, laid hands on her and commanded demon spirits to leave in Jesus's name. I didn't know much about the process at that time. But I can tell you as a fact that from that moment until the day she died almost three years later she did not have any more suicide attempts or heavy depression!

Some Things That Demons Don't Like

Demons don't like the name Jesus Christ. It is in His name that they are defeated. They retreat in His mighty name. They tremble. The mightiest of demons will bow at that name. You must remember that our authority is *only* in His name.

> And these signs shall follow them that believe; in my name shall they cast out devils...
>
> —MARK 16:17

> By stretching forth thine hand to heal; and that signs and wonders may be done by the name of thy holy child Jesus.
>
> —ACTS 4:30

> ...which he wrought in Christ, when he raised him from the dead, and set him at his own right hand in the heavenly places, far above all principality...and dominion, and every name that is named, not only in this world, but also in that which is to come: and hath put all things under his feet.
>
> —EPHESIANS 1:20–22

> Whatsoever ye shall ask the Father in my name, he will give it you. Hitherto have ye asked nothing in my name: ask and ye shall receive, that your joy may be full.
>
> —JOHN 16:23–24

> And the seventy returned again with joy, saying, Lord, even the devils are subject unto us through thy name.
>
> —LUKE 10:17

The blood is not authority. The blood is for forgiveness and cleansing: "And almost all things are by the law purged with blood; and without shedding of blood is no remission.... Having therefore, brethren, boldness to enter into the holiest by the blood of Jesus, by a new and living way...and having an high priest over the house of God" (Heb. 9:22; 10:19–21, cf: 1 John 1:9).

Demons cannot stand praise music, as I just mentioned. They are not only annoyed by it, but I also believe it torments them. You see, that used to be their job. They were once the angels of praise whose appointment was to sing and praise the Lord. It is a constant reminder that they made a fatal mistake in following Lucifer in rebellion. My experience is that you can praise your way through anything! Not only do demons detest praise, but also it invites the presence of the Lord, and He inhabits the praises of His people.

> For the Lord taketh pleasure in His people: he will beautify the meek with salvation. Let the saints be joyful in glory: let them sing aloud on their beds. Let the high praises of God be in their mouth, a twoedged sword in their hand.
>
> —Psalm 149:4–9

Praise did not get Paul and Silas out of prison, but it got God in with them! Praise loosed the shackles and kicked down the doors of the prison, and it does the same for those in demonic bondage. It brings God into the situation.

The blood will torment demons but they do not have to obey by the blood. The blood is for protection, cleansing, forgiveness, and healing. The holy, unblemished, spotless blood of the Lord Jesus will torment demon powers. However, it is the commands in the *name* of Jesus Christ that they must obey.

They do not like the anointing oil. I have experienced them scream and screech when anointing oil is applied to the one with demons. The anointing oil carries with it promises of healing, and demons are generally the source of sickness.

"Is any sick among you? Let him call for the elders of the church; and let them pray over him, anointing him with oil in the name of the Lord; and the prayer of faith shall save the sick" (James 5:14–15). Note here the authority for using the anointing oil is the *name* of Jesus.

They do not like the word holy. Anything holy will torment demon powers. Holy angels make demons nervous. Just the mention of the Holy Spirit makes them weak.

The name Jehovah *causes them to fear and tremble.* Often, I command demons to come before the throne of Jehovah God and speak truth in His presence. I have found they will not lie to Jehovah God!

The Word of God is the truth. Demons are all liars, and they hate the Word. The encounter is really a truth encounter anyway, not a power confrontation. You get the picture!

There is some useful information that I want to pass on to you. In one deliverance, the candidate was accompanied by a mutual friend. In the midst of the process, the candidate stopped and looked to her right where our friend was sitting. Then she said, "Your praying is distracting me. Please don't do that while Don is speaking to me." I thought this was very strange. I mean, I was in the midst of binding and commanding demon powers when she abruptly asked our friend to stop praying.

This is interesting because our friend was not praying, not out loud anyway! She was praying silently in the spirit. Apparently, the demons could hear the praying, knew it was "in the spirit," and were troubled by it. Good!

Our friend told the candidate, "I have not even moved my lips and not uttered one sound."

"I can testify that this is true," I told her. "She has not said one word, since we have started."

"Oh, my goodness," she said. "I was beginning to get very angry inside, and I was thinking how could she do this at this time?"

Well, something rose up in my spirit also. It appears demons can "tune in" to our prayers, perhaps even to the point of working against our very request. But, they are frustrated at "praying in the spirit" they are not able to bear it. It is one of the spiritual weapons given to us in Ephesians 6 as we do spiritual battle.

CHAPTER 7

A CASE OF MODERN-DAY DEMON POSSESSION

I N 1976 AND 1977 NEW YORK CITY WAS TERRORIZED BY A SERIES OF satanic murders. The entire nation was in shock over the bizarre occult crimes attributed to the "Son of Sam."

David Berkowitz was arrested and plead guilty to the historic crime spree. He is locked away deep in the New York Department of Corrections. He is serving more than three hundred fifty consecutive years. The so-called Son of Sam crimes are still among the most infamous in New York history. David was not the lone gunman. Being part of a satanic cult, others were also involved in the shootings. But David was the gunman in two of the eight separate incidents.

Today, David Berkowitz is my friend. He shared his testimony with me after our meeting in 1988. This is the account of God's more-than-amazing grace reaching into the depraved, dark world of David Berkowitz, freeing him from his torment, giving him forgiveness, eternal life, and sonship in the family of God. Here are a couple of his favorite scriptures.

> I will praise you, O Lord, with all my heart.
>   I will tell of all your wonders.
> I will be glad and rejoice in you;
>   I will sing praise to your name, O Most High.
>   —Psalm 9:1–2, niv

> If the Son sets you free, you will be free indeed.
>   —John 8:36, niv

David was born out of wedlock and given up at birth, but he was adopted by loving parents. He says that as a child he was vicious and destructive. I recall him telling me how he craved the darkness as a child. He says, "Like the psalmist says in one of the above passages, I must truly thank my wonderful God for His abundant love, grace, and mercy. You see, since my childhood, I have been tormented and victimized by demons. During all of my childhood and for much of my adult life, cruel demons had control of me. But thanks be to Jesus Christ, I was able to be restored in my right mind."

David's story has been chronicled by newspapers and other media outlets since the crimes took place in the mid-seventies. However, the complete truth has yet to be written, because the complete truth is known by David alone. He says, "There was a time in my life when I was living in complete rebellion against God. I was so wicked that I was actually worshiping the devil and I was involved with Satanism. Looking back at all that has happened to me, it is no surprise that I fell into such depravity. I was demon possessed.

"Let me tell you what some of my life was like when I was just a small child. When I was little, I would often have fits in which I would roll on the floor and knock over furniture. My adopted mother (who has long since passed away) would have no control over me. I was so vicious and destructive that I often caused considerable property damage.

"When I was in public school, I was so violent and disruptive that a teacher once grabbed me in a headlock and threw me out of his classroom. I was so much trouble that my parents were ordered by the school officials to take me to a child psychologist every week. But this had no effect."

David told me that he would get so depressed that he used to hide under his bed for hours. Then at other times he would lock himself in a closet and sit in total darkness from morning until afternoon. He said, "I craved the darkness and felt an urge to flee away from people."

"A FORCE THAT WOULD DRIVE ME INTO THE DARKENED STREETS"

"Other times I would wake up in the middle of the night, sneak out of the house, and wander the streets. I recall a force that would drive me into the darkened streets, even in inclement weather, where I roamed the streets like an alley cat in the darkness.

"Sometimes at 3:00 or 4:00 in the morning I would sneak back into the house the same way I left, by climbing the fire escape. My parents would not even know that I was gone.

"I continually worried and frightened my parents because I behaved so strangely. At times I would go an entire day without talking to them. I'd walk around our apartment talking to myself. My parents knew that I lived in an imaginary world, but they could do nothing about it. From time to time I would see my parents break down and cry because they saw that I was such a tormented person."

David said growing up was a nightmare and that thoughts of suicide plagued him continually. "I was so depressed and haunted that I would also spend time sitting on the window ledge of my bedroom with my legs dangling over the side. My parents would yell at me to get in, but I seldom listened to them. I would feel such an urge to push myself out the window that my body would tremble violently. And we lived on the sixth floor!"

"I Was So Wild, Mixed Up, and Crazy That I Could Barely Hang on to My Sanity"

His adopted parents did the best they could, but David was not able to respond to their love and direction. "My mom and dad tried to bring me up as best as they could. They loved me and gave me everything that good parents would give to their only child. But I was so wild, mixed up, and crazy that I could barely hang on to my sanity. Even when I would walk down the streets there always seemed to be a force that would try to make me step in front of moving cars.

"I was overwhelmed with thoughts about dying. And I wasn't even a teenager! I had no idea what to do, and neither did my parents. They tried to raise me in the Jewish faith, but they knew nothing about Jesus, the Messiah of Israel.

"Many of the things that happened to me might shock some people. But none of this was a shock to the Lord. In His day, when our Savior walked among humanity, cases of children being victimized and *possessed* by evil spirits was very common." (See Mark 7:24–30 and 9:17–29.)

David says, "In fact, childhood possession cases still happen today. But modern psychology tends to dismiss these disturbed children and blame their problems on some type of organic brain damage, family problems, something within the child's environment, etc.

"There were a few times in my life when I was at a stage of equilibrium. I managed to finish high school even though most of the time I was truant or in trouble. I also spent three years in the army. I was honorably discharged in 1974. But even in the service I had problems."

"I FELT AS IF I WERE BEING PULLED ALONG BY A POWERFUL FORCE"

David returned from his service in the armed forces to a lonely environment. The few friends he had prior had moved away. His adopted mother had died. His father had remarried and had also moved. He was invited to a party where he met some new friends. He didn't know they were Satanists, and it didn't really matter when he found out that they were.

"In 1975 I had become heavily involved with the occult and witchcraft. Looking back I cannot even begin to explain how I had gotten involved. It seemed that one day everything magically fell into place. Books about witchcraft seemed to pop up all around me. Everywhere I looked there appeared a sign or symbol pointing me to Satan. It felt as if a mighty power was reaching out to me.

"I had no peace of mind. I felt as if I was being pulled along by a powerful force. I had no idea how to fight it, and to be honest, I didn't try to. Why? Because things just seemed to be falling into place in a supernatural way.

"To someone who has never been involved in the occult, this could be hard to understand. But for people who have been involved, they know full well what I am referring to. The power leading me could not be resisted, at least not without Jesus. But I had no relationship with the Lord Jesus at this time, and so I had no defense against the devil.

"In the Bible, Jesus said about Satan: 'He was a murderer from the beginning, not holding to the truth, for there is no truth in him. When he lies, he speaks his native language, for he is a liar and the father of lies' (John 8:44, NIV).

"Well, he certainly lied to me! During the years 1976 and 1977, I had been lied to and deceived. And as a result of listening to him, I wound up in prison with a sentence of more than three hundred fifty consecutive years. I was charged with six murders and a number of other shootings and crimes.

"When I first entered the prison system, I was placed in an isolation cell for a while. Then I had been sent to Marcy Psychiatric Center. Eventually I went to Attica and Clinton prisons, and finally ended up where I am now, at the Sullivan Correctional Facility."

David has a large scar on the left side of his throat from an attempt on his life while at Attica. "As with many inmates, life in prison has been a big struggle. I have had my share of problems and hassles. At one time I almost lost my life when another inmate cut my throat. Yet through all this God had His loving hands on me.

"Over the years I have met a number of men who had accepted Christ. Many of them tried to witness to me. But because of the extent to which the devil had me bound, it was very hard for me to truly understand the gospel. However, about 1987 I did accept Jesus as my Lord and Savior. And today I cannot thank Him enough for *all* He has done for me.

"Presently the Lord is using me to teach Bible studies in the chapel, as well as to give words of encouragement during our services. In addition, I have the authorization to work with the men whom the Department of Correctional Services has labeled "mentally disturbed" or who are slow learners. I have been able to counsel these troubled people and help them with some of their spiritual and physical needs.

"One of my favorite passages of Scripture is found in the Old Testament Book of Micah the prophet. This passage has become to me something of my love song to the Lord."

> Who is a God like you,
>> who pardons sins and forgives the transgression
>> of the remnant of his inheritance?
> You do not stay angry forever
>> but delight to show mercy.
> You will again have compassion on us;
>> you will tread our sins underfoot
>> and hurl all our iniquities into the depths of the sea.
> You will be true to Jacob,
>> and show mercy to Abraham,

as you pledged on oath to our fathers
    in days long ago.

—MICAH 7:18–20, NIV

David calls me his pastor today. In 1978, I sent David a letter because I believed then what I believe now: God can save anyone! I told David that God still loved him and that Jesus could save him. He wrote me right back. His handwritten letter was wild, and the writing was scrambled all over the page. He said, "If I get out of here, I'll kill you!" I smile today when I say, "That ended our correspondence." Ten years later I met David in the Sullivan prison. He was in the worship service. He came up to me afterward and put his arm around me. He had a big smile on his face. (I didn't know who he was.) He said, "Brother Don, I just want you to know I appreciate you being faithful all of these years, going into these dark places with the light of the gospel. I appreciate you, brother, and I appreciated the service tonight." He stuck out his hand and said, "By the way, my name's David Berkowitz."

I said, "David, are you saved?" (I could tell by looking into his eyes that he was.)

"Yes, sir," he said. "I was saved a couple of years ago up in Dannemora, New York, at the Clinton prison."

From that night, for whatever reason, David and I have become very good friends. He has given much insight into the demonic realm, as he has been on both sides.

Demon possession is very real, but it cannot happen to a believer. David's testimony is that the more he filled himself with the Word of God, the freer he became. Today, he is demon free. The tormentors now can only influence his life and thinking. He can be "oppressed," but he was lost and "possessed"!

David's message today is summed up in this, one of his favorite scriptures.

To Him who loves us and has freed us from our sins by his blood, and has made us to be a kingdom and priests to serve His God and Father—to Him be glory and power for ever and ever! Amen.

—REVELATION 1:5–6, NIV

CHAPTER 8

A KILLER IN NEW HAMPSHIRE

NOT ENOUGH BELIEVERS ARE SPIRITUALLY AWARE OF THE POWER in the name of Jesus. Few believe or understand the extent of demonic activity. Others scoff at it. But be assured, it is real! Billy Graham has also written about the reality of demonic activity and the power of the name of Jesus Christ to combat it.

In the early 1990s, I preached at a prison on the East Coast. Alan Richards was an inmate in that service. I shared the testimony of former Satanist David Berkowitz. In the service, I told of David's conversion to Jesus Christ and his deliverance from the demonic. Alan was saved in that service, as were many others. He eventually got out of prison and back into trouble and is now confined at another state prison. Alan had maintained contact with me by letter, although I did not know he had been saved in our service. About three months prior to Alan's deliverance, I began to get letters from him describing torment in his life.

He wrote that he had been deeply involved with satanic cults. He told me that he felt something inside of him that scared him. He told me of horrifying nightmares, a strong sulfur smell in his nose, and that he couldn't read his Bible or even hold conversations with believers. He was very afraid and begged me for help.

"FEAR HAS TORMENT. HE THAT FEARS IS NOT MADE PERFECT IN LOVE"

There is no fear in love; but perfect love casteth out fear: because fear hath torment. He that feareth is not made perfect in love.

—1 JOHN 4:18

Fear is one of Satan's most popular weapons. Fear has torment. God's love will drive away the fear. I knew the things Alan shared with me were real. I have heard the story many times, not just from this former Satanist. I also knew that if he was genuinely saved, he could be free. I made arrangements to go see him on a clergy visit. I knew we would need privacy, but the prison would not agree to anything other than visiting in the visitation room. However, they did grant us an attorney's booth. There was a small measure of privacy.

Shortly before I left for the visit, I received another letter from Alan. It was filled with desperation. He told me that his nightmares were getting worse and that he could not stop seeing evil images from the sacrifices he had seen. He couldn't eat or sleep, and the name of Jesus burned on his tongue. He also mentioned dreaming of a creature with three Fs on its forehead.

Let me comment that F is the sixth letter of the alphabet. The demon had 666 on his forehead. *Malachi* means "messenger of God." It appears the demons were mocking him for being a Christian and telling the gospel story.

THERE IS POWER IN THE NAME OF JESUS

I arrived at the prison around 11:00 a.m. Alan was called to the visiting room, and we began our meeting.

I asked Alan to assure me of his salvation. He told me that I preached the night he was saved. He went on to tell me how he knew that if God would forgive David Berkowitz, the so-called Son of Sam, he would surely forgive Alan Richards. At this point, I was convinced that Alan was saved. I was also convinced that he was demonized!

Demonized is actually the most scripturally accurate description of demon invasion. Possession implies ownership. Christians are owned, bought with a price, and redeemed by Jesus Christ. He came to set the captives free! The woman that had an infirmity for eighteen years was a "daughter of Abraham" yet Satan had her bound. Jesus set her free (Luke 13). Alan was bound, though he was a son of God by the new birth.

As Alan sat across the table, I listened as he told me how much weight he had lost, and he complained of feeling very sick with a headache and nausea, and his eyes were glazed. I went through several scriptures with him, determining that he had no unforgiveness in his life and that he wanted to be free. I asked him to read a statement aloud, denouncing Satan, denouncing any and all ties with the occult, and proclaiming Jesus Christ as his Lord. He could hardly get the words out, but he struggled through the statement and had said to Satan and his demons, "You are not welcome in my life, and I am seeking to be free through Jesus Christ."

A DEMON IDENTIFIES HIMSELF

I began by binding all demon powers whether in him, attached to him, floating in free circulation or in any way connected with his life, in the name of Jesus Christ. I called the demons to attention and forbade them from hiding, leaving, calling others to help, or harming Alan in any way—always in the name of Jesus Christ. I commanded them to be obedient and to speak to me as directed. Alan began to tremble and lapsed into a sort of semiconsciousness. His eyes looked down and away from me as I spoke. With his hand, he spelled out a name. I asked if this was the name of a demon present in Alan. His voice began to mumble and eventually the demon spoke with harshness: "I am here!"

I asked the demon if there were other demon powers present. "No," he said. But I knew better. They are all liars and the truth is not in them. I knew he had brought other demons with him. I put him under oath and asked if that would stand as truth before Jehovah God? After a while, he spoke and answered no. After repeated questioning and demanding truth, I discovered he had five prince demons with him. (A prince is the "boss" of a kingdom, and each kingdom can be made up of many other less-powerful demons.) I asked the demon how he gained access. There was silence. I insisted, "Answer me in the name of Jesus Christ!" An abrupt response was, "I came in through hatred."

SEVERE AND REPEATED BEATINGS

Again I bound the demons to attention in Jesus's name, and I said, "Alan, I'm talking to you now." He looked up, and I asked him what happened during this time that hatred came in. He looked puzzled, but as he thought, he said, "I did something really awful to get into the cult. This is what they told me to do to become a member."

I asked if this event caused the hatred.

"No."

I said, "This demon says he came in through hatred. When did the hatred start?"

Alan told me that as a result of what he did to get into this cult he was sentenced to juvenile centers until he was twenty-one. He told of severe and repeated beatings by the officials. "I hated them," he said. "I hated them."

Once again I called the demon to attention and told him he was going to have to go in the name of Jesus. "No," he said. I began to cast this demon and his demon powers to the abyss. Alan placed the palms of his hands on his temples and began to writhe in pain and anguish. Fluids ran from his mouth, and his head tilted back with a few coughs as the demons left. I knew there were others. I called the demons again to attention and commanded their obedience in the name of Jesus Christ.

I asked for the name of other demons. There were several more who gave me their names, and each one had other demon powers with them. They all came out in similar fashion. Between each one leaving, Alan would tell me he was sick and didn't know if he could continue. The last demon was the most difficult. He claimed to be Satan. When he gave me the name, I said, "No, you're not Satan. I know you're not. You are a liar. I command you to give me your name in the name of Jesus Christ."

"I am he," the demon insisted.

"No, you are not Satan. Who are you?"

He blurted out angrily, "I am he, and I am too powerful for you!" Alan began to clinch his fists, and his face contorted somewhat.

"You are not too powerful for Jesus, and you will be obedient to His name. You will come out of him."

Still in an angry voice, "No, he is mine. He wants me here. I give him strength to fight. He is mine."

Again, I bound that demon to attention and spoke to Alan. He looked up and listened. "Alan, this demon says you want him here, is that right?" I asked.

He looked stunned. "No sir, I don't."

I told him that this demon said that Alan wanted him because he helped him to fight.

Alan confessed to his need to have the demon in his life to help him fight. I told him to confess that he did not want this vile demon. He said, somewhat weakly, "No, I don't want him, and he is not welcome in my life."

"YOU WILL COME OUT OF HIM NOW IN THE NAME OF JESUS CHRIST!"

I called the demon back to attention. "You are not wanted, and you will go in Jesus's name." He began to speak in another language—"tongues"—in a very threatening voice. Alan again was clinching his fists and looking angry.

I said, "In the name of Jesus Christ, stop speaking in tongues."

Immediately the voice stopped.

I said, "You will gather up all of your demon powers. You will leave no residue of your works. You will not harm him or anyone in the room. You will go immediately and directly to the pit, to the abyss, and you will go there now!"

Now the voice changed to a screech. "No, No!"

I kept the pressure on this evil spirit, "You will come out of him NOW, in the name of Jesus Christ."

Alan grabbed his heart and slumped over, then he arched back as fluids ran from his mouth and nose. After a few seconds, he straightened up in his chair and looked at me. His eyes were clear. I took his hands into mine; they were blood warm. I asked how he felt.

"I feel great!"

"You're not sick anymore?" I asked.

With a big smile, he said, "I have never felt so good." He was free. In the name of Jesus Christ, he was free.

Now, it is important to note that this is an exception to the many deliverances I have facilitated. Most are "regular" people like you and me. They have not committed violent crimes, and the only prison they have experienced is the bondage to Satan. Believers' bondage generally has more to do with what has happened to them than the things they have done wrong.

CHAPTER 9

A WEEKEND OF DELIVERANCES

M OST OF THE DELIVERANCE SESSIONS I HAVE ARE NOT MUCH more than discussion, prayer, and commanding evil spirits to go. It is low key and orderly. It is likely not what you think it is. There is no holding people down or yelling at the demons. Often this is an indication that the deliverance minister is not anointed or does not understand the process. I have shared a couple of exceptions, and I want to relate one more. The story is about a lady who is now an intercessor for our ministry and for me.

Jessica was a grocery store cashier. I had never met her until our appointment for deliverance. I drove to the city where she lived to meet with seven or eight other individuals who had requested a meeting for prayer and deliverance. I had not planned on meeting with Jessica. The lady who had invited me asked if I could possibly squeeze in one more. I decided to stay an extra night. Jessica and her husband, Chris, were to meet with me at 5:00 p.m. Several hours and many tears later, they were leaving and Jessica was free. But let me start from the beginning.

The session began, as always, with a brief discussion and then prayer asking the Holy Spirit to lead us to every area of bondage, acknowledging His presence and our inability to do anything without His assistance. Jessica was an attractive lady with a very pleasant personality. Her husband was quiet and very supportive. I had no idea how deep-rooted her bondage was. Tears came to my eyes as she began to share some of the possible areas for demonic strongholds.

She Was Familiar With Deliverance

One of the first things Jessica shared with me, as the three of us huddled around the typical little motel room table, was that she was familiar with deliverance and had been through one several years ago. I asked her a little about it, and she told me that she came under heavy attack from demons just a day or two after her previous deliverance. She offered that maybe the deliverance minister was not really qualified. I knew she had not received complete freedom when she told me a little more about it. It is fairly common that when demons remain, they often manifest as though they are angry about part of their kingdom being destroyed. It can be like stirring a hornets' nest.

She had experienced a measure of freedom, but still tormentors remained and had doubtless brought in others in the time since her first experience. I explained that we would just talk and search for some obvious areas or doorways for the enemy. I explained that she need not go into any detail about anything, but she said, "I've already shared it all many times with psychiatrists and psychologists..." Uh oh! I knew we would be dealing with some mental anguish tormenters.

I took out a note pad and began to take notes as we talked. I asked her about generational possibilities. She mentioned that both of her parents were alcoholics and that her father was involved in Freemasonry. Her mother was a nonpracticing Mormon. She said her parents fought all the time and were very angry people. "I never felt loved by either of them, though I'm sure they did love me." During the deliverance, she curled up on the floor in a fetal position and cried for her mother to hold her. She cried like a child needing her mom so desperately.

I Cried Too, Along With Her Husband

Her mother is now deceased, and Jessica said, "I don't ever recall being hugged by my mother." How sad! She told me that she had suffered many abuses from a past boyfriend. She eventually was admitted to a mental institution and was having so many psychological problems she could not take care of her everyday responsibilities. This was a horrible time in her life, she said.

I asked her about sexual abuse and other abuses that are often doorways for the enemy. She told me she was abused in all kinds of ways imaginable by everyone in her life—from relatives and counselors to school teachers and business associates. This was all very painful for her. We moved on to other possible areas, such as occult involvement. She had used the Ouija board earlier in life and may have been at some slumber parties where levitation games were played and horror stories were told. Also, she had seen many scary movies. She said she had been frightened as long as she could remember and that she was terribly insecure.

A History of Medical Problems

Jessica had a history of medical problems. She had been diagnosed with bipolar disorder and had been on antidepressants and mood-altering medication for many years. She also had experienced several major surgeries. She had constant back pain and chronic fatigue syndrome. She also told me that she had never been "diagnosed" but always felt she had a learning disability and that she could not retain much of what she read, especially the Bible. "I often feel very confused, and I struggle with decisions." I have heard this so many times prior to deliverances.

Well, there were obviously many opportunities for the demons to gain access to her life. She still had some anger, bitterness, and resentment toward all those who abused her throughout her life. But she said she could release that and confess it as sin. She also had unforgiveness for her first husband.

It was time to begin, and we prayed together affirming our salvation and then repenting of unforgiveness, anger, bitterness, hatred, resentment, and kindred sins. We also affirmed together that we received the full work of the cross, breaking the power of all curse and canceling the right of any demonic power to her life. Her husband prayed this along with us.

I explained that I would be binding evil spirits in the name of the Lord Jesus Christ and commanding them to be obedient in His name. I told her it might help if she closed her eyes so she would not be distracted. "Tell me what you feel, hear, or see when I am commanding the spirits."

She was already feeling nausea and trembling, she said.

I discovered a very powerful demon who made Jessica incredibly fearful, and I suspected that this demon spirit came in through Jessica watching scary movies. Very rarely does a person become somnambulistic (in a trancelike state where the demon speaks through them) during deliverance, but it does occur. The person will actually be unaware of what is taking place, and the demons will speak through his or her voice. This was not the case here. Jessica was in full control of her faculties, and as I bound the evil spirits in Jesus Christ's name, she dropped her head and closed her eyes.

I asked her to tell me what thoughts came to her mind, words or names, what she saw or felt as I commanded spirits to respond. She told me she was feeling very hot and had some tightness in her chest. She also mentioned tingling in her arms. I commanded, always in the name of the Lord Jesus Christ, that the "prince" demon, the boss, the demon power in charge, come forward and identify himself. Immediately she named the prince demon. I recognized the name right away. I run into this spirit quite often; there must be a million that carry that identity. This spirit boasted that there were too many for me to handle. The demon spoke through her, "You are too weary, and you will have to stop and rest. You will not be able to cast me out." This was a ploy to make Jessica believe she was being selfish by taking my time and energy, or that we would not be successful. I was tired, but I had no doubts about being successful because it has nothing to do with my strength!

The demon revealed his function and purposes in Jessica's life to be confusion, disorder, and death. One by one, we began to tear his kingdom down. This spirit was there by consent of the abuse she suffered as a child. Then a spirit who identified his function as confusion surfaced, and his work was to keep her unstable. There was also a spirit linked with this one with an assignment of instability and insecurity.

An interesting revelation was a spirit whose function was sexual abuse, not causing her to abuse others, but somehow it invited sexual abuse from others. I began to ponder the spirit. Was it seductive, deceptive, a coconspirator in murder? I had encountered this spirit before.

Another spirit identified itself whose function was denial. This spirit also came from humiliation as a child. A spirit identifying his function as dishonor came in through one of her cosmetic surgeries. This spirit often has a doorway of a "reprobate mind," according to Romans 1:24, choosing to "dishonour their own bodies." This falls in the same category as body piercing or tattoos. It is sometimes revealed as a demon spirit functioning in vanity.

Jessica said she wanted to move to the floor. So she left her chair and knelt on the floor, at times with her hands to the floor and her head down; other times, her body erect, but head tilted down and eyes closed. She raised her head and said, "I am so negative in my thinking and speech. There surely must be something there." Her mother was very negative and doubtful. She was right; there was a spirit there by permission of a generational curse from her mother and grandmother whose function was negativity.

Deliverance is so amazing. The Holy Spirit so wonderfully brings truth to us and forces the demons to react in obedience to commands in the authority of the Lord Jesus Christ. With each release, Jessica had deep sighs as the demons left and went to the pit of hell as commanded. Toward the end of this wonderful night, I commanded one of the remaining boastful demons to tell me where his master was. There was a weak response, "He's in the pit." That is exactly where he had been commanded to go earlier!

There were also spirits there by permission of her involvement with the Ouija board, and she had three separate spirits who identified their work as discord. Bitterness and unbelief demons had significant strongholds in her life. The bitterness was for her mom, and the evil spirit was there by that permission. This one refused to go, stating it had God's permission to be there. I told her this spirit would not leave until she forgave her mom and repented of the unforgiveness and bitterness. I asked her to confess this aloud. She did not hesitate but did break down during the prayer, saying, "O God, You know how much I needed her love and her approval."

She had been released of many spirits already, but still there were some that had to go. Once she confessed forgiveness of the bitterness toward her deceased mom, the stronghold was broken. The spirit of bitterness was eating away her joy and robbing her of the fruit of the Spirit. When this spirit was commanded to leave, there was some resistance, but it did not last long. She coughed and had several deep sighs. You could see her back and neck writhe a bit as the spirit released her. Then she settled back and fanned herself with her hands as though she was hot.

She felt there were still some there; I knew that also! We talked for a moment. She expressed how much resentment she had toward her mother. "She never hugged me. She never told me that she loved me. She was never there for me. I needed her so much!" She started to cry. "I need her now."

We dealt with resentment, and she knelt with her head buried in her hands as she confessed resentment and unforgiveness for her deceased mother. After she had completed this task, I bound spirits that were there by that permission and commanded them to come under the authority of the Lord Jesus Christ. As I did, she fell to the floor on her right side and began to weep. She curled into a fetal position and cried for her mother. "I need my mother. I need my mother." Both her husband and I were fighting tears as she lay like a small child and the demons tormented her. I commanded them to stop their work and to leave her immediately and go directly to the pit of hell. She screamed as the demons came out of her. She coughed and released them with deep sighs.

I wondered if her screams could be heard in the adjoining rooms of the motel. They were loud and high pitched, as if she were being harmed. But the most demonstrative release was still to come. Again, we talked, and though she was now somewhat calm, I knew the one spirit we had not dealt with might well be the prince or the most powerful of all. The spirit of rejection was a powerful spirit in her life.

Blood-Curdling Screams

Fear is a common spirit; there can be one or many. As soon as I mentioned fear, she began to tremble and her eyes began to twitch. Fear of "so many things." Failure, sickness, death, rejection, condemnation…this demon had been given much permission in her life. When I began to bind this spirit, she fell backward from her kneeling position and sat up with her legs extended forward on the floor. She look horrified! She was actually "seeing" this spirit. She scooted backward trying to retreat from what she was seeing until she was up against the bed. "It's so ugly. It's so evil. Oh, oh! OH!" Then she screamed one of those blood-curdling screams, "No, no, it's Charles…No, no!" I looked at her husband for some help. He said, "Charles is a man who Jessica works with. He'd been in the hospital for a long time, but he died a few days ago. She was visiting with him when he died."

It was *not*, however, the spirit of Charles. His spirit was somewhere in eternity, present with God or forever separated from God. Likely, it was the fear demons tormenting her. However, when someone dies, if they had evil spirits, those spirits go somewhere. The spirits no longer have a home when death comes. It is certainly true that evil spirits would be seeking a new home. Jessica did have open doors. This was a very unusual situation as she continued to scream. I was thinking maybe her husband should go to the front desk and explain just in case anyone was calling, but the Holy Spirit was in charge, and nothing came from her screams.

She looked frantically around the room for help. She was still saying, "No, no! Oh, it is so evil." She then crawled toward me as if she was escaping from something and grabbed hold of my leg, a powerful grip. She held on to me as though she felt something might pry her loose. She trembled. Actually, it was more than a tremble. Her whole body shook, almost out of control. I placed my hand on her shoulder and commanded the spirits to stop their torment.

"Oh, they are going to kill me. They're going to kill me!"

"No they are not going to do anything but come out of you. That's all they are going to do," I assured her.

Before I could assure her more, she cried, "They are going to kill my kids. Oh, no, they are going to kill my kids!"

I laid both hands on her head and commanded the spirits to leave her instantly.

"Oh, oh . . ." she said as she coughed. Softer words came each time she spoke, until she sighed deeply and said, "Oh, they are gone. They are gone!" She slumped forward, released my leg, and looked into my eyes. It was over. She was free. She leaned over toward her husband who had tears in his eyes. He gave her a big hug.

It was getting late. We had been in warfare for several hours. As we hugged and talked briefly, I was looking into different eyes than when they arrived. There was clarity, and there was peace and joy in her countenance. Another victory. Another captive set free by the power of the name of Jesus Christ.

I was so spiritually charged I thought I would never go to sleep. Spiritual adrenaline still was flowing. I was so tired, but I was filled with Holy Spirit excitement. Not only was I able to see the delivering power of the Holy Spirit at work, but I also had two new friends and two new intercessors. I am always seeking intercessors. Jessica has a new job now, and she often comes to the church when I am in her city to intercede as I lead people through deliverance. Again, I give Him praise and glory.

Interesting Weekend

Since 1999, I have been driving to different cities to meet with people who have requested deliverance. A friend of mine, who has also gone through deliverance, makes appointments for me. When I arrive, there is always a waiting list of ten to fifteen people who want to come. This is not something I tried to make happen. It has happened because one man experienced genuine freedom from the tormentors, and he told others, and…well, it doesn't appear to have an end.

It works like the salvation experience is supposed to work. One gets saved and tells another. Andrew finds the Savior and goes after his brother so that he may know Jesus also. When folks go through deliverance, and they find genuine freedom from the tormentors, they want others to know that freedom also.

I suppose I could report to you about any of those meetings that take place, but I want to share about one unusual weekend. It seemed that most all of the deliverance sessions were very visual in that the person being ministered to was able to "see" it take place and describe it vividly to me.

The first was a lady who had been in all kinds of trouble, more than I can tell in this book. She was, of course, from a dysfunctional family, ran away from home many times, and wound up in prostitution and drug addiction while still in her teens. She had been married a few times; dabbled in sexual perversion, sorcery, witchcraft, and white magic; had tattoos; and her ex-husband had a sex change. Does this give you an idea of her bondage? Wow! She was saved but, of course, in much bondage. Her pastor was there with her, and we met in the church where she was a member. After gathering some of the information from the lady, I could see there was going to be a battle. I leaned over to the pastor with a smile and said, "Thanks, pastor. Thanks a lot." The three of us all smiled and then went into a season of prayer.

What a powerful session it was. As the demons were bound and put under the authority of Jesus Christ, she was able to "see" the battle that was taking place. She reported, as her eyes were closed and her face in her hands, that she could see what looked like a cavern with stalagmites and stalactites and a precipice where there was nothing but darkness like a bottomless pit if you went over the edge.

One by one, the demons were identified and commanded to go to the pit. She described them hesitantly going to the edge and then plunging over into the darkness. The prince demon, or the "boss," she described as a large black, sort of prehistoric bird-looking creature. He went to the edge but dug the claws on his feet into the edge and sort of teetered there, refusing to leave. She said she could see a chain holding him and allowing him not to fall in. She said it looked like other smaller demons were holding on to the chain that kept him from falling.

Unforgiveness Gave Them Strength

At this point I asked her if she had any unforgiveness or bitterness in her life. She confessed that she did. I explained that this was permission for demons to stay and that she must forgive to be free. She bowed her head and prayed aloud, forgiving a sister-in-law. Then, I again commanded the demon to go to the pit of hell. She said the chain was broken, but still he clung with his feet. Then she said two angels came. One pried the claws loose, and the other swung with a big sword and knocked the demon over the edge. She then said, "The room is empty. The hordes of demons who were there are now gone. There is nothing but light shining in the room of the cavern."

Pretty amazing, huh? I didn't make anything up. There were two or three others that were very similar in the way they described what they were "seeing" as the deliverance took place. I must say, this was the most revealing weekend I have ever experienced. Many people I ministered to that weekend were able to give pictorial descriptions of the battle that was taking place. Amazing!

One man described seeing virtually the same thing, but it was a large room full of demons. He said, "As you bind particular ones, they start packing their bags, like suitcases, and they linger for a while. When you tell them to leave immediately, they hurry out the door. When you command them to not leave anything behind, to gather up all of their work and go directly to the pit, they look very sad, and they scurry around picking up papers and stuffing them in their bags as they hurriedly leave."

One lady who was having trouble with the spirit of fear said, "He's not going. He just stands there and is looking at me with this horrible looking, terrifying face."

I commanded the demon spirit to confess to her that she had authority over him in Jesus Christ's name.

"Defiantly," she said, "he says you [Don] have authority over him, but I don't."

Again he refused to confess that she had authority. She was crying.

I then said, "I loose the holy angels of God to torment you until you confess her authority over you."

Her face changed and she smiled, "I see two very large angels, and they are choking the demon. He is struggling, but he is still uttering, 'No, no, I won't say it.'" Then she related, the ugly creature said "OK, OK, she has authority over me in Jesus Christ's name."

As I then commanded the spirit to the pit of hell, she said the two large angels hurled him into darkness.

I heard reports like this for days! I was charged up to say the least. What insight the Holy Spirit gave me during these deliverance sessions.

A high school student came for deliverance. He was an unusually mature Christian for his age. He was preparing for college. Ray had experienced some "unusual" situations throughout his young life.

He told me of strange dreams he had as a child. "I remember dreaming about goats' heads many times when I was very young," he said. "I didn't know anything about demonic stuff then, but I do recall them as very scary dreams. I have always felt like there were supernatural things going on in my life. Almost like there was a battle going on concerning me. Do you know what I mean?" I did know what he meant. I had many people tell me something similar.

I had taken this young man through deliverance about a year ago when he lived in another state. I had traveled to meet with his family, and all of them went though the deliverance process. He was freed of many troubling spirits then, but he was still having some problems, so he decided to meet with me again. The Holy Spirit had shown him there was still something troubling him.

I really like this young man, and I expect he will someday be a successful businessman. He is very smart. Like always, we talked about possible consent or permission that demons might have. We talked about unforgiveness, bitterness, resentment, and similar doorways. We determined there were no open doors and had prayer. I then bound evil spirits according to the Word of God and commanded that every spirit be obedient. In the name of Jesus Christ, I commanded the highest ranking demon to identify himself to Ray and to make it very clear.

You could sense the stirring in Ray. He appeared to be very uncomfortable, and his brow was furrowed. He said, "Fear. It is *fear*." He had been previously released from the spirit of fear. I commanded the spirit, "Have you been commanded to leave him before?"

"No," was the response. It turns out that this spirit was not in him but attached to him. The spirit of fear that was cast out before was *in him*; this one was *attached* to him. He could "see" the spirit, and it was an octopus spirit with tentacles attached to various parts of his body.

There were spirits on the inside that identified their functions as envy and lust. They were bound, commanded to leave, and they did.

"There is something still here," said Ray. Again we probed, and a spirit came forth. He was a spirit of distraction and confusion. This spirit claimed to be on assignment from a territorial spirit named Ma Ha Bone. I had encountered this spirit many times. He is a high-ranking spirit over demon spirits who have ancestral Freemasonry as their permission. Ray said, "I keep hearing, *Ma Ha, Ma Ha*." I knew what was happening. This spirit was calling for help.

Ma Ha Bone showed up, and Ray said, "It's like he put a wall around these spirits." I recognized the presence of this spirit by saying that I respected his high rank but that I had authority in this situation and that Ray had authority in Jesus's name. I reminded this spirit that the permission of generational curse had been canceled and told him to confess that he no longer had any right to Ray's life.

Immediately, Ray reported, "He said he confessed that he did not have any permission to my life."

The Ma Ha Bone spirit departed, and I continued to deal with the other spirit. He was there by permission of an ancestral curse and claimed to have been in the family for many generations, having gained entrance through Druid worship. Interesting.

There were four other spirits in this kingdom that were present by permission of Freemasonry in his ancestry. One demon claimed to be responsible for betrayal and persecution, something Ray had struggled with for several years. There was a spirit that claimed his function was "removing him from where God wanted him to be and putting him in a different place." This spirit said he was to "rob his destiny." He had failed. God's Holy Spirit was leading us and revealing information so that Ray could be free.

Next a spirit claimed to function as *need*. This was a spirit of poverty, and I sensed the Holy Spirit was showing me it was also attached to his father. I commanded the spirit to reveal if he was also in the father. Ray said, "I can see this snake; part of it is in me, and part of it is in my father." In the name of Jesus Christ I commanded the spirit to become one spirit and go directly into the abyss. Ray said, "He's dead. An angel with a big sword just chopped his head off. He's dead!"

That left the final spirit. Ray said, "He's not in me. He is over me like an umbrella but attached to my body."

This was a hovering spirit. I commanded it to reveal its assignment in Ray's life.

"To hide him, to steal recognition," was the demon's response.

Ray said, "It's like people who are around me can see me if they are close, and on my level they can see under the covering, but other people can't see me. My face is hidden to them."

I commanded this spirit to, "like a magnet," attach any work of darkness to itself and to release Ray immediately and go into the abyss.

Ray said, "Wow! When you said to gather everything like a magnet, I could feel all kinds of stuff in my midsection moving to one point and then leave me. Wow!" he said. "This is wild."

Yeah, it is. It is also exciting to see God's hand at work and to experience the authority that has been given us by the Lord Jesus.

There are hundreds of such stories! Pretty awesome, huh!

CHAPTER 10

THE POWER OF THE TONGUE

CONNIE IS A WONDERFUL CHRISTIAN WOMAN WHO IS WELL-respected and serves her church tirelessly. She is Spirit-filled and solid in her walk with the Lord. However, this has come through overcoming much adversity in her life. Hers, however, is another story. This one is about her daughter, Rebecca. Connie has brought several people to me who were in need of deliverance. This day she brought her thirty-year-old daughter.

Rebecca was a recovering alcoholic about to come out of a treatment program. She had quite a story to tell about her bondage, bondage not to heroin, but to Satan and his demonic kingdom. She was saved when she was a girl and has clear memories of her salvation experience but has known torment most all of her life. It started right at her birth, through no fault of her own or her parents.

When someone comes to me seeking freedom from the tormentors, the format is much the same. I do my best to make them feel comfortable and see that the event is not threatening or intimidating. I have witnessed the deliverance, firsthand, of more than twenty-five thousand believers. There is much false teaching about this subject, but worse than that there is little scriptural teaching. There is plenty of truth in the Scriptures about the demonic but very little taught in our churches. I am puzzled by this. Most have a conception of demons that was birthed in Hollywood that is not anywhere close to what the Scriptures teach. There is mystique and fear whenever the subject is mentioned. If you want to be a conversation-buster, just mention demons. It won't be long until you are left all alone. Getting people beyond the false concepts of the works of darkness is one of the first works of the deliverance process.

"Apart From You I Can Do Nothing"

Rebecca and her mom did not fall in this category. Both were very aware of the scriptural teachings, so we started with a prayer something like this:

> *Father, thank You for Jesus and for our salvation. Thank You for this moment that we believe to be ordained of You. We recognize and acknowledge the presence of Your Holy Spirit, and we seek His guidance as we seek to break the bondage and free Rebecca from the tormentors. I am ever aware that apart from You, I can do nothing! Give us clear direction, and we receive anointing for this moment. We claim her complete freedom in Jesus's name. Amen.*

I got a notepad and said, "Let's begin with some discussion about possible doorways that may have given demon spirits access to your life. Mom, you help also. Possible generational curses, spoken curses, traumas, and so on."

We discovered that there was involvement in Freemasonry from both sets of grandparents and some adulterous acts in her ancestry. There was a lot of depression on one side of her family and anger and alcohol on the other. One of her grandfathers was a very violent man. One of her favorite relatives had severe depression and had many suicide attempts before succeeding. There were several possibilities that spirits would be there from the permission of generational curse. I noted this, and we continued our discussion.

"They Feared That I Might Bleed to Death"

Her mom told of her birth and some difficult and painful moments. "They thought I might die when she was born. There were some complications, and they feared I might bleed to death. My blood type is rare, and none was available at the hospital. It was a very traumatic time. Nurses took my newborn child to my husband and asked if he wanted to hold the infant. He was so upset about my condition he said, 'Not now!'" This seemed to be a pretty normal response from a concerned husband, but in this case, it was a doorway for the spirit of rejection. It is amazing and absolutely incredible the power of our words and actions. Demons jumped at this opportunity.

Obviously, Connie survived. Blood was found at another hospital, rushed to her, and she was eventually OK. Both parents had looked back on that moment and wondered if maybe a spirit of rejection could have come to the child through that trauma. The Holy Spirit had already revealed this to them and they had dealt with it, but the spirit of rejection was still there. Rebecca said, "My father has told me about the situation and asked my forgiveness, and I have forgiven him…but you know I never really felt loved by my father, even though I know he loves me very much."

I asked about any incidents when she was a child that she remembered as embarrassing or humiliating—sexual abuse by friends or words of condemnation, ridicule, and so on. Again, traumatic situations tend to be doorways for demonic entry. However unimportant it may seem to others, the event to us may be frightful enough to cause an opening in our life to receive a spirit from the enemy.

SEVERAL KIDS WERE MAKING FUN OF HER

Her mother told me she had always had stomach problems, very bad colic as a baby, and problems ever since. Rebecca had several situations she recalled as being traumatic. One occurred when she was in grade school. Several kids were making fun of her, and she ran and hid inside some tires on the playground that the children would crawl through. She said, "I remember hiding in there and them throwing sand in on me and laughing at me. They mocked me and made fun of me. I felt horrible." Later, we would find that a spirit of weakness came into her through that incident.

When in junior high school, about seventh grade, she said, "I lost all of my friends. This girl's boyfriend started calling me, and she got very jealous. She was one of the most popular girls in the school, and she was able to turn all of the kids against me. I became an outcast and was not allowed to socialize with any of them. That too was a horrible feeling." More spirits of rejection would come from this. She said, "I just felt worthless, and it was about this time that I became very shy. Maybe it was the fear of more rejection. I don't know." Her mother agreed.

By the time she was in ninth grade, she had a new set of friends. "I was finally accepted by others," she said. "But for whatever reason, I still felt rejected. It was then that I first experimented with alcohol."

Rebecca told me that she felt enormous guilt during this time in her life, because she knew better and knew she was disappointing her parents. She said that she was very lonely and depressed and even became suicidal with lots of anxiety and panic attacks.

She described a burning type of pressure on both sides of her back. The pain was there even as she arrived at our meeting place that day. I have heard this story many times: people getting sick or feeling fear prior to them arriving for deliverance. The demons know!

I AM DARKNESS

I asked if she ever had nightmares or felt a fearful presence in the room. "Yes! Once I awakened and felt, actually saw, this black mist hovering over me, and I asked, 'Who are you?' It replied, 'I am darkness...'" This was very frightening. When my favorite relative died, I started having feelings that I was going to lose my mind. They were very strong. [A demon of insanity tormented this relative and doubtless had left her at death and came to Rebecca.] I started being tormented to a greater degree since the night of my aunt's funeral.

"Once while sleeping in the guest bedroom where she often slept," Rebecca continued, "I actually saw a figure standing in the doorway, like a mist. It even moved to the staircase before disappearing. I was terrified."

"In a moment," I said, "we will pray a prayer repenting of things that could give permission to demons to remain. We will cancel their consent to be there. We will break their power and void their rights to your life." I told her she may very well begin to feel the evilness of their presence. She told me that she already did.

I have found that stirring in the midsection, nausea, headaches, temperature change, eyes fluttering, heart racing, burning, intense confusion, numbness or tingling, back and neck pain, tension, and so many different symptoms can occur once the demons are aware that their times is short. I reminded her of this and assured her they would not harm her but were merely grabbing hold. I encouraged her to not be alarmed and that she may begin to have some very unusual thoughts.

"They Hate You"

I have had people tell me, "Oh, I hear them screaming." "They hate you. They are saying some horrible things about you." "I hear them saying you don't know what you are doing, and I am only going to be embarrassed by coming here." "He doesn't have the power to make us leave." "Your child has just been hurt and needs you." So much garbage from their filthy mouths.

I explained to Rebecca the way in which demons generally come out of a person. "Most often you will feel them come right up out of your midsection and out on your breath. You may feel the need to belch, burp, cough, or you may even feel like you are going to throw up. Just release them. Sometimes the release is very simple and without any drama." I asked her to practice with a deep sigh. This would be helpful when the demons were coming out of her.

"Before we pray," I said, "let me ask you to tell me whatever you hear, see, or feel during the session. It will help me in the process. The Holy Spirit will give us discernment, and the demons will reveal enough for us to get them all. Don't be alarmed. They will not hurt you, and they will not leave you and go to anyone else. They will do as they are commanded because they are subject to the name of the Lord Jesus Christ.

"Now let's all three pray this prayer. Pray it after me. You can reword it if you like," I told her, "but the truth of what we pray is going to break strongholds. Say it after me out loud. We are confessing according to 1 John 1:9, and we are receiving forgiveness and cleansing."

Father, thank You for Jesus. I thank You for my salvation. You are the Savior, and I am the sinner. Thank You for receiving me into Your family by grace and through faith. I am Your child, and I qualify for freedom. Because You have forgiven me, I choose to forgive others. Everyone who has hurt me, lied to me, or disappointed me, I forgive. I repent of unforgiveness; I know it is sin. I put it under the blood of Jesus. I repent of anger, bitterness, hatred, rebellion, resentment and revenge, envy, jealousy and strife, lust, witchcraft, idolatry, and all the works of the flesh. I put it all under the blood of Jesus, and by doing so I break Satan's power and legal rights to my life. I break the power of generational curses and deny permission of any demon spirit to my life. I repent of and denounce any contract I made with Satan; since he is a liar, no contract is binding. By the blood of Jesus I free myself from any pact with the devil. I renounce all unholy oaths, vows, pledges, and ceremonies. I denounce and confess as sin all unholy soul ties, for Jesus is my Savior AND Lord. He is my deliverer and my healer, and He broke the power of curse! I choose to be free, and I will be free by the resurrection power of Jesus Christ according to His holy Word and in the authority of His name. Amen.

SHE SLUMPED FORWARD IN HER CHAIR

I then informed Rebecca that I was going to do as Scripture said to do: "I am going to bind the strongman, and we are going to get your stuff back and have a clean house. You just be honest and desire to be free. [For thirty years, this young woman had known torment from the enemy.] I am going to command the prince demon, the head guy, to come forward. You just tell me what you hear, see, or feel." As I began to bind evil spirits, she slumped forward in her chair and knelt on the floor in front of me, head bowed and eyes closed.

"I now speak to the prince demon, and I command you to come forward and reveal yourself to Rebecca now."

Immediately, Rebecca gave me a name.

I commanded that the demon reveal the names of the other prince demons. Again Rebecca gave me names instantly. We would find out later that one who identified himself as Jake was not a prince.

I commanded the spirit identifying himself as the prince and asked him to reveal his function. The immediate response was "kill." Well, that is the purpose of Satan, according to Jesus—rob, kill, steal, and destroy. He also revealed under examination that he was a multifunction demon and was responsible for rejection, addiction, and fear. He was also a gatekeeper demon.

This demon revealed that he came in by legal consent of a generational curse, likely from the violent grandfather. Since all demons are liars, it is often difficult to get truth from them. I have learned that no demon will lie to Jehovah God. While they would lie to me or you all day long,

I have found you can get truth by keeping them under oath in Jesus's name. While they continue to be very deceptive, I always remind myself that deliverance is a truth encounter, not a power encounter. It is the name of Jesus Christ that invokes fear in them. The presence of God's Holy Spirit and His holy angels enforce commands given. Commands given must always be based upon truth as defined in God's Word.

We found there were spirits there through permission of a generational curse from ancestral involvement with Freemasonry—a bloodless, Christ-less organization, a cult in its purist definition, with oaths and pledges that deny the deity of Christ!

"Depression, Depression, Depression"

I commanded one of the spirits who had identified himself to come forward and reveal his functions. Immediately Rebecca began to repeat, "Depression, depression, depression." We would also find that this demonic entity was a multifunctional spirit that was also there by permission of a generational curse.

He was building a kingdom of destruction in Rebecca's life. This demon claimed responsibility for not only depression but also headaches, sickness, panic, blindness, control, doubt, worry, fear, and death. But depression was this demon's primary focus and function.

Now the third evil spirit who claimed to be a prince demon identified himself as Rebecca. I have found that it is not uncommon for a spirit to take the name of the person he inhabits. It appears that this spirit came in through her relative's death and was likely a spirit that tortured her disturbed relative. Rebecca suffered many of the same things her relative suffered before she died.

Whenever someone dies, in whom spirits dwelt, the spirits are now without a body. Clearly, they prefer a body, a living organism. They had rather go into pigs than be cast out and commanded to the deep. (See Mark 5:1–22.) Rebecca had said that the night of this family member's funeral, she started having terrifying thoughts. She felt as if she would someday lose her mind. She thought she was going crazy. This "family" spirit found its way to Rebecca. Tormenting spirits left this relative and came to torment someone familiar.

This prince demon, Rebecca, claimed responsibility for anxiety, pain, allergies, and insanity. Rebecca had been a victim of all of these since her relative's death. These spirits were quickly dispelled and sent on their way. There was little resistance as they came out on her breath. There was some slight body convulsion and tremors as they came out with deep sighs. With each release, her body became less and less tense.

Three princes—head, lead, or chief demons—had been exposed, and two had been commanded to leave taking all of their works with them. Only one remained. I had learned that the demons are deceptive enough to sometimes make you believe a response is a yes or no by saying something other than a direct answer. I had seen many times when the prince demon of all others would send some spirit forth to act as prince while the real "head guy" would hide behind something yet unexposed. That seemed to be the case with this last prince demon. There was also one more spirit who had identified himself as Jake but was not a prince. Interesting. Rebecca thought for a moment as I asked her if the name Jake meant anything to her. She had a somewhat puzzled look when she revealed that Jake was an older guy who would buy alcohol for her and her friends because they were underage!

Her Decision to Purchase Alcohol

I commanded the spirit to reveal how he gained access to Rebecca, and the spirit confirmed what we now suspected. He came in through Rebecca's decision to purchase alcohol. This spirit was responsible for unbelief, resentment, and rebellion. These spirits left on Rebecca's breath when they were commanded to and with little resistance.

Now I went back to the one who had claimed to be "the" prince. I asked again before Jehovah God if he was the prince demon. There was no response. The Holy Spirit had revealed to me that there were many others there and that this demon was not in charge. In the name of the Lord Jesus Christ, I bound this spirit and commanded him to gather up all of his works and go immediately and directly to the pit of hell. This one was a bit more intense, but with some great heaves and releases of breath, this spirit and all the ones he had brought in left.

I knew the prince had yet to be revealed, so again I commanded in the name of the Lord Jesus for the prince spirit to speak his name immediately. Rebecca gave me a name without delay. None of us had ever heard the name. It was surprising to learn that according to the dictionary the word means "to occupy." Interesting.

This spirit was there through a generational curse and was there by permission of both grandfathers' Masonic affiliation.

"I'm Feeling Very Nauseated"

Now Rebecca was beginning to feel ill and asked if there was a trash basket where she could vomit. Now the spirits were nervous and aggravated. We were in the process of tearing down a kingdom that had been thirty years in the making. Rebecca was also getting a headache, and the burning in her back intensified. Her neck and back were getting really tight and tense.

I immediately bound this spirit and commanded him to go to the pit of hell and to leave her without incident. The spirit came out with some gagging and was released on Rebecca's breath. I knew there were others, and we would get them one by one.

The next one would cause the most resistance. Another prince surfaced when commanded to and identified himself. At this time, the pattern of destruction for Rebecca's life unfolded. This demon's purpose throughout Rebecca's life was to torment her as a child, get her into addictive bondage, drive her crazy, have her wandering the streets as a homeless woman, and perhaps commit murder and suicide. Wow! What revelation the Holy Spirit was giving to us.

We Were Digging Up Roots Now

As I said, one of the functions of this demon was to get Rebecca to wander! This has scriptural significance. Remember, Cain was banished to wander because of his murder of Abel. (See Genesis 4:11–12.) A spirit of wandering was taking up roots in Rebecca and did not want to leave. Thank God this is not a negotiable process. Demons who have no permission to be there must leave when commanded. Now, I believe this spirit of wandering has only the pits of hell in which to wander. He has been banished to the abyss. We were digging up roots now, entrenched spirits, that tried unsuccessfully to remain. Rebecca expressed that she felt they were like tentacles wrapped around her insides.

This wandering spirit was also a prince demon and had three spirits under him—anger, guilt, and fear. The Holy Spirit showed me that this spirit was somehow related to the alcohol. When put under oath before Jehovah God, the spirit of wandering confessed that it, fear, anger, and guilt were all connected to alcohol.

Spirits of worry and tension were also there. When I commanded a spirit of tension to come forward and reveal his function, Rebecca said her back was burning near the points of her shoulder blades and she could hardly turn her neck for the tightness. When commanded, this spirit also left her, and her body sort of slumped in relaxation. Other spirits would be found somewhat easily as this kingdom within her was getting weaker and weaker.

TIGHTNESS IN HER CHEST

Next would come a spirit of confusion. And I had bound this spirit from the beginning, commanding that it must be completely inactive during the deliverance process. I asked Rebecca how she felt. She said she still felt some stirring within her and some tightness in her chest, sort of like heartburn. We talked some and asked her mom to offer any insights she might have from the Holy Spirit. She said she felt there might be a spirit of a reprobate mind. This is a somewhat common spirit and is revealed in Romans 1:28: "And even as they did not like to retain God in their knowledge, God gave them over to a reprobate mind, to do those things which are not convenient." This spirit comes when a person knows God and chooses to live as though he doesn't know God. Rebecca knew alcohol would lead her into trouble, she knew becoming addicted to it was wrong and would displease God, but she did it anyway. The reprobate mind spirit came in through her willing walk of disobedience.

Other spirits were there with this spirit. There was a spirit of lust, which was a prince demon. Perverted thinking was there, a spirit of humiliation, a spirit of deception, and a spirit of murder, which had come in through a generational curse. The kingdom was crumbling, the enemy was retreating, and Rebecca was about to be free. Each of these spirits was bound and was commanded to leave. In some of these cases, I had to ask Rebecca to repent of the act that allowed these spirits permission to her life and to denounce their works. As soon as she did, their power was broken, and each left without incident.

After a few hours, she was free! Her countenance had changed. Her eyes glistened and were not glazed. There was evidence to her mother that her appearance was changed. She knew she was free.

A TEN-YEAR-OLD WITH MANY PROBLEMS

Before I close out this chapter, I would like to report on a recent deliverance that was quite special. It was with a ten-year-old boy named Brandon. He had experienced many problems in his young life and had been diagnosed with attention deficit disorder (ADD) and depression. He was very disturbed, angry, and unhappy. The school nurse had once called home and told Brandon's mother that he was saying some very strange words and felt his parents should know.

He also had once chased a kid down the street with a bat threatening to kill him. He terrorized the neighbors and destroyed private property. I asked Brandon if he knew why he did that. "Yeah, I wanted other people to feel as bad as I do," he said. "Sometimes at night when I try to go to sleep, I pray and tell God I love Him, something tells me, 'No, you hate God.' I am tired of feeling like this."

Brandon had spirits by permission of a generational curse and had been tormented all of his young life. Some of the permission was from ancestors involved in Freemasonry. The spirits spoke through him, and he did not seemed surprised. I commanded the spirit responsible for ADD to confess that he would not have any need for medication once it left. The voice from the little boy said, "I can't confess that. I don't know anything about physics." Amazing.

Brandon had a dark countenance about him and an anger that furrowed his brow. When all of the spirits had been cast out, he had a big smile on his face, as did his parents. When I asked how Brandon felt, he said, "You know what? I feel like yelling real loud. I feel so good!" He had a desire to shout! I sensed a calling and anointing on Brandon for intercession. I asked him if he would pray for me every time he took his shoes off. "I sure will," he said. "I promise you I will."

"I HAVE NEVER FELT LIKE THIS BEFORE. I'M SO HAPPY!"

The next day, I was the guest preacher at his church. As I was waiting in the pastor's office just prior to going to the pulpit, there was a little knock on the door, and Brandon came in dressed in his Sunday best and with a big smile on his face. He just grabbed me and hugged me for several seconds. "I have never felt like this before. I am so happy." He just thanked me and thanked me. I didn't need to tell him to thank Jesus instead of me; he knew that, and he thanked Him as well. He said, "You know what? I took my shoes off all day long yesterday just to pray for you." What a mighty God we serve.

CHAPTER 11

BRAIN TUMOR HEALED

D<small>O YOU BELIEVE THAT THE PRAYER OF FAITH WILL BRING</small> healing to the sick? Are you afraid it might not happen? Are you fearful of being embarrassed?

Allow me to give you an example. Several years ago, I was asked to fill the pulpit for a pastor friend of mine. I had to rearrange my schedule to do it. He was going to be out of town and needed me to preach for him. I gladly agreed to do so. There was a member of that congregation named Donna Motley. She and her husband, Mike, had really been facing some problems. Donna had been plagued with headaches and fainting spells. She had been to five neurologists and two neurosurgeons. The conclusion was that she had a brain tumor, a pituitary adenoma, and that it must be removed.

Several people had been praying for Donna. She was scheduled to have surgery the Thursday following the Sunday I was to preach. All week long as I studied for the message, she was continually on my heart. I kept "hearing" the Holy Spirit tell me to lay hands on her and pray for her—in the service. I wanted to resist this because I had never seen it done at this church. I didn't know how they would receive it. But I knew God had spoken to me, so the only thing that mattered was being obedient to Him.

I was at the close of the message, and the music director got up to lead in an invitation song. "No," I said. "I don't want any music now. I am going to do what the Holy Spirit is urging me to do. I don't know what anyone will think about this, but I'm going to do it anyway. I am going to ask Donna and Mike Motley to come forward, and I am going to pray for Donna's healing." Now, virtually everyone in the church knew about her condition. "I am going to lay hands on her and ask the Lord to heal her. I want everyone who still believes that God is still healing people to come and gather around her also to pray." The entire church came. There was no hesitation.

The next day Donna went in to see her neurosurgeon for a presurgery MRI. She was scheduled to have her surgery on Thursday. She wore a T-shirt to her doctor that day with words across the front that said, "My God is an awesome God." Donna said that after they performed the MRI, she and Mike waited an unusually long time to see the neurosurgeon. She began to wonder what was taking so long.

My God Is An Awesome God

Finally, the doctor emerged with a perplexed look on his face. "Mrs. Motley," he said, "we have made a mistake. You don't have a brain tumor. There is nothing there." Donna had believed all along that she would be healed and had told her unbelieving doctor that. After the doctor continued to try and explain how seven doctors could be wrong, Donna said, "Doctor, the mistake you have made is not giving God the glory for my healing!"

She now has in her possession MRI films that show a brain tumor before prayer and films that show NO tumor after prayer. Our God is an awesome God!

Anointed, Appointed, Ordained Times

I once heard former Memphis pastor Dr. Adrian Rogers describe anointing. He said that it is "a special touch for a special task." I would add to that, "for a special time." Actually, it is much more than that. I want to share a special moment that happened a few years ago. I believe it was an anointed time. I was scheduled to preach in several prisons and decided to stay in a town central to all of them.

I love to fish but didn't think I would have time because of the many services I had planned, but I took my rod and reel just in case. When I got there, I called the chaplain of the prison where I was to be that evening. "I'm so glad you called," the chaplain said. "I tried to reach you, but you had already left home. Brother Don, we got a new warden on the unit today, and he canceled all weeknight activities. I'm so sorry, but we can't have church tonight." Well, I know those things happen. It is just part of prison ministry. So I decided to go fishing.

Generally, I fish from the marina area where there are "T" and "L" heads that allow you to drive out and fish from a parklike area. I bought my bait from one of the shrimp boats in the area and headed for my fishing spot, but I absentmindedly drove right past it. By the time I realized it, I was already a few blocks past and decided to continue along the bay side drive for a while because I had spotted a pier in the distance. I thought I would try the pier first. When I arrived at the little public park, I could see one person on the pier. I gathered up my fishing gear and headed to the end of the pier. As I got closer to the end, I could see that the person was a woman. She had no fishing gear and was just gazing into the bay waters.

I wondered why a woman would be out there alone and with no fishing equipment, but I didn't really want to know. I just wanted to fish. I went to the opposite side of the pier about one hundred feet from where she was. As I began to fish and was reeling in one small fish after the other, I could see her making her way, little by little, over to where I was. I just wanted to fish, so I more or less ignored her. Shortly, she started a conversation. "You sure are catching a lot of fish. Do you always put them back?" I confess I was not overly friendly as I told her I always put the fish back. I was not interested in conversation at that point.

I didn't know at this time that this was an anointed, appointed, ordained moment from God. God has arranged this meeting! I just kept fishing.

She continued to talk, and as she did, I began to listen with more interest. She told me she was a doctor. I just listened, but in my mind I was saying, "Yeah, you're a doctor." She told me she couldn't practice because she had been admitted to an institution for psychosis about a year earlier. She told me she had attempted suicide a couple of times. I listened more intently. I asked her why she was on the pier. She said, "I just seem drawn to the water. There's something final about the water. You can cut your wrist and survive, you can overdose and survive, but there's something final about the water." I looked at the choppy bay waters and glanced back at the shoreline—a pretty long swim. She explained how despondent she was and how terribly depressed because of her situation. She was there to commit suicide!

I KNEW THIS WAS AN ORDAINED MOMENT

I began to put away my fishing gear, because now I knew why the service had been canceled. Now I knew why I had "absentmindedly" driven past my fishing spot. I knew this was an ordained moment! I was going to do some different kind of fishing! Just as I was ready to witness to her, other people began to show up and spoiled the private moment. I understood that too.

I said, "Ma'am, I don't want you to misunderstand this, but would you mind walking back to my car with me and sit for a few minutes in the front seat of the car? I want to talk with you and pray for you." She did not hesitate stating that she knew she needed prayer.

As we walked toward the car, I talked with her about her salvation. She assured me that she was saved and was confident of her relationship to Christ. Even though she did not attend an evangelistic church, she remembered the day she asked Christ to be her Savior. I asked her if she believed in angels. "Oh, yes, I do. I believe they have intervened many times in my life." I then asked her if she believed in demons. She hesitated a moment, then said, "Yes, I suppose I do."

GOD HAS HEARD YOUR CRY

We arrived at the car and sat in the front seat. I said, "I don't think you are psychotic, though that may have been your diagnosis. I believe you are tormented with evil spirits of depression and suicide. I further believe God has heard your cry for help. I believe that's why we are seated here at this moment."

I told her if she wanted to be free and she had no unforgiveness, anger, or unconfessed sin in her life, that in the name of Jesus Christ I could rebuke the demons. She was ready! "Please do it!" she said. First, I had a word of prayer acknowledging and thanking God for His presence. I asked the Holy Spirit to give me direction and accomplish her freedom through biblical deliverance.

I explained to her that I was going to bind evil spirits in the name of Jesus Christ, and when I did so, she might experience some physical sensations such as nausea, stomach tightness, tingling sensations, eyes fluttering, burning in parts of her body, and so on. She nodded that she understood. I took authority over the evil spirits and bound them in the name of Jesus Christ. I commanded that they could not split, divide, hide, or use any form of trickery. They could not harm her or go to anyone else. I commanded them to attention and that when commanded to go, they would go immediately and directly to the abyss.

After the evil spirits were bound, I asked if she experienced any unusual feelings or symptoms. "Oh, yes, my lips are burning, and my hands, both hands, are tingling and burning." The demons were nervous, and they knew what was about to follow. They manifested through the discomfort she described. I told her she might feel them come up and out of her mouth when I commanded them to go. I could see her body heaving from deep exhaling as the demons were expelled. I could see and hear the deep sigh of relief! I asked her what she was feeling.

"The fog is gone. [It had not been foggy.] Oh, I can even see more clearly. Things are sharp and distinct," she remarked. "I have never felt such peace in all of my life!"

I talked with her briefly about what had happened and encouraged her to go to a Bible-teaching church. Then I had prayer with her again. She was free in the name of Jesus Christ! Appointed, anointed, ordained time!

When I got back home, I sent her some materials to read and a letter of encouragement. A few weeks after that she called our home and spoke to my wife. I was out of town. She told my wife what had happened to her life as a result of this moment ordained by God. She was doing fine. I went back a couple of years after this incident, and I called to check on her. Her husband answered. I introduced myself and said, "I don't know if you know who I am..." He interrupted me with, "Yes, yes, I know who you are." He told me his wife was not at home, but that she was a different person. "Thank God, her life is different now," he said.

CHAPTER 12

MORE PERSONAL ACCOUNTS

THIS COULD BE A VERY LONG BOOK IF I INCLUDED THE TESTIMO-nies of all who have gone through deliverance. It would also be a very interesting book. From all walks of life, people have come to me requesting to be free of demonic oppression. To me, it is very sad that our churches don't address this. The people come like Nicodemus—they come by night, under a cloak of secrecy because of the stigma that goes with deliverance. They know there is something wrong, and often they even know what it is. But they can't go to their pastor because he doesn't believe it. They won't tell their friends because they don't want to be humiliated. Like Nicodemus, they know there is something more for their lives.

Hollywood has created such false images of deliverance. It has given the demons too much power and has made people fearful of the very thought of the demonic. We must forget Hollywood and focus on the Holy Word. The truth is, every believer has been given authority over every demon power, including Satan himself! We have been given authority over "all the power of the enemy" (Luke 10:19). So, I wonder why the church won't step up and deal with this? Every church should have an active deliverance ministry, and every pastor should be able to lead someone through deliverance! I also believe that every pastor should go through deliverance as well!

Some time ago, I was scheduled for chapel services at women prison in the southwest part of the country. As usual, the chaplain met me at the front gate. He confessed that he had made a mistake in his sched-uling and another group was there for ministry also. He asked if I wanted to share the services with the other group. I have found that never works very well. He apologized for the mistake. I told him I understood and it was no problem. Out of courtesy he said, "Since you are here, is there anyone you would like a personal visit with?" "Yes," I told him, "There is a lady who has asked to see me when possible. I'll see her today."

The chaplain took me to a private room near the cafeteria and sent an officer to the dorm to call the inmate out for the special pastoral visit. I will let that former inmate tell the story from here.

"A Day I Will Never Forget"

Well, first, I want to thank Don for his passion to see souls set free from the grip of Satan. Oh, dear reader, Satan is real. He wants to destroy each life God has created and take us all to hell when we die. I am about to share a day that I will never forget.

On January 26, 1997, the Lord sent Don to me to continue the process of setting me free. I was in prison, but God had already begun a work in my heart. Meeting with Don was the next step in delivering me from the kingdom of darkness.

It was a beautiful Sunday morning at the Hilltop prison unit in Gatesville. I was usually in church and had plans to go that morning. The chaplain called my dorm and sent word that Don Dickerman was there and would like to see me. I was so eager to see Don. I knew he could help me with the awful nightmares I was having. I knew he understood the warfare. My nightmares were so horrible that I would wake the entire dorm with horrible sounds coming out of my mouth.

I had accepted Christ and lived for Him with all my heart, but the residue of my sinful life still lingered with much demonic presence. I told God, "How can I witness for You during the day and terrify people at night?" I didn't know what to do. I didn't realize at that time that I had authority to come against these powers in Jesus's name. God was faithful and sent Don to me.

We Caught the Demons by Surprise

The chaplain arranged for us to meet in a small quiet room, and there were no officers present. We caught the demons by surprise. I didn't know Don was coming, and Don didn't know he was coming to minister to me. The demons were caught off guard. They had no chance to plan a defensive strategy.

I had to be totally honest with Don that I still had tremendous unforgiveness against my parents. I didn't know that unforgiveness was giving the demons permission to torment me, but Don did. He helped me in prayer to release that unforgiveness, and immediately I was unburdened by the tremendous weight I had carried.

We began the session with prayer to acknowledge the presence of God's Holy Spirit and to ask His anointing and guidance for what was to follow. Then, Don bound evil spirits in the name of Jesus Christ and gave them specific instructions—commanding them that they could not hurt me, that they could not go to anyone else, that they could not split, divide, or multiply....Many direct instructions he gave them and the final command that they must leave and go to the abyss when commanded to and would never return!

It Angered the Demon to Be
Put Under Oath Before Jehovah God

Don commanded the prince demon to identify himself. He demanded the name of the demon who claimed to be in charge. The demon said his name was Anvil, and this demon actually spoke through my mouth. Don then commanded this spirit to reveal how many demons were present. The demon lied several times, and Don kept commanding, "Will this stand as truth before Jehovah God?" It angered the demon to be put under oath before Jehovah God, but it finally confessed that there were six hundred demon spirits present.

Then Don commanded the spirit to reveal how it gained entrance into my life to live its heinous personality through me. This spirit had come into me at birth along with another spirit that went by the name Wind. These two demon powers had permission to my life through the sins of my ancestors. (See Exodus 20:5.) The consent was from my grandfather's involvement in the occult. He was very active in Freemasonry, a secret society that involves many unholy vows, oaths, pledges, and ceremonies.

As Don commanded Anvil and Wind to leave, I grabbed my stomach and wrenched in pain. They had dwelt in my stomach all these years. They had controlled my life of sin—alcohol, poverty, lust, anger... They did not want to leave, but they came up and out of my mouth. I could feel them depart from my body.

There were six other "prince" demons, and each one had a kingdom of many demons under its authority. I recall demons that specialized in the works of confusion, death, and murder. I was in prison for attempted murder. This demon had almost accomplished its filthy work in my life. Thank God for His mercy and grace.

It Had Tentacles Going All Throughout My Body

Then there was a demon who called himself Octopus. I was able to somehow see this spirit. I could see that it had tentacles going all throughout my body. It was a demon tormenting me in the area of lust and had so consumed me all of these years. As Don commanded these spirits to leave, I could feel these beings literally depart from me out of the back of my neck and through the pores of my skin. As he commanded them to go directly into the abyss, I felt them leave me!

The next demon that came forth was a prince of confusion. These unholy creatures were causing me to be very nauseated and sick at my stomach. They were stirring all inside my body, fighting not to depart. They knew they had to leave, but they were clinging, striving to remain in my body. There was a war going on inside of me, and I could feel their resistance to the power of Christ in Don. As they left me, I could "see" them flying away, and they were screaming. The noise was horrible. It must be what hell sounds like, just incredibly terrible sounds.

As they left me, I could see them leaving through a dirty funnel that was narrow at my body and expanded out toward the end. As they were leaving, I had this overwhelming desire to lash out at Don and hit him. The demons wanted to kill him, but I could not move. He was destroying their kingdom they had established in me, and they could no longer control my life. Though they hated Don, it was really the Holy Spirit that they hated. They knew they had to leave!

I could see them as they left like a flock of black birds. They were ugly, horrid, dirty, disfigured creatures screaming as they left out of the top of my head. There were hundreds of them. I feel there is no way to adequately describe what took place, but what I shared is an accurate description of what happened.

I Felt Like I Had Taken a
Shower From the Inside Out

Finally it was over. It was over! I slumped forward on the desk and was exhausted. I remember telling Don that I felt like so much dirt and filth—gritty, grimy dirt—had been washed out of me. I felt like I had taken a shower from the inside out. For the first time, I felt free and clean inside, and it was the first time in my life that demonic beings did not live inside my body and have some measure of control over my thoughts and actions. Finally I was free from their powers and influence over me and could live my life totally for Christ.

I had the authority all along but did not know it, nor would I have known how to use it. Satan had so deceived my mind. I could not see this truth in Scripture even though I was saved and serving the Lord the best I knew how. Now I know how to fight, and I understand who I am in Christ. The war for my soul still rages, but now the demons must battle me from outside of my body. I am no longer held captive by Satan and his demons. I am free inside my body, and I choose to remain free from their torment from the outside.

I was set free from the physical prison I was in the next year. Thank God when the gates were opened for me to come home, I was also free on the inside. That has been several years now, and my life has not been the same. My life today is a praise and proclamation of the victory we all have in the mighty name of Jesus. Praise Him, just praise Him!

And then there was Kay, who had already been delivered from many demons. I had seen her on at least three prior occasions. She had been sexually abused as a child, had been treated for seizures, and experienced much trauma in her early years. She was a beautiful young lady with two children but recently divorced.

After the first session about a year prior she had been delivered of sexual perversion spirits that had come through the abuse she received as a very young girl. Fear spirits were also cast out of her, and she received freedom from the seizures. The choking sensations she would have at night stopped, and her life began to show much improvement. She was active in Bible studies and intercession.

I saw her again at her request when she was experiencing bitterness and some irrational fear from her ex-husband. She suspected that he might be trying to hurt her or cause her mental anguish through phone calls and implied threats. Again she had a measure of deliverance and was freed from spirits of doubt and confusion. She began to show more improvement and testified of it. However, the next time I saw her, she said, "Don, there is still something. I can't put my finger on it, but something is still there."

About six weeks later I was in another city for a series of deliverance sessions with various people. Seems like it was thirteen different individuals. It was Sunday afternoon, and the sessions ran all the way to near midnight. One of the candidates for deliverance did not show up, and the coordinator said, "Kay is in church, and she has been wanting to see you again."

Soon the coordinator returned with Kay. She was so happy, she said, "This morning the Holy Spirit told me today would be a date with destiny for me. I didn't know I was going to get to see you, but I know this is what the Holy Spirit had in mind."

Kay had always been subject to believing everything that happened meant something spiritually. She actually was plagued, to some degree, by trying to make spiritual sense out of things that to you and me would be just everyday occurrences. I was thinking maybe this was another of those situations. I was wrong, and thank God I was. It was her date with destiny. Her life was about to be forever changed.

We began with prayer. Then I bound evil spirits with a general command and demanded that if there were any demon powers present, the prince of those demons identify himself. Kay smiled, actually more of a smirk, and said, "Just Jesus." It did not ring true to me, and I suspected this was a deceiving spirit. I demanded, "Are you Jesus Christ? Are you the Lord Jesus Christ?" Kay began to growl. I had never seen her do this before. Her head turned slightly to the side, and she lowered her face to the table and growled.

It was a deceiving spirit. It had taken the name Jesus (Christ's earthly name) and was deceiving her. The spirit claimed to be "anti-Christ" and said he was on assignment as the territorial prince of the town Kay lived in. Kay was seeing as in a vision everything she was telling me. "The demon is a green and orange dragon, and he spews fire from his mouth." I commanded the territorial spirit not to lend any assistance to the kingdom established in Kay. Again, she growled. This spirit called Jesus had twin kingdoms! Another spirit was there by permission of Druid worship and had come into the family in Scotland several centuries ago. He called his function darkness.

One demon defined his work as "death wish." He claimed to be there by permission of words spoken by her mother. These underlings were cast out, and I called the prince Jesus to the front. I demanded that he reveal how he gained access to Kay's life. "Electrodes," was his response, "when she was ten years old." Kay remembered they were testing for the seizures then. An incubus demon that came through sexual abuse brought this spirit in. He was a vile spirit, boasting of his anti-Christ duties. I said, "You know your time is short, don't you? Jesus Christ is returning soon." The spirit spoke through Kay, "Yes, we must be diligent!" Still there was some "growl" as the voice came from her.

I commanded this spirit to reveal his assignment and functions in Kay's life. "Destroy, deceive, mental psychosis, to make her think she's crazy, death…" Mental psychosis! That explained her confusion with trying to spiritualize everything that happened, and she did often think that she must be losing her mind. I commanded this spirit to leave and go immediately into the abyss. There was much coughing, gagging, and growling, and soon she appeared free. But not completely; there was a hidden kingdom, yet to be discovered.

I was scheduled to leave and return home on Tuesday. The coordinator called and said, "Kay needs to see you again and is driving up to meet you." I thought she would just be giving me a good report of her freedom. Wrong. "Don, the strangest thing happened when I got home. My left leg just started twitching and got all tingly. I think there is still something there."

"Well, let's see," I said.

Again we prayed. I bound evil spirits and commanded the prince of any demonic kingdom to come forth and identify himself. "I am Jesus."

I hesitated and asked the Holy Spirit to help me, "Are you the same spirit that was cast from her on Sunday?"

"No, I am his twin," and again there was a growl that continued after each response.

I had run into this before, that is, twin spirits, twin kingdoms. Then a spirit surfaced and called himself Satan. I knew it wasn't, but he kept insisting.

I humiliated the spirit, saying that Satan must be a fool to waste his time in a little blonde in Texas when he could be in a vast place of importance in the world. "You're just a liar," I said.

The spirit then confessed he was a replica of Satan, and I said, "You are a poor imitation." There was much growling.

Two more spirits identified themselves. One was a prince, and the other was a spirit of deception. I commanded the anti-Christ spirit to gather up his kingdom and to become one spirit. Mental psychosis was in this kingdom as well. I commanded him to retrieve every seed that had been planted, uproot everything that had been planted, clean up the mess completely, and go into the abyss.

Kay was able to see this all happen in her mind. "Oh," she said, "I can see him pulling things up by the roots. The roots are so long. Each time you let up on the commands, he puts some of them back." So I kept the pressure on.

"He's pulling them all up and putting them in a bag. Now he's picking up what looks like seeds on the ground and putting those in the same bag." As I continued to command, she said, "Now I see a dirty rag, a filthy rag, and it is being squeezed by two powerful hands. The dirt and grime is running from the rag. Now the hands are squeezing it more and all the dirt is gone. The rag is shaken straight, and it is clean." Kay was crying, tears running from her face. "Oh, thank You, Lord. Thank You. Praise You, Jesus. I am free!"

Our righteousness is as filthy rags. Thank God that Jesus came not only to forgive us and cleanse us from sin but also to free us from the filth of demonic oppression!

AN IRISH PRISONER

Eddie Ferncombe with Don

On the other side of the Atlantic, I would also encounter demons in the life of an inmate. In October of 1999, I made a trip to Ireland to see my new born-again brother, Eddie Ferncombe. Eddie had a notorious reputation in Ireland. He was well known for his criminal activity. My friend David Berkowitz (the Son of Sam), who has been a believer since the late 1980s, read about Eddie's escapades in Ireland and asked if I would write to Eddie and witness to him as I had done with David many years ago. New York inmates are not allowed to correspond with other inmates, or David would have witnessed to Eddie himself.

I wrote to Eddie and shared the gospel. He wrote me back saying that if I knew who he really was, I probably would want nothing to do with him. He felt he was too bad for God to love, and surely Jesus couldn't save someone like him. I continued our correspondence, and one day Eddie accepted Christ by mail! Our friendship grew, and he asked if I had any cassette tapes I could send him as he was allowed to have a small tape player in his cell.

I gathered up some tapes from prison services here in the States and mailed them to Eddie. On one of those tapes, I was ministering deliverance at the end of a service, commanding spirits in the name of Jesus Christ to leave certain inmates. When Eddie listened to this particular tape, it riled the demons in him. Just the commands in the name of Jesus on audiotape snapped the demons to attention! He said that as I was commanding spirits on the tape, he began to get very hot. "It was the middle of winter, Don, and I had stripped down to my shorts and was splashing water in my face from my wash basin. I had never felt anything like it." Eddie realized that he had demons.

"DON, CAN YOU HELP ME?"

The next day, he called for the chaplain, a Catholic priest. "When I told him about my experience and asked him to help me, he laughed at me. Don, can you help me?" I knew God was calling me to make the trip and minister to my new friend in Christ. Now, I didn't know anyone in Ireland and was not sure how I would get there, since it is a very expensive trip. I only knew I was supposed to go. Here is Eddie's story.

> I was born in 1972, and as I look back on my life, I never thought I'd reach this far and become the man I am today. Since birth, it seemed I was born to die young from my own self-destruction. So I lived fast and came very close to death many times. Now things are different, Satan's grip on my life is broken, and Jesus Christ is my Savior! The "power" I once knew was violence and crime. That is now gone, along with its pain, anger, hurt, frustrations, blood,

sweat, and tears. The Lord and my new Christian friends have helped me break this vicious cycle of self-destruction and harm to others. So what they gave to me I now give to you, my brothers and sisters, to help inspire hope and change for you also. I give you love and truth.

I could easily blame my childhood for how I turned out, but my brothers and sisters didn't turn out like me. It must have been something else. I was born and reared in a working-class ghetto, riddled with drugs, crime, violence, and youth crime gangs. I witnessed violence at a young age. I came from a broken home. We barely had enough money for food. I have little education, and while my upbringing had some effect on me, I now accept responsibility for my actions, my crimes, and my mistakes. My mother and grandmother raised me since I was two and a half years old. My mom was twenty-five when she had five of us kids. I also have four half-brothers. We moved a lot when I was young, from flat to flat. My mom worked hard to provide for us, and we got lots of love and affection, which is better than material things.

I Craved Revenge

Moving around a lot left me to run the streets and "hook up" with the bad boys. We committed violence as children. I soon learned that my violent ways could be a powerful weapon over people. I loved to hurt people who had done me harm or had done harm to my family or friends. I never let anyone get away with doing me over. I craved revenge, and I always got it. I was always in trouble in school, expelled often, and eventually at thirteen, I was thrown out of school. I never went back.

At this time, I was in and out of the children's court for crimes such as car theft, robbery, and assault. I stole anything I knew I could sell. First it was for drinking. Later it was for drugs. I was becoming very violent. Anyone who got in my way I either stabbed or used hammers or hatchets; it didn't matter. By age fifteen, I had become a professional car thief and burglar, and I had become notorious for stabbing people.

I Was Feared by People

I was a member of a youth crime gang. We had about forty members, and we controlled the crime in our "hood." I was feared by people two or three times my age, and this made me feel powerful. To keep this power, I felt I had to get more violent. The home for troubled kids would not accept me. Eventually one did but threw me out for stabbing two people in a fight. At sixteen, I was sent to a youth detention center for twelve months for an assault and for escaping from lawful custody.

While in the detention center, I was in and out of solitary for assaulting inmates and officers. I was only out for five days when I was arrested for robbery and received another sixteen months for three counts. I was doing drugs pretty heavy at this time. I did this sixteen-month sentence the way I did the first—violence against authority and other inmates. Three months after this sentence, I stabbed a man to death during a street robbery. I was using heroin, crack, and cocaine. I was messed up at this time. I was seventeen and had already stabbed twenty-five to thirty-five people, and that doesn't include the others I hurt with other weapons. For the most part, it was rivals that I hurt, those who would have done the same to me.

I Was Charged With Murder

I was charged with one count of murder at age seventeen. (Later this was reduced to manslaughter because of my age and drug dependence.) I was given a ten-year sentence. I had always hated authority, so I was in trouble from the start. I wouldn't obey orders from anyone. I assaulted officers and went on all sorts of protests, which caused me to be sent from prison to prison. I was in all of Ireland's prisons and punishment blocks three or four times over. None of this helped. I kept rebelling at any chance because my hate only grew over the many beatings I was given by eight, ten, or twelve guards. In more than eleven years of incarceration, I have only spent about ten months in general population. As the case is now, I spent my time in isolation. Along the way I even dabbled with the occult and have "666" tattooed on me. I had tattoos about hate for everyone! All in my anger for authority.

I hated the system and the system hated me. I did have the respect of other inmates because I fought the system. I earned my way here to Ireland's toughest prison, housed in the defaulters wing. In 1996, while in the Mounty Joy Prison in Dublin Prison, me and five other inmates took five officers hostage. We held them for three days in what has been described as the worst crisis in prison history. We were all sent to the Portlaoise prison, Ireland's most max facility. I am now in a prison within a prison. This is my fourth time here, and three times previously I was on the "gangland" wing. The guards here wear riot gear any time the doors are opened. I am always cuffed before leaving my cell and no less than six officers go with me. I received an additional six-year sentence for the siege, and that's why I am on the defaulters' wing.

Someone Did Care For Me

Two years ago, I started writing to some Christians, and they showed me love and respect as a human being. They showed me that someone did care for me. They trusted me and took me into their confidence as an equal. This all felt strange to me as I hated society and thought society hated me, but it also felt good. I wanted what they had. I accepted Christ by mail! I wanted change. I really did, but I did not know God loved me so much that He sent Jesus to save me. Save me?

I was writing to Don Dickerman in Texas. He sent me the salvation prayer and words of encouragement. I read some of the Bible, and as I said the prayer of salvation…BANG! With tears in my eyes I began to loudly scream and shout. A feeling of calm came over my thoughts, and I knew something was really happening. The Holy Spirit came into MY body. Wow!

I wasn't tripping; this was real! Don sent me some cassette tapes of prison services he conducted in America. As I listened to one of the tapes, he was ministering deliverance to inmates. He bound evil spirits in the name of Jesus, and as he did this on the tape, my body began to get hot and there was stirring inside. It was the middle of winter, and I could not cool off. I stripped to my shorts and splashed water from my basin in my face. As he commanded spirits to leave, I started doing the same. I knew now I had demons but couldn't find release. I told my chaplain about it the next day, and he laughed at me. I wrote Don and told him about it and asked him to help me. Don told me that when he read my letter he felt the Lord telling him to come to Ireland and to minister deliverance to me.

That is a day I will never forget. First he came to see me on Monday to discuss what I needed to do and said he was going to come back on Wednesday to do the deliverance. He talked to me about the necessity of forgiving and that I could not be free until I did. Wow, this was difficult. I had so much anger for the beatings I had taken, for the man who had "snitched" on me and was now out selling drugs to kids…so much hate! How could I forgive? He told me it had to be like God forgave me, not based upon them deserving it. He told me to read Matthew 18:23–25. He said, "Forgiveness is not saying what happened is OK. That's not what Jesus said when He forgave me. He didn't say sin is OK. Sin is ugly, and it sent Him to the cross. What He said was, 'I love you anyway.' When you forgive, you are not saying what happened is OK. It was painful then, and it is painful now. What you are saying is, 'I wish no harm for you. I want God to love you just like He loves me. If vengeance is in order, I release that to God because He says, "Vengeance is mine, I will repay, saith the Lord" (Rom. 12:19).' You can do that, Eddie. You have to if I am to help you."

When I left the prison that day and drove back to Dublin, I wondered if Eddie would forgive. I wondered if he could. I knew that my trip would be in vain if he didn't. I prayed for him and asked God for extra measures of grace in Eddie's life. My contact in Dublin had driven me to Portlaoise and waited while I visited with Eddie. She was not going to be able to drive me there on Wednesday as I was headed for southern Ireland to preach in a few churches.

On Wednesday, I was to be at the prison about 10:00 a.m. because of the limited one-hour visit and no visits after noon. Well, it was a Murphy's law day! It seemed everything that could go wrong did go wrong. There was a massive traffic jam. I was stranded in traffic in Dublin, not to mention driving on the left side of the road with the steering wheel on the right. Time seemed to race as I watched the clock and tried to maneuver the roads. It was noon when I finally arrived at the prison. Portlaoise is about fifty miles south of Dublin, and it had taken me almost three and a half hours to drive it.

As I arrived at the prison to visit, others were coming out because visitation was over. I was so discouraged. I had been binding Satan all the way from hindering this visit. I still was expecting victory even though it was not looking good. I explained to the visitation officer that I had come all the way from Texas. "I remember you from Monday, lad," he said. "I am going to lunch now. Come back at 1:00, and I will ask the governor (warden) if he will grant you special permission."

I went to get something to eat and prayed for God's intervention during the hour. I remember it was somewhat cool, dreary, and rainy that day. It seemed like the entire ten days I spent in Ireland were that way. I went back to the prison in anticipation of special permission. Surely I would get one hour with Eddie. I was wrong! I got three hours! And I got it in a special area with no one else present. All the visitors had gone, and the officer told me I could have until 4:00. I headed back to see Eddie escorted by a kind Irish officer. He asked me, "Are you like David Wilkerson?" (David Wilkerson was a well-known pastor of the Times Square Church in New York and former street minister.) I knew what he meant. I thought for a minute and said, "Yes, yes, I am." The officer said, "You are welcome here, lad!" Look how the Holy Spirit had prepared everything. I wondered now if Eddie had been able to forgive.

IT WAS A STRUGGLE

Eddie continues his story:

> It was a real struggle turning loose of my anger and forgiving those I felt so much hate for. But I realized I must do it because the forgiven must forgive. Those who have received grace must be gracious to others. When I did forgive, I knew something had happened. I knew I was ready for demons to be driven from me. I could hardly wait until Wednesday. When Don came in that day, he told me of many obstacles he had endured that morning. He even arrived too late for visiting time (one hour is all we are allowed). However, in God's plan, because Don had arrived late and had come from Texas, the governor (warden) gave us a three-hour special visit. The extra time was necessary. I was a little nervous as the time approached. I wasn't sure what to expect. Don said he felt it might be wise to alert the officer, who sits in a Plexiglas box and observes the visit, about the upcoming deliverance. When he told him he was going to be praying deliverance over me, the officer just nodded and said, "'elp yourself, lad, 'elp yourself."

Jesus Came to Break Sin's
Shackles as Well as Forgive My Sin

They brought me into the visitation chamber, shackled as always. Four officers escorted me. I think Don could tell I was ready to experience deliverance by the look on my face. We talked some, then he prayed, acknowledging the Holy Spirit's presence and our need for His direction for me to know complete liberation from the enemy. He explained to me that when the evil spirits were bound in me I might very well feel their presence by some kind of manifestation. I already knew that from just listening to the tape. The name of Jesus Christ is powerful. He explained that demons must have permission to be present through a generational curse, abuse, trauma, immorality, occult, and other things. We prayed a prayer thanking God for salvation and then repenting of unforgiveness, anger, bitterness, hatred, and so on, and received the full work of the cross to break the power of any curse.

He also explained to me that while I was previously possessed by demons, I was now possessed by the Holy Spirit of God; I was redeemed, bought with a price, purchased—God's possession! He explained that the demons were now intruders and their only work now was oppression, that they were in my flesh and soul, *not* in my spirit. He began to bind the evil spirits in the name of Jesus Christ. I felt all kinds of stirring inside of me—nausea and headache, burning… I became very tensed up. He began to rebuke spirits and commanded them to leave me. Man, this was some experience! I felt them leaving on my breath, sigh after sigh, release after release as he commanded spirits to leave—spirits of hate, anger and bitterness, resentment, spirits of rebellion, spirits of murder and death.

For about two hours spirits were leaving me until finally the last one was gone and I sort of slumped in my seat. The tension was gone, and I felt peace. I remember I felt "high," high on God, not drugs. I felt a peace and a calmness I had never felt before. All of my inner battles were gone. All of my hate and my anger, my pain and frustrations, they were all gone, gone, man!

I had always told Don in letters that I could never forgive the system and some people, never, ever! But now, not only could I forgive, but I could also love. I could truly forgive people, and wow! What a powerful weapon that is. I loved it, and I have never looked back. That was October 26, 1999, a day I will never forget.

The Lord now lives in me, and I feel He is using me to reach others who were and are in my old situation. I love Jesus so much now. He died for our sins. Take time to think about that. I want to make the Lord proud of me and reach as many people as I can. I believe He will open the right doors for me, and I will follow Him without questions. I want all of my Christian friends to be pleased with my life, and I want this testimony to be a big thank you for their love.

The Scowl Is Gone From My Face

My family and my girlfriend have been waiting all of my life for me to truly come home. It won't be much longer now. I have been off drugs totally for over four years, having been a heroin addict for seven. I have finally beat that. I am now placid, peaceful, and calm—a happy man. The scowl is gone from my face. The hate is gone from my dark eyes, and now they shine. I am hoping this helps anyone who reads it, and I will try to help anyone who writes to me.

While writing this portion of the book, I was interrupted with a phone call. It was from a man who now lives in Texas. He said, "Brother Dickerman, I know you don't remember me; to be honest, I didn't remember your name. I had to call one of the prisons you ministered at and get your name from the chaplain. After I described a little about you and the ministry that took place in a service I attended a few years ago, he said, 'You are talking about Don Dickerman.' He gave me your phone number, sir.

"I want to tell you something to encourage you," the man continued, "and to keep you ministering as you do. You mentioned in that service that God was still healing people and that demons were still retreating in the name of Jesus Christ. I'll have to tell you that I was a little skeptical, because I had been prayed for before and nothing had happened. You see, I had been shot and was paralyzed in one of my arms and had a very weak back. I could hardly move."

He asked if I remembered the service. I didn't, but I was sure it was like many of our other services.

He said, "After you had prayed for men for salvation, you asked men to come forward that needed healing. I almost didn't come because my injury seemed too bad and because others had laid hands on me. I guess it was the devil telling me not to come, but I did.

"You prayed for me a very simple prayer, and the pain and restriction in my arm released immediately. I could move my arm, and it did not hurt. I have no problem with it today, many years later!"

I thanked him for his call and for the praise report.

Then he said, "But, sir, that's not all. You also bound evil spirits in me and commanded them to go. My momma had always told me I had an evil spirit and needed deliverance. I spent many years in prison for a terrible crime I committed. Something left me that day, and my life changed!

"I had been going to church and trying to get right, but it just seems after that day that I had a hunger for the Lord. I couldn't get enough of Him or the Word. Since I have been out, I have held a full-time job and have started a ministry. I too now minister in prisons. I send them books and buy things for the chaplains who need equipment and such. The Lord is blessing my life, and it all started that day when you touched me in Jesus's name. I just want to say thanks and keep on doing what you are doing."

Pretty exciting! I just thought I would include that as a bonus.

A Baptist Deacon With Demons

There is one story that I want to share about a friend I met in Oklahoma. He and his wife have since moved to Texas. They are both on my advisory board. I asked if he and his beautiful wife would share their story, and they graciously agreed to do it. Here it is in their words:

> I have a vivid memory of this day. It was the first of October in 1999. It was a typically beautiful fall afternoon. We had been home from church a couple of hours when we heard a car drive up to our home in Oklahoma. My wife went to the door and greeted our guest. He was a very soft-spoken, humble man, named Don Dickerman. It was our first time to meet. As we visited, he told us a little about his life and how God had called him to minister in prisons. These folks were literally behind bars! He told us how he had seen so many of them set free from bondage by the power and authority of the Lord Jesus.

I knew his being there was of the Lord. One of the things Don talked about that afternoon was how God "orchestrates" things in our lives. Ever since that day, I have become more aware of that divine "orchestration" in my life, and I am amazed and so grateful. On that first encounter, I felt an incredible bond to Don. I knew help had arrived.

It Was Truly a Miracle

You see, though I was not behind the bars of a prison cell, I had been in bondage for years but didn't realize it. It was truly a miracle when God brought Don into our situation so that Jesus could set me free. God used this anointed man in such a mighty way in my life, and I thank God for his willingness to be used. It's hard to summarize my life story in a short space, but I will share what I believe is necessary. It is my prayer that as you read this, God will touch your heart with the knowledge of who He is and just how awesome He is! To His name be glory!

My wife and I had each been saved as children and had faithfully served in church for all our married life. We had taught Sunday school, sung in the choir, been on various committees, led Sunday school departments, been on prayer teams, and attended workshops, seminars, and discipleship training. I had even been an ordained deacon since the age of twenty-nine. We had never even heard of deliverance ministry until about a month prior to meeting Don. Certainly we never thought we would be in need of it. We both loved the Lord, and we taught our children to love Him. God has blessed us with a good life and with children and grandchildren who all know Him as their personal Savior. We have a loving family and enjoy each other's company. As in most families, there have been trying times, but, thank God, He has preserved our family unit through them all. What I'm trying to say is that I am a normal person with a normal life. I am a Christian!

I knew there was a devil, but I thought his job was to tempt me to sin. I had no idea of the control that the demonic world could and did have in my life. Praise the Lord for His beautiful plan for each of us and for the way He brings us to the place where we call out to Him and He never fails to be there.

For several years, the Lord had been drawing us closer to Him through some studies that were offered at our church. We had gone through five or six years of discipleship training where God was preparing us for what was to come. These studies were all about how to experience God in a deeper way. We studied the characteristics and attributes of God, how to develop the mind of Christ, how to pray, how to forgive, and how to submit the hurts and sins of the past to Him. We learned that life for a Christian means warfare, and we learned what Scripture says about our victory through Jesus Christ.

We Were Going Through Some Difficult Times

One of the things He used to prepare us was the Walk to Emmaus, a seventy-two-hour retreat that concentrates on Jesus Christ and His great, unconditional love for us. Promise Keepers is also a ministry that God used tremendously in my life. I heard men talk of their love for Jesus, and I saw them cry in gratitude when they spoke of His love for them. All of these things and more, the Lord was using to get our eyes on Him while we were going through some difficult times.

The Lord had blessed me with a job with one company for more than thirty-six years. The company had been through some major changes in upper management over the last several years, and as a result, I had been demoted for the first time ever in my career. This was a real blow, bringing on a period of depression and suppressed anger. It was during this time that God began to move in our lives in a big way. The day after I got the news of the demotion, a large pay cut, and transfer to another state, we were using a devotional book that we had also given to our married children as a gift.

I Will Do a New Thing

On that day, our daughter called to check on us and asked if we had read our devotional that morning. (Of course we hadn't. We were feeling very sorry for ourselves at that time and hadn't opened our Bible.) She said, "I think today's scripture is for ya'll." It was Isaiah 43:18–19, which says "Do not remember the former things, nor consider the things of old. Behold, I will do a *new thing*. Now it shall spring forth: shall you not know it? I will even make a road in the wilderness and rivers in the desert" (NKJV, emphasis added). This should have been a clue that God was in control of the situation. We did acknowledge that He wanted to make some changes in us, so we reluctantly began to take the necessary steps to make the move.

It was in the *new place* that He began to do the *new thing*. It was to be one of the greatest challenges and also one of the most blessed times we had ever experienced with Him. I was humbled in many ways, not an easy thing for someone who had never even had serious criticism on the job. All I had ever experienced were promotions and compliments. I would not have admitted it, but my job was my life and my identity. I did a good job and was proud of it. I look back on my life with much more understanding than ever before. The Lord has shown me many things.

That Was a Very Sad Time in My Life

Even though my parents didn't attend church regularly, they saw to it that we did. We attended a small Baptist church in the neighborhood. My father and mother were addicted to alcohol, and both experienced battles with depression at times, especially my mother. She spent weeks at a time in hospitals being treated for depression. I hardly saw her at all during my senior year in high school. That was a very sad time in my life. Years later when she died unexpectedly, I had a hard time expressing my grief. My emotions were locked up deep inside. My childhood and teenage years were a succession of embarrassing moments and disappointments.

On the outside, my family appeared to be OK, and I do have some good memories. But I knew the truth and determined not to be "that way." As a result, I had many casual friends but not any really close ones. I wanted to prove something to my dad, because I never really felt his approval, though I know he loved me. One of the things I now understand is that both my parents were bound up by the chains of the same enemy who had been stealing from me all my life. I can now see that these same strongholds had been in their families for generations. I never talked about my home situation with anyone.

These Hurts From the Past Seemed to Be Surfacing

I didn't even discuss this with my wife for many years. My sisters may have seen things differently, but this is the way I saw the situation. I believe there is a certain amount of denial and hiding from the truth that we all do. There were personality traits in both my mom and my dad that I saw in myself and that I now know were demons in my life by permission of a generational curse. (See

Exodus 20:5.) I never had a problem with alcohol, but I decided at an early age not to do certain things. This became a matter of pride in my life, which gave the enemy a stronghold. It wasn't a bad thing to choose to do right, but the way demons work is that they twist things, and if there is pride, they can sure use it. These hurts from the past plus some fresh ones seemed to be surfacing and needed to be dealt with.

About the same time, the Lord began to place in me the desire to retire from my job. I knew I had put my job first for all these years. Although I had brought this before God and asked for forgiveness before, I came once more to Him, confessing that I had not put Him first in my life and I sincerely committed my life to Him. I told Him that I wanted what He wanted for my life and that I would do whatever He said. I believe this is when God began to put into action His plan to expose the demons causing bondage in my life and bring me freedom to experience true joy. The enemy had robbed me of that for so long.

I Don't Ever Remember Being That Free

Only my wife realized that there was a lack of genuine joy in my life. One of the things I shared with Don was a memory I had from about age thirteen when, at the beginning of summer, I was at the movie theater in our small town. I remember being so excited to think I had the whole summer ahead of me, three whole months of freedom! I don't ever remember feeling that free again, until now.

I decided to retire and made a trip to discuss this with my supervisor. While I was on this trip, in a state of severe depression and confusion, I experienced what I now know was the manifestation of evil spirits. I must say here that I was never depressed or confused about my decision to retire. In fact, it was as if a burden was lifted in that area. I believe that was confirmation from the Lord that I was doing the right thing. The depression was related to personal things that had nothing to do with my job. One night in the hotel, I was awakened by tremendous shaking all over my body. It was as if I would be thrown out of the bed, and I held on to prevent that. This shaking lasted for what seemed like a very long time but was probably only minutes. I called my wife the next morning and told her about the incident. She recognized this as a spiritual battle, but at the time, I did not.

She had become hungry for things of the Lord and was being filled up through the Bible studies and also through spending more time with Him in prayer. She had been responding to the Holy Spirit's drawing her to a different place in her spiritual walk. She had fallen in love with Jesus as never before and was learning to listen and be obedient to Him. I, on the other hand, though I had gone through the motions of attending class and attempting to do the homework, had always had a problem with concentration, especially when it came to spiritual things. It was as if there was a fog or a cloud over my mind. I was very easily distracted. I never finished any of the studies completely. It was a kind of hit-and-miss thing with me. I didn't retain much of what I read, but I thought I was making big points with God by attending class.

I'm so grateful that even though I wasn't getting all that I should have out of the studies, God was using them to turn my heart to Him. I was so deceived. I would sit in church, and instead of listening to the sermon (even though I tried to concentrate), I would solve work-related problems in my mind. Or even if I listened closely, I could rarely remember anything the pastor had said. As with so many other things, I soon learned that this lack of ability to concentrate and comprehend was a work of the enemy. He is also an expert at distracting us from what the Lord has for us.

I Suffered From a Terrible Depression

For weeks after the incident on the trip, I suffered from a terrible depression. I lost all interest in my job, which was not at all like me. I have always been very aggressive in my work, and even when I experienced the demotion, I had determined to do the best job possible. I had succeeded in turning a bad situation around. I learned to love the people who worked for me, and they loved me. It had turned out to be a real blessing, and I knew that. But I was not myself. Not many weeks after the trip, I was awakened again in the night with the same jerking and shaking in my body. This time it was accompanied by strange sounds coming out of my mouth.

My wife immediately started to take authority in Jesus's name and rebuke the demon spirits. Eventually, the loud noises and the shaking stopped. But it wasn't over. For nine straight days and nights, we went through much of the same thing over and over. When she would speak the name of Jesus or read Scripture, especially from

Psalms, or speak of the blood of Jesus, the demons would leave. We
began to realize not only just what we were dealing with, but we also
began to see the power that is present in the holy name of Jesus and
in His Word.

We Were Overwhelmed

Even though this could have been a frightening situation, my wife
says she was never really afraid because she felt the very presence
of the Lord and knew it was His battle. I felt His presence too.
It was as if God opened up a way for us to see into the spiritual
world and revealed to us the truth of what really goes on in that
invisible realm. We learned that even though that world is invisible
to our human eyes, it is very, very real. We were overwhelmed and
confused, but God was working. I guess this was all a part of that
new thing He told us about.

My wife had made arrangements days before these things started
occurring to meet with a friend at our house one morning. She
is a very strong Christian with whom we had become close. On
the day she came to visit, we shared with her what had happened
and she prayed with us. She understood! We had thought no one
would. God is so good to put the right people in our lives at just
the right time! She put us in touch with some other people who
understood and who began to pray for us. I was getting some relief,
but stranger and stranger things began to happen.

There were times when my body would go into all kinds of
contortions. I would gag and dry heave for long periods of time,
and I also began to speak in a really strange-sounding "language."
These things would happen as I was being taken through deliverance by either my wife or the others. Once when I tried to reach
for my Bible, my hands became so contorted that they looked
deformed and even caused me pain. When the demons were bound
and rebuked, my hands became normal again. I believe demons
were leaving at these times when they were commanded to go, but
we couldn't figure out why it wasn't over. We had begun to read
about spiritual warfare and to ask questions about it. This wasn't
happening like the books said it would. That's when the Lord
brought Don into the picture.

I Was Even Healed of a Thyroid Condition

As I said before, it was a miracle. I won't go into the details, but it was a "my friend's brother knows a guy whose brother has a deliverance ministry, and I believe he deals with that sort of thing." We called Don, and he came to our house. Don has taken me through numerous deliverance sessions, with many of the same strange things happening. Through discernment from the Holy Spirit, he was able to identify the controlling evil spirits and to order them to go into the abyss in the name of Jesus. Each time, there was more freedom. I was even healed of a thyroid condition!

He says mine is an unusual situation in the fact that it took so long, and there were so many areas of bondage, but he also says that the strongholds the enemy had in my life are very common. We have found that much of my bondage was from generational spirits. Some of the same spirits had wreaked havoc in my parent's lives. Others came through trauma and hurts in my life, and there were some that were given permission by my own choices and actions. I am learning that there is not an easy fix to this situation. By that I mean that you can't just call on someone like Don to come and bind demons and cast them out and never expect to have any more trouble with the enemy.

I Now Know What to Do

It is an ongoing battle that we must be prepared to fight. I have found that it is necessary for me to be in very close communication with the Lord at all times. I am learning to "pray without ceasing." I am learning to discipline myself to get into the Word on a regular basis and to be sure my body, soul, and spirit are in alignment with and in submission to the Holy Spirit. I have learned to recognize the enemy's subtle attempts to regain strongholds in my life. When I do recognize them, I now know what to do about it. I recognize, rebuke, and remain (as Don says). My wife has also been through deliverance with Don, and so have other family members.

Here's another thing I must share with you about how our Lord so beautifully "orchestrates" things in the lives of His children. When Don came to our home that first time, he didn't know anyone at all in the town where we lived, not even us. Today, Don goes to that town on a regular basis to minister deliverance to anyone who wants it. Hundreds have been set free because of God's mercy and because of Don's dedication to the ministry God has called him into. Praise the Lord!

I Feel Freer Than I Have Ever Felt

It's difficult to record in a few pages everything that has happened over a period of years. Actually, it's been throughout my lifetime that God's been bringing me to this place. I may not feel thirteen years old now, but I feel freer than I ever felt at any age! God has restored real joy to my soul. I'm a free man. I am free to love, free to serve, and free to worship my Lord. He has done and is continuing to do wonderful things in my life. He has allowed us to share our experience with others who need to know that they are not alone in the battle.

My mind is much clearer now, and I can hear from my Lord without interference from demons. He speaks wonderful words of encouragement and instruction to me. I now know my true identity, and it's who I am in Jesus. There will never be an end to the battle, at least not in this life, but I know Jesus has already won the victory. I also know where my freedom comes from. It comes from Jesus Christ who "came to set prisoners free." Praise His name!

Night Terrors Turn Into
Daytime Terror for a Four-Year-Old

I received an e-mail from a friend and ministry associate asking me if I ever ministered to children. She said she had met a couple who were having extreme difficulty with their four-year-old son. They sensed it was spiritual but didn't know how to proceed.

I told my friend that we do minister to children, actually quite often. I did explain to her, however, that the parents must first go through the deliverance process in order to break any legal permissions that demons might have to the child's life through a generational curse. She said she would speak to the parents, since they attended the same church, and have them contact me. Here is an account of what happened. This is in the parents' own words.

My husband and I have a happy marriage and have sought hard after God over the course of our seventeen years of marriage. We both grew up in Christian homes and have a nurturing, loving, peaceful home for our own children. To begin our story, I want to describe our son, Seth. He is an extremely sweet, affectionate, loving child. He is very obedient and showed a deep sensitivity to the Holy Spirit at a young age. We were always cautious of the influences in our home and were diligent to keep a clean spiritual environment. When he was two or three years old, if he had disobeyed, it was not uncommon for him to come to us and ask for a spanking.

When he was eighteen months old he had what the medical world refers to as a night terror. We recognized this experience as demonic torment. Seth experienced these night terrors periodically for a couple of years. He also manifested demons when we were with my husband's family at various times. We prayed and commanded evil spirits to leave when these bizarre episodes would occur. These episodes were infrequent but very disturbing when they would happen. Seth had not had any sort of manifestation for several months, and we thought he was free from any generational demonic spirits.

In February 2005 my husband and I went on a trip. My sister kept our kids while we were out of town. Once we returned, our reunion with the children was wonderful. It was so great to be home. (Seth was four years old at the time.) However, the next morning all hell broke loose when our son started manifesting demons as my husband was leaving to go to work. As these foul spirits manifested, we prayed in authority and commanded them to go. They were growling, and the look in his eyes was *not* Seth. Later in the day, Seth became very violent and aggressive toward me, which was completely out of character for him.

Over the next two weeks these demons continued to manifest. Demonic spirits were obviously operating in Seth; you could see it in his eyes. It was as if a dark presence was suddenly upon him. The spirits would scream horrible things at me, kick, hit, spit at me, and even threw things at me once. One day a spirit spoke through him and said, "I'm going to get a knife and kill you." (Our child did not have an aggressive bone in his body; we *knew* this was *not* him.) Most of the manifestations would occur when my husband was *not* home. Several times Seth would be manifesting demons in a completely agitated and aggressive state, and then it would cease seconds before my husband pulled into the garage. These demons were obviously trying to destroy my relationship with my son. We prayed, commanded, and sought counsel from our pastor, but still the evil spirits continued to manifest. We knew we had the victory in Christ but were not getting the breakthrough with our son. We were completely desperate for help.

A friend at church got us in touch with Don Dickerman. Don required that my husband and I go through deliverance in order to break off any generational spirits before he would see our son. So we filled out the paperwork to go through deliverance. My session was first. Don ministered deliverance to me and also dealt with evil spirits that were operating in Seth. While Don was dealing with a spirit that operated in our son, I felt half of my face contort into a snarl. I heard a growling sound come out of my mouth—very weird but very real. I would love to report that everything was suddenly back to normal after that first deliverance session, but it was not. However, the intensity level of the demonic manifestations was greatly decreased. Satan was trying to destroy our family, but God was raising us up as warriors in His kingdom.

Two weeks later, Seth and I met with Don while my husband had his deliverance session with another couple on Don's ministry team. My husband was about as "squeaky clean" as you can get—he never drank alcohol, did drugs, or even had a rebellious stage. We were even virgins when we got married. We knew that his grandfather was involved in Freemasonry, which we discovered were the main spirits operating in Seth. During my husband's session this Free-masonry spirit actually spoke through his mouth in a hideous voice saying, "He was mine." It was referring to Seth. The spirit was very angry and reported that Seth had "the high call of God on his life." These generational spirits were assigned to our son to block God's destiny for his life.

As my husband was in his deliverance session, Don humbly ministered to Seth and cast out more demons that were at work in his life. Seth was quiet throughout the session, but at one point said, "Back to headquarters," as Don commanded a demon to leave him and go into the pit. Don and I looked at each other and smiled.

Over the next two months, Seth continued to manifest demons, but the intensity level was greatly decreased. It was a long four-month battle for his freedom, but the Lord wanted to train us in some intense hand-to-hand combat with the enemy. We knew he would be totally free from demonic torment; we pressed in and battled on a daily basis for our son's freedom. When he would manifest demons, we would command them to leave, and Seth would begin to cough, gag and thrash about. God was showing us the reality of evil spirits and teaching us how to battle in the spirit realm.

At the end of May 2005, I had another ministry session with Don to deal with the remaining demonic spirits that were operating in Seth. Soon after that session, he was free! Seth came downstairs one morning, and the darkness was gone from his eyes. His freedom was confirmed to my husband as the Lord spoke to him, saying, "He is free." Praise God!

Seth is now seven years old and walking in victory! What Satan meant for harm, God has used for good. As a result of the battle we walked through, we sensed God calling us to minister deliverance to others. We trained under Don for a couple of months, and now we minister deliverance to others on a regular basis. It is truly a joy to not only walk in victory in our personal lives but also to be used by the Lord to help others walk in freedom. Thanks be to God who gives us the victory through Jesus Christ our Lord!

Pretty neat, huh! It's just an amazing story, and as a result, there are a couple of additional deliverance ministers out here who totally understand the process and have an anointing upon them to minister.

I Thought I'd Never Be Free:
Ron Cummings's Story

I was a career criminal. I couldn't stay out of trouble. That story is long and not relevant to this part of my testimony. I was in and out of prison. I was helpless and hopeless. I escaped, but they caught me. When I was sent to the Eastham prison after my escape, they put me in the cellblocks to live. This prison has been called America's toughest prison.

It was in those cellblocks that late at night I began to suffer some of the most horrific nightmares I had ever experienced in my life. In the nightmare I would find myself buried alive underground in a casket. It was so dark and so claustrophobic. I couldn't breathe or see anything. I vividly remember that I would kick and thrash about in that casket trying to force my way out. I would claw at the lining of this casket just trying to escape, just claw and claw and claw. But it was no use. I was trapped! Just buried alive! On one particular occasion I remember kicking and thrashing about and clawing at the top of the casket. I suddenly just bolted straight up.

It was very dark. I was out of breath, and I felt a wetness on my fingers. I reached over and pulled the string on the light in the cell. When the light came on, I saw there was blood all over my fingers and on the bedsheet. I glanced up at the wall next to the bunk and there were claw marks in blood where I had scratched my fingers down to the quick trying to escape from the casket. It was just horrible. So real and so demonic. Such a blackness had enveloped me to my innermost being. There was no life in me. I knew I was dead. I was just waiting on my heart and breathing to stop.

Medication didn't help! The nightmares would not stop. I became more aggressive and I was eventually sent to the Ellis III Psychiatric Unit where they stripped me down to a pair of white boxer shorts and placed me in a padded cell. It was just a cement slab, with a hole in the floor that served as a toilet. I remember being so cold in that cell. I had goose bumps all over me. That cell was so cold!

Once every four hours they would open up the little food slot in the cell door to medicate me. I got so bored. During one of my more lucid times, I asked the guard on one of his rounds if I could just have something to read. When he said no, I went into an absolute rage. I eventually passed out on the floor. I had lost my wife, my children, my life, my freedom, and now I had a 125-year sentence. I was losing it! I was going crazy! I don't know how long I was passed out, but then I saw a little pocket Bible that had been laid on the food slot of my cell. You know I couldn't take my eyes off of it. I just laid there and stared at it. I opened the Bible from the back (God knew what would reach me). There were three words that just jumped out at me. They said, *"God loves you!"*

I didn't think anyone loved me, much less God. I hadn't had a visit in years, and I hadn't had a letter in years. I hadn't had anyone just reach out and touch me and tell me, " Ronnie, I love you." But here it was. God was telling me He loved me. I fell to my knees right there and just cried out to God. I said, "God, I have made such a mess of my life. God, I have hurt so many people. God, all my great plans and schemes have all crumbled and come to nothing. I have failed at everything I have ever tried to do. God, I am so sorry. Make the voices stop. Please make the nightmares go away. God, make the pain stop. God, please stop the bleeding."

And you know in the corner of that cell, up high near the ceiling, a little light about the size of a pencil just suddenly appeared. It was so bright, the brightest light I have ever seen. In a fraction of a second, it just illuminated and filled the whole cell. That light pierced me! It seemed like every cell in my body came alive. I felt a warmth sweep over me and through me, and where I had been so cold, I now began to sweat profusely. The sweat just literally dropped on the floor until there was a puddle. And I just began to cry and cry and cry. I couldn't stop. You know, the Spirit of the living God came into that cell, and Jesus just came into my heart that day. I felt stuff leave me, man! It's like it was just pressed out of me. Whoosh! Bad stuff. And Jesus just loved on me and loved on me and loved on me. I don't know how long this lasted.

I got better and better, and a couple weeks later they transferred me back to the Eastham Unit. I immediately asked to see the minister there. I told him that I was a nut and that I had just returned from the psychiatric unit, but that I had had an experience with God while I was there. I related to him about the nightmares and the voices. He said, "Ronnie, when you cried out and asked Jesus to come into your heart, He did. You have been reborn. You are a new person in Christ. What can I do for you today?"

"I don't want to lose this peace," I said. "Tell me how to keep it! Tell me how to keep this peace inside of me. Tell me how to keep this joy. Tell me how to keep the love of God in my life." Jesus not only wants to be Lord and Savior of your life, but He also came to be the best friend you ever had. He wants relationship with you. The minister advised me to start reading and studying the Word of God, to start coming up to the chapel services and sitting under anointed preaching and teaching. He told me to get with a group of believers to fellowship and pray together. He told me to spend quiet time with the Lord every day. And you know, as I began to do all of those things, I began to get grounded, and even more healing took place in my life. It just got better and better.

We would gather around the benches or table in the dayroom area every day for study, worship, and prayer. It was always noisy, but we would come together as believers, and the presence of the Lord would always meet us there.

I never received letters, but one day at mail call they called my name. People had stopped writing me. I had burned all my bridges. I had not received a letter in seven years. I went forward, and they gave me a letter. Actually, it was just a piece of paper that had been folded four times and stapled. As I opened it, I noticed the state seal of Texas and the words *Board of Pardons and Parole*. It said I had been granted parole. I was stunned. What a miracle! I did not ask for it, and I sure didn't expect it!

It seems like yesterday, but now I have been out of prison since 1991. God restored my marriage and my relationship with my four children. I have my wife and family back. I have a life I once thought was impossible. I went to church every Sunday, and often many times during the week. As I continued to learn who I was in Christ, I began to see that I still had some areas of bondage. I was a heroin addict before I got saved in prison. I didn't know it, but I would find out through a doctor's visit in 2004 that I had hepatitis C. The doctor gave me five years to live and said the last two years would not be very good.

I had become a Gideon and was so blessed to share my testimony all over the state and eventually the nation. But I still had something inside of me that troubled me. I could just see a commercial on TV about not doing drugs, see a needle, or sense a certain smell, and it was like my veins would rise up in my arms crying out for the heroin. There seemed to be a pull to certain parts of town. While I didn't yield, it really troubled me that the thoughts and struggles were still there.

A friend invited me to go hear Don Dickerman speak. When he mentioned his name, I remembered Don coming into the prisons all those years to preach. I knew him, and I loved and trusted him. My wife and I attended the meeting. Don was having meetings on a quarterly basis. The meetings were held at a local community center where the focus was deliverance and healing. He called them Nights of Ministry.

On one of those nights, he did a corporate deliverance for the entire congregation. I didn't really feel anything happen at the time, but afterward my wife and I went to a restaurant. Something started to happen. I could feel "stuff" leaving me, like spirits coming out of the pores of my skin. My wife asked me what was happening, and I said, "I don't know, but I think we better go home." She told me, "Ronnie, you are being delivered. Demons are leaving you!" She was right. It happened for about two hours. It was not painful or anything; things just left, and I felt lighter. Heaviness just left me. I began to notice the cravings that came ever so often were gone—completely gone. It was like phase two of a miracle in my life.

A few months after this experience, I was getting sicker and sicker, but I didn't know why. The doctor told me I had hepatitis C. I didn't know how bad this was until he told me I only had about five years to live. I took the interferon treatments. I had not told Don about my experience or about my physical condition. But I finally mentioned it in an e-mail to him, and he told me he had seen people healed of hepatitis C and that he had found that demons can be responsible for it. I remember telling him that I was responsible; I had done the drugs. He said, "Yes, Ronnie, you opened the door for it. You invited them in. Let's close the door. All you have to lose is a couple of demons."

We made an appointment, and I came in knowing that Jesus is the deliverer and healer. I confessed all of my involvement in drugs and received God's forgiveness and cleansing. Afterward Don began to bind evil spirits in the name of Jesus and specifically addressed demons associated with disease to my liver. Names of demons came to my mind, and I passed those names on to Don. There were five demons who took responsibility for the liver ailment. The evil spirits referred to themselves as "liver beetles." They were eating the life out of me. Don very simply commanded them to repair their damage and to leave me totally and completely. He commanded them into the abyss. Something happened. Spirits did leave me, and I felt it. That was in 2004. Since then I have had two blood tests with no hepatitis C detectable.

Did God heal me? I believe He did. Were demons there with an assignment to kill, rob, steal, and kill? Absolutely, but they are gone. I guess only time will tell what all took place. Right now, I can only praise Him for all He has done in my life! I am now able to minister with Don, both in the prisons and in the office doing personal deliverance with others.

CHAPTER 13

ALL THAT JESUS DOES HAS PURPOSE

WHAT WONDERFUL INFORMATION IS PROVIDED TO US IN Mark chapter 5 concerning demons. Jesus had made a special trip to see a man tormented with demons. We don't know what prompted the journey across the Sea of Galilee. As the scripture reads, it seems unplanned and without prior arrangements. Jesus had been teaching in parables on the west side of the sea when He spoke, "Let us pass over unto the other side." It was seven miles to the "other side."

It was evening, and He doubtless was tired and weary from the day. The disciples "took Him even as He was in the ship." It seems that almost immediately He retreated to the back part of the ship to sleep. I have often wondered if Jesus was going to the "other side" in response to someone's prayer. All that Jesus does has purpose! Unfortunately, we are not always privy to that.

I believe Jesus was responding to the prayers of someone in Gadarenes. In this country, He would encounter a man so desperate for help that he lived in hopelessness among the tombs. We have no background information on this fellow except that he had an unclean spirit, he lived among the tombs, and all efforts to help him had failed.

The work of the demon spirit is partially revealed in the bits and pieces of information that we do have. The account in Luke 8 tells us that the man had been possessed a long time. It tells us that he wore no clothes and had no home. We also learn that the demons had driven him into the wilderness. There was no rest for him. Night and day, he was in the mountains and in the tombs crying and cutting himself with stones.

Let's look at some of the characteristics of people who have demons revealed in this one account:

122

1. The person is "driven." I have found this to be a consistent mark of demons, especially in the area of compulsion and obsession. There are certain areas in the life of the oppressed in which no victory can be found.

2. There was no peace or rest. Always, night and day, he was roaming, controlled by restlessness. He searched for peace and found none. The pain of the tormentor is so great, only those who have experienced it can relate.

3. There was self-hatred and self-mutilation. Often, those so tormented tell me that the pain of hurting themselves actually relieved the greater pain they felt.

4. There was no help available from mankind. No man could bind him and no man could tame him. Man did not have the answer then and does not have the answer now. Spiritual problems must have spiritual solutions.

5. There was confusion and mental anguish. "Tormentors" is one description of demon powers given by Jesus in Matthew 18:34–35.

6. He wore no clothes. He was not able to function as a normal human being. His godly instincts were suppressed. He intimidated others with his uncouth actions. People could not be comfortable in his presence. Others avoided him.

7. He had physical strength beyond his normal abilities. I believe this often indicates rebellion.

8. He was rejected by society. He did not fit in. He did not measure up. Most likely, he had been "run out of town."

9. People had given up on him, and he was banished to suffer alone. He had his own prison, his own asylum.

10. He knew that Jesus was God's Son and deserved to be worshiped, but the demons would not allow it. He knew there was a better way but did not know how to obtain it.

THERE IS ALWAYS A KINGDOM

There was a demonic kingdom in this man's life. Scripture declares in Mark 5:2, "And when he was come out of the ship, immediately there met him out of the tombs a man with an unclean spirit." "An unclean spirit" seems to indicate there was only one devil (demon) present. But we find it was a demonic kingdom of many spirits, and the prince demon of that kingdom identified himself as Legion. There is, virtually, always a kingdom, and sometimes more than one kingdom, in those who experience demonic oppression.

Let's back up and try to understand why Jesus made this journey to the other side. And why was there such opposition to Him getting there? Why was this "castaway" such a priority to Jesus? We can only guess. And why was the man in such a bad state? My experience has shown that the man's condition could have been caused by parents who did not care. Maybe he was born under a generational curse. Maybe he was conceived out of wedlock. Perhaps his ancestors had been idolaters. Maybe his mother and father fought and argued while he was in the womb. Maybe his dad left his mom and had affairs with other women.

Could it be that his mom gave him up at birth? Were his parents killed in some tragedy? Maybe he was abused sexually and physically. Possibly, they told him he was unwanted, and demons were given permission to his life through no fault of his own. I have encountered all of these things to be consent for demons to enter someone.

I would guess that this man was eventually expelled from school and had a criminal record. Probably, at best, he would have been a "latch-key" kid, in today's world. He was troubled for a "long time" and was eventually banished to live among the tombs.

Now it could be that his parents were good people and loved him dearly. They may have tried their best to control him but did not know how to deal with the demons. More likely, they did not even believe that it could be demons. Maybe they were praying for him. I want to believe that his mom cried out each day and night, "God, help my son!" The father too, asking for God's mercy, must have cried out to God, "God, help my son."

I Can See Him Sitting Up Against a Tomb

Maybe it was their prayer that Jesus heard. We don't know, but something happened that caused Jesus to decide to go to the other side. Perhaps it was the young man himself. Maybe in a moment of sanity, he looked at the cuts and the dried blood on his body and cried out, "My God, look at me. Look at my life. God, help me!" I can see him sitting up against a tomb with tears streaming down his bearded, dirty face. Maybe he tugged at his long, matted hair and cried, "God, help me." His cry is the one I think Jesus heard. The pain of the heaviness and depression and the horrible feelings of rejection and abandonment oppressed him and everyone whom he touched. Maybe it was a combination of all of their prayers. Perhaps it was just God's sovereign mercy!

The man needed help and could not find it in this world. He had no medicine for his migraine headaches and for his tormenting thoughts of worthlessness that weighed upon him continually. He could not take an antidepressant. He suffered alone, and I believe the merciful Lord Jesus was moved with compassion to go to this one man.

What believer has not heard this story? Which of us has not had hope rise up in us when we read about the One who speaks peace to wind and waves? It seems to me there was a concerted effort on the part of demon powers to prevent Jesus from reaching this man. We know from Job chapter 1 that Satan's kingdom of darkness can cause storms of destruction. Lightening was used by demon powers to destroy Job's sheep and servants. Job 1:16 says, "The fire of God is fallen from heaven, and hath burned up the sheep, and the servants, and consumed them." It was a great wind from the wilderness, perhaps a tornado, that he used to destroy Job's children. Job 1:19 says, "And, behold, there came a great wind from the wilderness, and smote the four corners of the house, and it fell upon the young men, and they are dead."

STORMS OF OPPOSITION

After Jesus had declared that they were going to the other side of the sea, something began to take place in the heavenlies. A scheme, it seems, was devised to destroy the ship or at least to cause them to turn back. I have found that demons are always scheming, always trying to hinder the work of the Lord Jesus. Opposition often comes in the form of "storms." They come to instill fear and hopelessness. They come with attempts to discourage and to defeat. They make the way seem so difficult that it appears it would be best to give up. This seemed to be working with the disciples.

But Jesus had spoken. The Word had been declared. If Jesus says it, then we may stand upon what He has spoken. He had declared, "Let us pass over to the other side." He was on a mission! Evidently, the disciples did not know about the mission; they did not know the purpose of the trip. They did not know it was urgent! They had not seen the affliction or heard the cry as Jesus had. They reacted as most of us would have. They did not yet understand that fear and faith cannot peacefully coexist. They did not know that fear is a spirit and that God does not give that spirit to us. It seems from Jesus's words that He was telling them, "With faith you could have rebuked the storm also, simply by placing faith in that which had already been spoken."

I have a visual picture of the blackness of that night, the howling winds and the waves that tossed the boat and beat against it. Great splashes of water covered the disciples. The wind was threatening, and they felt helpless to change it. It's like the words of the songwriter who said, "Master, the tempest is raging."* This was without a doubt a raging storm. The disciples feared they would die. They probably did what they should have done in the midst of the storm—call on Jesus!

Jesus, with sleep in His eyes, looked the storm in the eye and commanded, "Peace, be still!" I see the waves drop immediately and lay flat on the waters. I see the wind gently blow the dark clouds away, and then great calm. The stars and moon that were hidden in the darkness now shine upon the glistening sea. Oh, what a moment that must have been! The disciples could only say, "Wow! What manner of man is this, that even the wind and waves obey him?" The once-troubled boat now glides on the calm waters directly toward a desperate man filled with hopelessness and despair. It seems the Navigator knew exactly where to land the boat.

JESUS GETS HIS FEET WET

The boat eases up to the shore, and I hear Jesus say to Peter or John to get Him an extra change of clothes. He throws the clothes over His

---

* Horatio Richmond Palmer and Mary Ann Baker, "Peace Be Still." Public domain.

shoulder and hops from the boat into the shallow waters. Probably he told them that He would be back shortly. Personally, I believe He was answering the demoniac's prayer. Isn't it something that Jesus makes so many special trips throughout the Gospels? Here it was for someone whom society had thrown away just as we toss an empty soft drink container. Thank God Jesus has been in the reclamation business for a long time. He salvaged me!

As He came out of the ship, the man from the tombs met Him immediately. There is an interesting exchange of words. "When he saw Jesus afar off, he ran and worshipped him" (Mark 5:6). It was the demons in the man that recognized Jesus; they knew who He was. Apparently, the demons communicated that to the man, for he wanted to worship Jesus. Just the presence of the Lord Jesus demands worship. Jesus commanded the demonic kingdom to come out of him. And amazingly, the demon spokesman responded with, "What have I to do with thee, Jesus, thou Son of the most high God? I adjure [command] thee by God, that thou torment me not" (v. 7).

This is one for the books. The demon was giving a command to Jesus! The demons were afraid. They always are. They knew it was about over for them. In Luke's account, the demons begged Jesus that He would not command them to go into the deep (the abyss). (See Luke 8:31.) The tormentors were pleading to not be tormented. Those who instilled fear are now overcome by it. It seemed to be understood that if demons are cast out, it would be into the abyss.

Jesus commanded the demon spokesman, the prince of the kingdom, to identify himself. "And he [demon] answered, saying, My name is Legion: for we are many" (Mark 5:9). "And he besought him much..." (v. 10). Demon powers are such sorry creatures and such enemies of mankind. Their hatred for Jehovah God and the Lord Jesus is vented toward God's special creation—*man*. Here, the merciless creatures beg for mercy. Incredible.

Now, I have tried to get a mental picture of the country of the Gadarenes, because there is a strange encounter next. "Now there was there nigh unto the mountains a great herd of swine feeding" (v. 11). The demons wanted to go into the swine on the way into the abyss. Think of these lying, ugly spirits who claim to have such power. They are begging to go into swine!

There are some in deliverance ministry who believe that deliverance should be done by discernment only. They teach that it is wrong to confront and command truth from demon powers. Jesus asked this demon to identify himself. I would say the reality is that no anointed deliverance minister is going to carry on a conversation with demon powers. It is not conversation, but rather it is confrontation. Why did the demons request permission to go into the swine? Why did Jesus allow it? What can we learn from this?

They knew their time was up. It is clear that demons would prefer the body of a pig to nothingness. There seems to be some truth here concerning the abilities of an evil spirit to enter into animals. I think this was one last attempt at destruction, to rob life, even the life of the swine. Remember, the demons have the same functions as Satan. He is a liar and the father of lies. He was a murderer from the beginning. He has come to steal, kill, and destroy. All demons are thieves. I have yet to encounter one that did not fall in the category of steal, kill, and destroy.

Near the scene of this miraculous deliverance, there was an unusual number of pigs. A very large herd of about two thousand pigs. They were being fed. Picture this in your mind. I recall my grandparents talking about "slopping the hogs." Many of you have heard that term. Well, that's what was happening. I imagine there was a lot of snorting and grunting as the pigs pushed and shoved to get their share of the food.

What we can know is that the owners of the swine were not Jewish. But they likely were wealthy; that's a lot of bacon. This pig farm was on a mountainside that must have overlooked the Sea of Galilee. I'm not sure the smell was very good, but it seems somewhat picturesque.

As the Legion of demons was cast from the man, the swine began to screech. The pigs were experiencing the same torment that the man had known. The noise from the swine must have been disconcerting, perhaps frightening to those who fed the pigs. Perhaps the soul God has breathed into man was strong enough to resist the suicidal demons. The pigs immediately plunged to their death because of the torment. The men feeding the swine could not control the herd. The pigs hurt each other. They trampled upon one another and bit each other as the demons entered into them. They ignored the commands of their keepers. Not only were they out of control, but the tormented swine also committed suicide. They ran headlong down the mountainside and into the sea. I'm sure the swine were knocked over by others, and many of them tumbled over the rocky mountainside and over a cliff into the "deep."

SUICIDE WAS DOUBTLESS A PLAN FOR THE YOUNG MAN

Demons have come to kill, steal, and destroy. I could only speculate as to why Jesus allowed this mass suicide of the pigs. Perhaps because the swine themselves had been declared unclean. Regardless, the demons not only destroyed the swine, but they also brought hardship to the community that raised the swine. It had an economic impact on many people. The pigs went into the deep, committing suicide, and the demons went into the abyss. Doubtless, suicide was a plan the demons had for the young man who had just been freed.

Look what happened when genuine freedom came to this man. This was the man that no man could tame. This was the man who had no social skills and could not be taught. This man was made a missionary on the spot. Jesus anointed him and ordained him. He commissioned the man to go home and tell his friends what great things the Lord had done for him. Remember, this man was previously not "in his right mind." He wore no clothes and had no control over his life. Now they find him "sitting," not wandering, and clothed, maybe in the extra set of Jesus's clothes. Maybe Jesus took an extra robe with Him because He knew what He was about to do. More so, He was clothed now in the righteousness of Jesus Christ. His mind had been restored!

I feel certain the demons understood that they had to put things back in order when Jesus spoke. They had stolen the man's peace and joy. They robbed his self-image and worthiness. They created disorder in his mind and were planning to kill him. Then Jesus came!

You know, I see the same things happen on a regular basis. I see demons putting back things they have stolen at the command of the name of Jesus Christ.

The church needs to get ready because a new anointing is coming—a new and fresh understanding of spiritual warfare and of the believer's authority. Pastor, get ready. Get your deliverance team ready. God wants His people free, and He has commissioned us to act in the name of Jesus Christ. Demons still bow and retreat in His mighty name.

Jesus is still speaking peace to the storms!

PART II

THE NUTS AND BOLTS OF DELIVERANCE

CHAPTER 14

TURMOIL IN THE TEMPLE

And [Jesus] said unto them, It is written, My house shall be called the house of prayer; but ye have made it a den of thieves.
—MATTHEW 21:13

WHAT FIRST COMES TO YOUR MIND WHEN YOU THINK OF there being "turmoil in the temple"? Do you think of the many conflicts that arise within organized religion? Do church splits come to your mind? What about the restless congregation that is never satisfied with its pastor?

However, that is not my subject. What I do want to discuss might well eliminate some of those problems within the organized local congregations. I am talking about *your* temple and my temple. "Our earthly house" as Paul calls it in 2 Corinthians 5. He also refers to us as a tabernacle. "For we that are in this tabernacle do groan, being burdened…" (v. 4).

In 1 Corinthians 3:16 the Word declares, "Know ye not that ye are the temple of God, and that the Spirit of God dwelleth in you?" Clearly this scripture indicates that we, as believers, are indwelt by the Spirit of God. Where does He live? I mean, does He occupy our entire being? Where does the Holy Spirit abide in us? We are a trinity, a spirit that has a soul that lives in a body.

Does the Holy Spirit live in our flesh or our body? Does He live in our soul; that is, our mind, our will, and emotions? Does He live in our spirit? Clearly He lives in our spirit. That is what is born again. Our spirit is eternal.

Liken the spirit of man unto the holy of holies in the temple or tabernacle. Only a high priest with a blood sacrifice could enter the holy of holies. To enter with sin in his life would be certain death. He was entering into the very presence of Jehovah God. Nothing unclean could be in God's presence. The Holy Spirit of God lives in our holy of holies—our spirit.

The soul of man, which is our mind, will, and emotions, can entertain sin. Certainly uncleanness can and often does live in our soul. Obviously our flesh can indulge in sin. Uncleanness and unholiness must abide in the soul and flesh if it is in the human body. Our soul and our flesh would be the equivalent of the outer court and the holy place. The flesh must die daily. Our mind, will, and emotions must surrender to the Holy Spirit's direction and conviction in order to live a pleasing life unto the Lord. The blood of Jesus must be applied to our sin, cleansing and covering it. The turmoil in the temple is the conflict that rages within us. The Holy Spirit cannot participate in our sin and evil deeds.

Paul describes this conflict in Romans chapter 7. He describes a war raging within him—the Holy Spirit showing him what is right, just, and holy, and the soul and flesh desiring that which is not. There is turmoil in the temple. Frank Hammond called it "pigs in the parlor."

Often people ask me how a demon could possibly be in a Christian if the Holy Spirit is there. My response is with a question, "How can sin and evil thinking be where the Holy Spirit is?" Sin is in the flesh, the mind, will, and emotions. Turmoil is the result. Demons cannot enter the spirit of man, just as sin could not enter the holy of holies. But demons can and do gain access to the flesh and soul of believers! This is a battle, and it is not being disclosed by most preachers. Hence, many Christians live defeated because they are not even aware of what the battle is.

Demonic oppression or demonization is common among believers. Obviously, it is not demon possession. Possession is ownership, and we are owned by the Lord Jesus. We have been bought and purchased with a price. Possession is not the question! Demons gain access to the body or the soul by many different doorways. My experience is that they stay until they are commanded to leave. They enter by deception and become "squatters." They take and take, until in the name of Jesus Christ someone puts an end to it.

Jesus dealt with "turmoil in the temple." Remember when He went up to Jerusalem at the time of Passover and found the temple in turmoil? This was the time of celebration for the deliverance from Egypt, the commemoration of the shedding of innocent blood to bring protection for the people, and the most holy of times for the Hebrews. And the temple was in disarray.

I want you to know that Jesus exercised His authority! He called the temple "my Father's house." That makes it His house. He did not *invite* those who defiled the temple to leave. He did not suggest that it would be a good thing if they did. He demanded it! With force and heavenly authority He commanded the thieves to leave. He upset the place they had assumed in the temple. The Word of God says that *He drove them all out!* (See John 2:13–17.)

Luke's recording of this event quotes Jesus as saying, "My house is the house of prayer: but ye have made it a den of thieves" (Luke 19:46). Luke also said that Jesus cast out them that bought and sold! "A den of thieves"? Indeed!

I have found many such dens of demons. They have all come to rob, steal, kill, and destroy! Demons in believers are exactly that—a den of thieves. They steal joy and peace. They rob relationships and health. Spirit fruit is squelched. Demon spirits in believers must be dealt with just as Jesus dealt with those who caused turmoil in His temple. They must be driven out. They cannot be medicated out or counseled out. He did not say to pray them out or read them out, neither did He suggest we sing or worship them out. He said to "cast them out"!

Jesus was offended that man would defile the very temple of God. It was the place for worship. Once the offenders were driven out, the blind and the lame came and were healed by Him. I find that healing often takes place in the temple once it is cleansed. (See Matthew 21:12–15.)

Many are sick and are experiencing turmoil and defeat because of the unclean spirits that have invaded their temple. The conflict is real. The ugly, defeated demons are stealing from God's people. They have set up a kingdom of destruction in the very temple of God, the soul and flesh of believers. A nest of iniquity! A den of thieves! There is turmoil in the temple, and Jesus came to drive out all that defiles His temple. Know you not that we are the temple of God!

Believers don't have to take it. I pray this book has been an eye-opener for you so far. I pray truth has been revealed so that you no longer have turmoil in the temple and that you can bring others to freedom in Christ Jesus.

CHAPTER 15

ARE WE DOING WHAT JESUS DID?

... God anointed Jesus of Nazareth with the Holy Ghost and
power: who went about doing good, and healing all that
were oppressed of the devil; for God was with Him.
—ACTS 10:38

I DON'T KNOW THE NUMBER OF CHURCHES IN THE WORLD; I'M SURE the number is staggering. In each congregation there is an assigned preacher. In the pews of most churches there are several other ministers who have expressed the call of God on their life. I wonder among this great number of servants how many have encountered evil spirits. Even more, I wonder how many resisted them in the mighty name of Jesus Christ.

I am well aware that pastors must preach a balanced message and that there are varying degrees of spiritual maturity in each congregation. I totally understand that deliverance is not "the" ministry but it certainly is *part* of "the" ministry.

Some have referred to healing, deliverance, and gifts of the Spirit as "apostolic doctrine," meaning that those gifts were for the apostles, not for the modern believer. I would simply say to that, then being born again was only for Nicodemus and the Sermon on the Mount was only for those present. The argument that healing, deliverance, and gifts of the Spirit is "apostolic doctrine" is weak and only reflects the disbelief of the one making this claim.

I would guarantee every pastor that someone in your congregation needs deliverance. My guess is that in every congregation there is someone who is in need of "oppression healing." The above scripture is a wonderful description of what Jesus came to do. He came to bring relief from the oppressing powers of Satan. That includes more than forgiveness of sin.

While pastors have for the most part ignored this message, it is nonetheless true. The church today is weak, anemic, sick, and in bondage. We are just like the unsaved when it comes to sickness, divorce, and other areas of bondage. The reason for this I believe is simple: the message of freedom from demonic powers is not being preached.

Pastor, what will you do when your members start to come to you to ask for help in this area? If it has not already happened, it will. The numbers will increase, and I assure you that you will not be able to escape it. Sure, you can send them to a counselor. You can recommend a Christian psychologist. But Jesus did not say, "Counsel them out" or "Medicate them out." Neither can you get them out by being more religious. You can't wish them out or will them out. Jesus said to cast them out, and that is the role of the church!

The battle is heating up. You cannot lead your church where you have not been. You must bring your people out of spiritual bondage and teach them to walk in freedom and boldness. That's why I have written this book. I wish my pastor had taught me. I could have avoided so much pain. I could have helped my mother who was tormented with demons. I could have helped my brother who was in the grips of sickness and debilitating bondage from the enemy. I could have made a difference in so many lives...but no one told me. No one taught me. If Jesus came to "heal all that were oppressed of the devil," should we not let that Jesus come alive in us? Should we not be advancing against the kingdom of darkness with the authority Jesus has given us? Have we not been silent long enough?

From the pulpit, a pastor recently said, "My son has been waking up every night in horror; he cries out in such fear. My wife and I would go to his room to try to calm him and talk him back to sleep. Sometimes he would walk in his sleep during these times of fright. I was downstairs studying one night when I heard his scream. As I walked to the stairs, it seemed the Holy Spirit said to me, 'How long are you going to take this? You know what it is. Deal with it.'" The pastor said he climbed the stairs and picked up his screaming son. He cuddled him in his arms and addressed demons, "This is *my* son. I command you in the mighty name of Jesus Christ, leave him alone! Leave now and never return in Jesus Christ's name."

He went on to say with a big smile on his face, "Ever since that night it has been nothing but z's. Just peaceful sleep."

Why don't we teach the people what kind of authority we have in Christ? Pastor, I urge you first to get in the stream; get more than your feet wet. Jump in headfirst. Plunge into the river! Experience firsthand who Jesus is and who you are in Christ. You can't teach it until you experience it. Spiritual warfare is more than knowing about Ephesians 6 and 2 Corinthians 10:4–5.

Power of attorney is legal, recognized authority one has received from another. Prior to my father's death he gave me power of attorney, legal, court-recognized authority to act in his behalf. His authority became my authority. I could sign his name, make decisions in his name, and it was honored! Jesus has given us power of attorney.

> Hitherto have you asked nothing in my name: ask, and ye shall receive, that your joy may be full.
>
> —JOHN 16:24

He sent out the seventy with power of attorney. He told the church gathered after His resurrection, "As my Father hath sent me, even so send I you" (John 20:21). How did the Father send Him? With all power in both heaven and Earth. All power was given unto Him by the Father. He gave it to us as well in regards to the spiritual world on this earth! Power to speak with authority to demon powers and make them retreat. Power of life and death in our words. Authority over all the power of the enemy. I urge you to jump into this stream of anointing. It may cost you something, but it is worth it, whatever the cost!

God's people are sick. They are in spiritual bondage. I believe God is looking for deliverers, for men who will stand unashamed in the power and authority of the Lord Jesus and speak to set His people free!

CHAPTER 16

WHO IS SATAN ANYWAY?

Be sober, be vigilant; because your adversary the devil, as a roaring lion, walketh about, seeking whom he may devour: whom resist stedfast in the faith, knowing that the same afflictions are accomplished in your brethren that are in the world.
—1 PETER 5:8–9

HAVE YOU EVER REALLY GIVEN MUCH THOUGHT TO WHO SATAN is? He is very likely not who you think he is. He has many names and titles given throughout Scripture. I'm not going to give you all of that here. I just want you to know he's a liar and a deceiver and likely has you fooled about who he is. He has had some bad days in history, and he has some bad days to come.

Knowing who we are in Christ is absolutely necessary if we are to be successful in spiritual warfare.

The above scripture reveals quite a bit of information. We are to be on guard at all times. We are to remain alert and aware because the kingdom of darkness is looking for those who can be devoured! The demons are looking for whom they *may* devour. Since I am in Christ and have been given authority in the name of Jesus Christ, I will not grant him permission to devour me. Who is he anyway, seeking to devour God's children?

As we discover who Satan is, let's first look at who he is not. Satan is not the opposite of God. We have a real adversary, a very real enemy, in the devil. He is a liar and a loser, and the power he has over believers is only in lies, threats, and deceits. I am going to share a little of that message with you as an encouragement. If you asked the average man on the street who Satan is, you would likely hear that he is the opposite of God. He is evil, God is good, and there is a conflict in the heavenlies that involves mankind. One or the other influences us. This is a gross misconception. It is not even close to scriptural truth.

Satan is not the opposite of God; he is not even close. He is not omnipotent, omniscient, immutable, or omnipresent. GOD IS. God has no counterpart. Lucifer is the opposite of Michael, not God. God is in a league all by Himself. Satan is a created being, a fallen angel, and is very limited in power. He was created as an archangel and was a magnificent creation called Lucifer and possibly one of three archangels that included Gabriel and Michael. That he was an astounding creation is doubtless.

What is Satan's origin? It was God who was in the beginning, not Satan. God made everything. Satan created nothing—except rebellion! Is not the creator always greater than the creation? Read the account of Lucifer in the following scripture.

> Son of man, take up a lamentation upon the king of Tyrus, and say unto him, Thus saith the Lord GOD; Thou sealest up the sum, full of wisdom, and perfect in beauty. Thou hast been in Eden the garden of God; every precious stone was thy covering, the sardius, topaz, and the diamond, the beryl, the onyx, and the jasper, the sapphire, the emerald, and the carbuncle, and gold: the workmanship of thy tabrets and of thy pipes was prepared in thee in the day that thou wast created. Thou art the anointed cherub that covereth; and I have set thee so: thou wast upon the holy mountain of God; thou hast walked up and down in the midst of the stones of fire. Thou wast perfect in thy ways from the day that thou wast created, till iniquity was found in thee. By the multitude of thy merchandise they have filled the midst of thee with violence, and thou hast sinned: therefore I will cast thee as profane out of the mountain of God: and I will destroy thee, O covering cherub, from the midst of the stones of fire. Thine heart was lifted up because of thy beauty, thou hast corrupted thy wisdom by reason of thy brightness: I will cast thee to the ground, I will lay thee before kings, that they may behold thee. Thou hast defiled thy sanctuaries by the multitude of thine iniquities, by the iniquity of thy traffick; therefore will I bring forth a fire from the midst of thee, it shall devour thee, and I will bring thee to ashes upon the earth in the sight of all them that

behold thee. All they that know thee among the people shall be astonished at thee: thou shalt be a terror, and never shalt thou be any more.

—Ezekiel 28:12–19

Ezekiel speaks in this passage of the king of Tyrus. However, the passage has a double meaning. It describes the literal king of Tyrus, but it also describes Satan. God, the Creator, made (literally "set") Satan to be full of wisdom and perfect in beauty. He was complete. God also set him in the Garden of Eden. Remember, he was kicked out of heaven, he rebelled against God, he fought to be like God, to take over, and he lost his first estate. He was kicked to this earth and was already present when man was created.

God covered him with every precious stone. Actually this list is the same as for the stones on the apparel of the high priest with the exception of three stones. The gold is specifically representative of kingly apparel. The mercy seat in the temple was made of pure gold. The idea of "workmanship" indicates that God made Satan for a specific service. Satan had tabrets (timbrels) and pipes (flute or horn, or organ) built into his body. The idea of "prepared" indicates these were designed by God with a specific purpose. Satan was to use these to lead the heavenly hosts in worshiping God. God designed music for the purpose of worship. Satan was heaven's worship leader. I suppose with Satan's firing that there's an opening in heaven for a worship leader. How would you like to have that job? We should practice for it while we are here. Worship Him from where you are.

Satan was the anointed cherub. The concept of "anointed" meant to be set apart for service unto God. (See Exodus 30:26.) The concept of "covered" may be compared to Isaiah 6:1–3 and Exodus 25:20. God said, "I have set thee so." Please notice who is in charge. God said that Satan was upon the holy mountain of God. This was the place set apart or exalted for God. Satan was in the presence of God walking up and down in the middle of the stones of fire. What an awesome sight this must have been!

"I will cast thee as profane out of the mountain," says God (Ezek. 28:16). Satan was perfect in his ways, thoughts, and actions from the time God created him. Then iniquity was found in him. The word *iniquity* means "perverseness" or "wickedness." Iniquity, we will learn, is different from sin. We will see iniquity is also a spirit of evil. It is wickedness, the spirit, that leads to sin. It is that same spirit that is passed to others through the permission of a generational curse. Jehovah God bluntly says that Satan has sinned because iniquity was found in him. God is always in control! "I will cast thee as profane out of the mountain of God," God said. "I will destroy thee." Why? Satan began to look at his beauty and focus his attention on himself. Once, he had seen from God's perspective (true wisdom), but now that wisdom became darkened when he looked at himself.

Again, God declared His sovereignty. "I will cast thee to the ground, I will lay thee before kings, that they may behold thee" (v. 17). Because of Satan's pride, God says that He will bring judgment upon Satan. Because of Satan's iniquity (perverseness and wickedness) and his spreading of that iniquity, God will judge him with fire. Satan's kingdom is made up of fallen angels—iniquity spirits! This is important to note in dealing with generational spirits (Exod. 20:5).

People who have given their lives to Satan, even some who have worshiped him and who once admired the beauty, power, and work of Satan will someday be astonished at him. People who also feared him and Christians who refused to fight against him will see the horror of his shame and humiliation. They will see that he will never be as he once was.

> How art thou fallen from heaven, O Lucifer, son of the morning!
> How art thou cut down to the ground, which didst weaken the
> nations! For thou hast said in thine heart, I will ascend into heaven,
> I will exalt my throne above the stars of God: I will sit also upon the
> mount of the congregation, in the sides of the north: I will ascend
> above the heights of the clouds; I will be like the most High.
> —ISAIAH 14:12–14

Lucifer is the original name given to the devil. The name Lucifer means the "shining one." This is interesting because we can see that God created Lucifer (Satan) to reflect God's glory. However, now he only "appears" as an angel of light but actually is the angel of darkness.

THE FIVE FOOLISH BOASTS OF SATAN

Satan in his pride and rebellion made some foolish boast. Most preachers have spoken from this passage and called these boasts "The Five 'I Wills' of Satan."

1. "*I will ascend into heaven.*" This is perhaps the first seed of iniquity. He decides he will be like God and assumes to take the abode of God.

2. "*I will exalt my throne above the stars of God.*" This is likely when he attempted to take control over all angels (Isa. 14:13).

3. "*I will sit also upon the mount of the congregation.*" Could this be a reference to the temple of God? (See Daniel 11:37; 2 Thessalonians 2:4.)

4. "*I will ascend above the heights of the clouds.*" This is likely reference to the cloud being a covering of God (Exod. 13:21).

5. "*I will be like the most high.*" This is a pretty strong boast for a created being; he would assume to take the place of God.

It is interesting that in Ezekiel 28, God says what *He will* do as a result of Satan's rebellion. The Word says:

> I WILL cast thee as profane out of the mountain…
>
> —EZEKIEL 28:16

> I WILL destroy thee, O covering cherub…
>
> –EZEKIEL 28:16

> I WILL cast thee to the ground…
>
> —EZEKIEL 28:17

> I WILL lay thee before kings, that they may see thee…
>
> —EZEKIEL 28:17

> I WILL bring thee to ashes in the earth in the sight of all them that behold thee…and never shalt thou be any more.
>
> —EZEKIEL 28:18–19

God's simple response to this foolish boasting and rebellion is recorded in Isaiah 14:15–17:

> Yet thou shall be brought down to hell, to the sides of the pit. They that see thee shall narrowly look upon thee, and consider thee, saying, Is this the man that made the earth to tremble, that did shake kingdoms; that make the world as a wilderness, and destroyed the cities thereof; that opened not the house of his prisoners?

When Satan's judgment is revealed, people will marvel not at his power but at the deceptiveness in appearing to have power. He was perfect until iniquity was found in him! He was an awesome creation of God, but that is all he is—a created being. He is one angel! Just one fallen angel! Since he is not omnipresent, he cannot be where I am and where you are at the same time. He is not a spirit that covers the earth. It is a grievous error to believe otherwise. God can and is everywhere present at all times.

Do you think Satan has ever been to your house? I seriously doubt it. It is important that you read carefully what I am about to say. Since Satan can only be in one place at a time, I doubt that he has personally been to my home or to yours. While I am certain my name is known in the kingdom of darkness, I doubt that Satan knows my name. He cannot be but in one place at one time. My guess is that most of his time is spent in Washington DC and other influential capitals of the world. He is *not* omnipresent! But his demon powers roam about as a roaring lion. When Satan came before God concerning the life of Job, he confessed that he had been "going to and fro in the earth...walking up and down in it" (Job 1:7).

He is *not* omnipotent, or all-powerful. As a matter of fact, he is very limited in his power and always in subjection to Jehovah God. He had to ask God's permission to touch Job because there was a hedge of protection that he could not penetrate. Not only did he have to seek permission, but also God set the limitations as to what he could and could not do. It is important to know he is not God's equal opposite! He's not even close.

Satan is *not* omniscient, all-knowing. His knowledge is limited and cannot know what God has not revealed to him. He can only know what is revealed in Scripture or what Jehovah God allows him to know. Certainly demon powers know our tendencies and our past failures, but they can only know our thoughts if they have access to our mind by dwelling in our soul. I actually doubt that even then can they "read our mind." Do they know what you are going to do or are about to do? Think back to the times you have started to pray or read your Bible and there was some distracting activity that took place.

Satan is *not* immutable; rather he is the opposite. He is always changing, lying, and deceiving. What we must logically and spiritually deduce from this is that it is not Satan himself that we deal with; it is his demons. There is obviously a demonic hierarchy, and we deal with some of the lowest-ranking soldiers. You can imagine a line of reporting that goes through many demonic powers before it reaches Satan himself. Demons we deal with likely report to regional or territorial spirits—spirits over communities, cities, counties, states, regions, countries, nations, hemispheres, and the world system. They are likely more complex than we can comprehend.

Without doubt there is a system of rank and power in place. The powers that we deal with are on assignment from higher-ranking evil spirits. But let it suffice here to say that Satan is not who most people think he is. He is a defeated foe, right now, this moment. He is defeated. It is important that we remember that Satan only has power over us that we give to him, that we yield. He was disarmed at Calvary, publicly humiliated.

> And having spoiled principalities and powers, he made a shew of them openly, triumphing over them in it.
> —Colossians 2:15

"He made a shew of them openly." This is what the Romans would do when they returned victorious from a battle. They would display the enemy in humiliation. They would glory in their victory by showing the enemy soundly defeated. Many times the victorious chariots would return with leaders of the opposing army strapped to the wheels as the chariots came into the city. They made of show of the defeated enemy. They gloried in their triumph. So did Jesus with the shed blood and glorious resurrection! Jesus, in defeating Satan, made him like Barney Fife, the feisty deputy of *The Andy Griffith Show*. He had lots of boasting of power, but he had no bullets for his gun. He is a threat and no more. Fear, lies, and deceit have become his power concerning believers. The power he has over believers is the lies we believe and the biblical ignorance we tolerate.

Seven Bad Days for the Devil

Satan has had some bad days in his history, as I said at the beginning or this chapter, and he has more to come. Let's review seven of those bad days.

Satan's first bad day is recorded in Isaiah 14:12–17. He was kicked from heaven to this earth. In all of Lucifer's magnificence, pride found a way into his life. It seems clear that he was the praise and worship leader in heaven. One-third of the angels made up his heavenly choir. He deceived himself. He forgot he was the created and not the Creator. He actually made a decision to be like God, but has the clay power over the potter? Ridiculous is his self-deception.

The five "I wills" of Satan as referred to earlier indicate that Satan was given a will and made a very foolish choice. This makes me believe his own deception and pride blinded him. Regardless, it got him booted from heaven! Talk about a bad day! Kicked from heaven to this earth. This was more than a "bad hair day"; this was a bad day! There is no real evidence when, in history, this event took place. Likely, Satan's arrival on Planet Earth was the cause of the darkness. It is clear that he was already here when man was created.

You see that while Satan is extremely deceptive and clever, he lacks real wisdom and understanding. In his foolish boasting, he actually said that he would be like God. That is part of his lie today—seeking the worship of men and luring them from the worship of God. He still wants to rule! Someday when we see him for who he really is, we will proclaim, "Is this the man? This is the one we feared? This is the one who caused all of the havoc? This is the destroyer?" (See Isaiah 14:16–17.)

Notice also in the last phrase of verse 17 that he does not open the house of his prisoners! If he, through his demonic kingdom, gets a person into bondage, there is no parole, there is no mercy, and he does not open the house of his prisoners. This is another reason Jesus came and took the keys from Satan. Jesus holds the keys of death and hell, but He also took the keys of the prison (bondage to the kingdom of darkness) and gave them to the church. Any believer who stays in bondage does so through ignorance or a choice to remain in the bondage.

But, back to Satan's dismissal from the heavens. Talk about a demotion, he was reduced to the god of this world. His domain was greatly diminished, and he became the prince and power of the air, the ruler of darkness. He was greatly reduced in power when God booted him from His presence.

Look at this and rejoice. Jesus was present when Satan was booted to this earth. He told the seventy, who represent the church, in Luke 10:18: "I beheld Satan as lightning fall from heaven."

Do you realize what Jesus is saying? "I know who he is; I know his power. I saw him fall. I was there when he was cut down to the ground and greatly reduced in power. I know all about him and his fall!" Likely, it was Jesus who kicked Satan from heaven to this earth. Now understand the impact of His next words in Luke 10:19: "Behold, I give unto you power to tread on serpents and scorpions, and over all the power of the enemy: and nothing shall by any means hurt you."

Pretty awesome, isn't it? "I know who he is," Jesus said, "and I am giving *you* authority over him." This is absolutely an incredibly overlooked verse of Scripture, but more on that later.

Satan's second bad day came when he began to mess with God's creation. Apparently it really disturbed him that we, not him, were created in God's own image. I like it that it bothers him. He was already seeking whom he could devour. He was lurking about to destroy God's plan and purpose. He is called "the destroyer." You see, he was already on this earth when man was created. He used his powers of deception and lied to Eve with the same lie he is spreading today. You will be like God. The seeds of New Age and humanism were planted in the garden. The message is not new at all. It's the oldest of all lies.

> And the LORD God said unto the serpent, Because thou hast done this, thou art cursed above all cattle, and above every beast of the field; upon thy belly shalt thou go, and dust shalt thou eat all the days of thy life: and I will put enmity between thee and the woman, and between thy seed and her seed; it shall bruise thy head, and thou shalt bruise his heel.
>
> —GENESIS 3:14–15

After man's fall, God showed up in the garden and cursed the serpent. He gave the promise of a Savior who would crush his head. Genesis 3:15 tells of the second bad day for the devil!

The bad day was a promise for mankind that a Savior would someday crush Satan beneath His feet, a promise of a woman giving birth to the Son of God, God in the flesh. I'm sure Satan understood what was going to happen, but he did not know when. He didn't know how soon, and he didn't know how to prevent it. This bad day lasted four thousand years—wondering and waiting. He likely did not know until prophecies dating the Messiah's coming were revealed through the prophets.

He had four thousand years to anticipate this day, the day he would bruise the Savior's heel but would be crushed in the head beneath His feet! He knew it was coming and couldn't stop it. Oh, that was a bad day when he deceived man and received the promise of a Savior to be born who would crush his head.

I'm sure each time one of God's prophets told of the Messiah's coming Satan had nervous tremors. I believe he is having those now, knowing that his demise is getting closer with each passing day. For when Jesus returns for His bride, Satan's days are literally numbered. He will have 1,007 years before he is forever banished in the lake of fire. He gets a little more desperate with each day that brings us closer to the Rapture!

The third bad day was not the birth of Jesus but the baptism of Jesus. Many unusual events surrounded the birth of the Lord Jesus—an increase in heavenly activity with visitation from holy angels, a similar atmosphere that we will likely experience prior to His second coming. When Jesus was born, Satan used Herod to tried to kill the long expected Messiah, but this was not possible. And I can tell you with great confidence that he cannot prevent what God may be birthing in your life! If you are anointed by the hand of God, what God has promised you will come to pass. Satan may hinder but never thwart the plans and purposes of God.

The third bad day, when Jesus was baptized, was the beginning of the end for Satan, and he knew it.

> And Jesus, when he was baptized, went up straightway out of the water: and, lo, the heavens were opened unto him, and he saw the Spirit of God descending like a dove, and lighting upon him: And lo

a voice from heaven, saying, This is my beloved Son, in whom I am well pleased. Then was Jesus led up of the Spirit into the wilderness to be tempted of the devil. And when he had fasted forty days and forty nights, he was afterward an hungred. And when the tempter came to him…

—MATTHEW 3:16–4:3

I can see this take place: the Holy Spirit coming upon Jesus with power and directing Him to the wilderness for a face-to-face confrontation with Satan. It was like Satan was offering a challenge, saying, "OK, let's you and me just get it on. I've been waiting four thousand years for this day. I've got my best spiritual weapons ready for you." I imagine Jesus replying with something like this: "Yeah, well, first let Me fast for forty days and forty nights to make Myself weak as humanly possible, so this will be a little more even, because I'm about to beat you up one side and down the other! It won't even be close. It won't go into overtime. There will be no extra innings. I am going to beat you like the dog that you are!"

Jesus fought Satan on neutral ground in Matthew 4:1–10. Look at the result of that skirmish; that's all it was to Jesus, a skirmish. "Get thee hence, Satan," Jesus said. After Satan fired his best shots trying to defeat Jesus by causing Him to sin, Jesus spoke to him like the dog that he is: "Get out of here!" He beat him up with the Word of God, and on the way to the main event at Calvary He stomped on him time after time, healing the sick, casting out his demons, raising the dead, giving believers authority over all demon powers (including Satan himself), preaching the gospel to the poor, and so much more. This was on the way to the main event. Third bad day for the devil! I see Satan leaving that confrontation with his ears laid back, his tail tucked between his legs, and his rear dragging the ground, Jesus spoke to him like he was a dog. Get out of here!

Jesus defeated Satan with the Word. You too can know that when Satan fires his best shots at you and you stand on the Word, victory is assured. When we resist, demons retreat. Not only that, but after this skirmish, the angels of God came and ministered to Jesus. They will come to you also. Keep standing on the Word. The Word defeats him because the Word is truth and demons are liars.

Every day, as the time got closer for Jesus to go to the cross, He was virtually beating on Satan and the kingdom of darkness daily. Three times He slapped death right in the face and spoke life to corpses! He raised the dead and proclaimed that He would rise from the dead. All the way to the cross Jesus demonstrated that He alone is Lord. He conquered disease, demons, and death and demonstrated His authority that would soon be given unto believers.

He revealed His authority over wind and waves, He walked on water and calmed seas, He spoke a curse to a tree and it died, and He spoke to Lazarus and he lived. He said:

> Have faith in God. For verily I say unto you, That whosoever shall say to this mountain, Be thou removed, and be thou cast into the sea; and shall not doubt in his heart, but shall believe that those things which he saith shall come to pass; he shall have whatsoever he saith.
>
> —MARK 11:22–23

What awesome words He spoke. Have faith in God. If you can believe, *you* can receive. Please note that the "whosoever" in the above verse is the same "whosoever" that calls men to Christ. It includes any believer, not "special" believers. He poked at Satan all the way to the cross.

When the seventy had returned from their appointed, anointed mission (Luke 10:1–7), they marveled. Now you must know these were not the twelve disciples, nor were they their relatives. They certainly were not apostles. They obviously are representative of the church today. They were "whosoevers," and He gave them authority. Look at the transaction in Luke 10:17–22.

> And the seventy returned again with joy, saying, Lord, even the devils are subject unto us through thy name.
>
> And he said unto them, I beheld Satan as lightning fall from heaven. Behold, I give unto you power to tread on serpents and scorpions, and over all the power of the enemy: and nothing shall by any means hurt you. Notwithstanding in this rejoice not, that the spirits are subject unto you; but rather rejoice, because your names are written in heaven.

In that hour Jesus rejoiced in the spirit, and said, I thank thee, O Father, Lord of heaven and earth, that thou hast hid these things from the wise and prudent, and hast revealed them to babes: even so, Father; for it seemed good in thy sight. All things are delivered to me of my Father: and no man knoweth who the Son is, but the Father; and who the Father is, but the Son, and he to whom the Son will reveal him.

Do not dismiss this; do not try to keep yourself in the restrictions of a church doctrine. Receive this wonderful truth and be part of freeing God's people from bondage.

Have you ever considered Jesus's job description? Have you given much thought to what He said He came to do? His anointing was spoken of by Isaiah and received and confirmed when Jesus stood in the little synagogue where it was His custom to worship there in Nazareth. As a matter of fact, it is the event in Scripture that follows His water baptism and the Holy Spirit baptizing Him with power. After He trounced on Satan in the wilderness, He returned to Nazareth, His hometown.

Jesus gave His job description. For maybe twenty-five years Jesus had been attending the synagogue, listening to the teachers. He listened and learned in silence, worshiping and learning from the rabbis. This day would be different. Today, Jesus would speak. Thirty years after He was prophetically born of a virgin, the Lord Jesus would speak. I can see the gentle, quiet Lord Jesus rise from His seat and call for the scrolls of Isaiah. What anointing and power must have come from His lips as He quoted from Isaiah's prophecy and announced His job description.

> The Spirit of the Lord is upon me, because he hath anointed me to preach the gospel to the poor; he hath sent me to heal the broken-hearted, to preach deliverance to the captives, and recovering of sight to the blind, to set at liberty them that are bruised, to preach the acceptable year of the Lord.
>
> —LUKE 4:18–19

Amazing! The Bible declares that He closed the book and sat down.

What have we missed here? I don't hear this being proclaimed as the job of the church, yet Jesus said in John 20:21, "As my Father hath sent me, even so send I you." Why is that not the job description of every pastor?

Not only do our people need the gospel of salvation, but hearts are also broken and need mending. Jesus came to bind and heal the broken-hearted. People are sick and blind, and He came to restore what the enemy has taken. People are bruised from life, some scarred since child-hood. He was "bruised for our iniquities." That is why He can heal our bruises that came through iniquity. He came to break the bonds of captivity. Salvation is eternal, but it does not bring healing or break Satan's bonds. I honestly never understood this. Salvation was the only message I knew!

I discovered I had been living in only one room of a really big house. I camped out in the salvation room. I invited many people into that room, and over the years more than one hundred thousand have joined me. I really give praise to God for that! One day the Holy Spirit invited me to other parts of the house. I could hardly take in all that I saw as He took me to other rooms. One room right by the salvation room was the healing room. He anointed me to go into that room.

I had believed that this room was closed, that it was no longer open. I saw in the hallway leading to this room many other rooms, all with names of spiritual gifts. But I had always heard that these rooms were closed after the Bible was given to man. They told me not to even look for these rooms. Why did they do that? What man had told me was off limits the Holy Spirit was now inviting me into. Wow! I heard some rejoicing and praise coming from other rooms and the healing room too as God's people gave praise for various healings.

I saw the room where demons were being run off, and I wanted in that room. People were in such peace and fulfillment as the robbers and thieves were being kicked out of their lives. It's a big house I was discovering, and I still haven't been in all the rooms yet. Everything starts in the salvation room, but it leads to many other areas of the house. This is the way I felt when I began to see people healed and delivered. Why had I been so long in the salvation room? Because I didn't know the other rooms were open. I had believed a lie!

One of my mentors in deliverance ministry was Rev. Frank Hammond, who wrote, among other books, *Pigs in the Parlor*. There is an account in Matthew 15 of a Canaanite woman, a Gentile, coming to Jesus for help for her little girl who was "grieviously vexed with a devil" (v. 22). Jesus told her that He had come for the lost sheep of Israel. She was a Gentile; therefore, she did not qualify. She pleaded and Jesus said, "It is not meet [right] to take the children's bread, and to cast it to dogs [Gentiles]" (v. 26).

She was not one of the children of Israel. She was out of bounds. So desperate was she that she fell at His feet and worshiped Him, "Truth, Lord: yet the dogs eat of the crumbs which fall from their masters' table" (v. 27).

Uh oh! Now she had made a statement of faith, and Jesus said, "O woman, great is thy faith: be it unto thee even as thou wilt" (v. 28). Her faith got her in. She now qualified as one of the children, and she got what she came for.

What she came for was healing and deliverance. Jesus called it children's bread! This is another instance where Jesus slapped Satan on the way to the cross: a Gentile received salvation, healing, and deliverance.

The fourth bad day was at the cross. Every drop of blood paid for something. Not only was salvation's work finished at the cross, Satan was finished there also. The innocent spotless blood of Jesus streamed from the stripes on His back in the judgment hall. In that instant, our healing was being paid for! The first drop of blood that oozed from the beating had sufficient power to bring healing to all suffering mankind. Prophecy was being fulfilled. While Satan thought he was having victory, his doom was being forever sealed.

> But he was wounded for our transgressions, he was bruised for our iniquities: the chastisement of our peace was upon him; and with his stripes we are healed. All we like sheep have gone astray; we have turned every one to his own way; and the LORD has laid on him the iniquity of us all.
>
> —ISAIAH 53:5–6

1. Wounded—for our transgressions!

2. Bruised—for our iniquities!

3. Chastised—for our peace!

4. Stripes—beaten for our healing!

Four separate things were paid for in this one verse: sin, evil spirits, peace, and healing.

Satan did not even recognize that this was a bad day. He deceived himself. But the blood that was shed will never lose its power! It will never lose its power to cover sin, to expose wickedness and darkness, to bring peace, and to afford healing. It will never lose its power.

The fourth bad day continues into the resurrection! No resurrection, no victory. "If Christ be not raised," Paul says, "[I am] of all men most miserable" (1 Cor. 15:17–19). Oh, but he is risen indeed! Matthew 28:6 declares: "He is not here: for he is risen." In Revelation 1:18, Jesus said, "I am he that liveth, and was dead; and, behold, I am alive for evermore, Amen; and have the keys of hell and of death." Every drop of blood He shed at Calvary was crushing the serpent's head. Every drop of blood paid for something and gave us authority over the devil. A bad day for the devil!

When Jesus descended into hell, He went to Satan's house and beat him up again. I can also visualize this happening. Maybe the demons were having a party, celebrating the death of Jesus. Maybe there was a card table where Satan, Beelzebub, Abaddon, and Belial were playing poker. The doorbell rings and Satan says, "Abaddon, get the door." I can see this ugly demon strolling to the door, somewhat cocky. He looks through the peephole and immediately passes out. He hits the floor with a thud! Beelzebub rises from his chair and says, "I'll get it." He goes to the door, and as he glances through the peephole, he grabs his heart and starts stumbling and stammering. He can't speak. Satan jumps up in disgust and opens the door. There stands Jesus! "Oh no, no, no," cries Satan.

Jesus says, "I've come for the keys! Give Me the keys." He punches him one more time. He took the keys from Satan, and now He has the keys of hell and death. He ripped the stinger out of him, taking away death's sting forever for those who believe. He jumped up and down on the grave, robbing it of its victory, and He is alive forever more. That was a bad day for the devil!

The fifth bad day occurred only fifty days later. Jesus walked on the earth and showed Himself alive for forty days. The church was told to go into all the world and preach the gospel, to cast out demons in Jesus's name and to lay hands on the sick and they would be healed. But they were not to go until…until the power came.

They waited in prayer for ten days. Have you ever prayed and nothing happened? Keep praying until the answer comes! They prayed one day, then two, then three, four, five, six, seven, eight, nine days, and nothing happened. Nothing. Do you suppose there was any talk of not continuing? Do you think maybe some suggested that they had prayed and tarried long enough? I feel certain that they did.

But on that tenth day, Acts 2:2, says, "Suddenly there came a sound from heaven..." The power came! When the power came, they were energized to fulfill the commission on their life. Now go, now preach, now witness. Multitudes began to accept Christ. The gospel was being spread all over and was being received all over. Jesus had already spoken, "And I, if I be lifted up from the earth, will draw all men unto me" (John 12:32). I can see Satan tremble at another of his mistakes and must have said, "Oh, my! Oh, no! I had one Jesus to deal with. Now I have little Jesuses everywhere!"

Christians were beginning to understand the principle of binding and loosing. The words that Jesus spoke were coming alive to them. "Behold, I give unto you power...over all the power of the enemy" (Luke 10:19). It is a bad day for the devil when that truth comes alive in believers today. Speak to those demons in the name of Jesus. Tell the demons that you face, "You are defeated. I have victory in Christ Jesus. I am in Him, and He is in me. And He that is within me is greater than he that is in the world. YOU back off; you are the one going to hell, not me. You are the one with a problem, not me. I have eternal life living in me. You have a bad future ahead of you, and you and your principalities and powers are all under the feet of Jesus. You back off! Go in the name of Jesus Christ. I overcome you by the blood and the power of His name. I resist you, I rebuke you, and you must be obedient!" We have been given power of attorney; use it. Do it. Give him a bad day.

The sixth bad day is on the horizon. Revelation 20:1–3 tells us that he has a couple of bad days coming too! Someday *one* angel will bind him for one thousand years, and while Satan is bound, we will rule and reign with Jesus on this earth for a full one thousand years! Think about it; one holy angel will bind him. "Is this the man?" Lies, deceits, threats. He has some bad days coming. Remind him occasionally.

The seventh and final bad day is recorded in Revelation 20:7–10. The devil, the beast, and the false prophet—the unholy trinity—will be cast into the lake of fire and brimstone and shall be tormented day and night forever and ever! He has a *bad* day coming. Every time he reminds you of your failures, your guilt, and your past, remind him of his future! "Is this the man?" Stand on the Word. We have victory, and he is defeated. Jesus has given us power over all the power of the enemy! Praise God!

During the time Satan is bound for one thousand years we will rule and reign with Jesus on this earth. We who are saved, that is. If you are not saved, then you have a bad day coming also. Your fate will be the same as Satan's. But because he is defeated, you can have life everlasting through Christ Jesus. Believers have some great days ahead. There is a day coming when God Himself will wipe away all tears, and there will be no more sorrow, heartache, or pain because the former things will be no more.

It is the former things that we deal with now.

CHAPTER 17

WHAT EXACTLY IS SCRIPTURAL DELIVERANCE?

ELIVERANCE IS PROBABLY NOT WHAT YOU HAVE HEARD THAT it is. It is not like the movies. It is not like Hollywood; it is like the *Holy Word*! It is for believers! It is nothing to be afraid of and is totally nonthreatening to the individual. It is simply inner healing by removal of the cause of the problem. Remember what Acts 10:38 says? "... God anointed Jesus of Nazareth with the Holy Ghost and with power: who went about doing good, and healing all that were oppressed of the devil." That is what deliverance is, breaking the oppressing power of the enemy!

Why could Jesus do all that He did? The simple answer is that He was God's Son sent into this world to do all that He did. God sent Him with power and authority, right? God gave Him authority, and Jesus gave us authority. Scriptural deliverance is relieving spiritual oppression!

Demons can possess *areas* of a Christian's life; that is, once they are in the soul and flesh, they can control areas not submitted to the Holy Spirit. Complete possession of a believer is not possible because the Holy Spirit lives in our spirit, that part of us that is eternal.

Is it correct to say that deliverance ministers are exorcist? In the proper definition of the word, yes. The goal of the deliverance minister is to expel the demon from the soul and flesh of the individual; however, it does not happen the way movies and the media have depicted exorcisms. It is often without any significant manifestation and is completely nonthreatening to the one receiving the ministry of deliverance. It is not much more than praying for the individual in terms of what goes on. The "deliverance dramas" are rare, though they do happen.

The most common misconception I encounter is that *only evil people have demons*. Somewhere in church history the notion was presented that Christians could not have demons. Nothing could be further from the truth! If you are alive, you are a candidate.

The average believer has either been taught or has come to a "logical" conclusion that demons and the Holy Spirit cannot coexist in the same body. That's what most people struggle with.

Demons take up residence in the body and the soul but not in the spirit. The Holy Spirit abides in the spirit of a believer. If you have believed this because of a "logical" conclusion, then you must account for how sin dwells in a person where the Holy Spirit abides. How does evil manifest in believers if we use that logic? Where do the anger, hatred, and bitterness live? Where does lust manifest if not in the body? It is a foolish conclusion. Demons can and do live in believers if they have been granted legal permission.

A second mistake I see when the word *deliverance* is mentioned is that people want to think "demon possession." It is *not* possession. Possession implies ownership. We are owned by the Lord Jesus! We are purchased, redeemed, and bought with a price. We are possessed by the Holy Spirit of God who lives in our spirit. Oppression takes place in the soul and in the flesh. The soul—mind, will, emotions—is the area of torment, and that is where the demons do their misdeeds. This is the warfare that Paul so often talks about. In Psalm 116, David describes oppression and deliverance perfectly. David said, "The pains of hell gat hold upon me; I found trouble and sorrow.... [He] loosed my bonds" (vv. 3, 16).

Demons must have legal rights to one's life. They cannot intrude at will. It always involves legal consent from either the individual or from God. A generational curse, of course, does not involve our will, but it does grant permission to evil spirits through the sins of the fathers and mothers for three to four generations, meaning *anyone* born could be born with a spirit that has legal right according to Exodus 20:5. This is the most common entryway for demon spirits, and for you to think it could not happen to you is evidence of the power of their deception.

Entryways many times are there not because of sin committed but because of things that happened. Trauma is a very common doorway. To believe that torment is sent by God is borderline blasphemy. God sends good and perfect gifts. Demons are tormentors. Coming to a scriptural understanding of this is the first step toward release.

Demons, evil spirits, unclean spirits, devils, spirits of infirmity, principalities, powers, and the like *must have permission* to be in someone's life. Jesus had to have permission to be in your life. God requires our permission. Jesus says in Revelation 3:20, "I stand at the door and knock." Why does He knock at our door? Because He must have our permission to enter our lives!

Demon or evil spirits must also have our consent, and permission is granted in many ways through each person's life. The Holy Spirit honors our will; demons must also. They cannot intrude without some kind of consent. (Consent can be as simple as being in the presence of a Ouija board, a childhood abuse or trauma, periods of anger or unforgiveness, and so on.)

When people come to me for deliverance, I ask them to complete a questionnaire. The questions came after years of deliverance experience and noticing common doorways for spirits. I ask people to pray after completing the form that I give them and ask the Holy Spirit to bring to their remembrance anything that may have given access to the demon powers.

Once consent is granted, the demon takes up residence in the soul or flesh and begins to build a "kingdom" bent on destruction. Jesus says that Satan works to kill, steal, and destroy (John 10:10). I have yet to locate a demon power with any other function. Now, the oppression begins because the demon has been granted permission to be there.

Part of the deliverance process is to determine what doorways or entryways were granted to evil spirits. That is, what permission or consent do the demons have to be there. The fact that they are there indicates they had consent. The question now is, do they permission to stay?

You may wonder what would give a demon legal consent to stay in a believer's life. Consent to stay could be, for example, unforgiveness in one's life. Unforgiveness is God-given permission for demons to torment. (See Matthew 18:23–35.) If unforgiveness is in a believer's life, demons do not have to leave! They have God's permission to stay—and permission to torment.

Another example of permission to stay would be sin in an individual's life that he or she is unwilling to surrender to the Lord. That will block deliverance because the demon has legal rights to stay.

If all consent to be there, and to stay there, is canceled, then the demons must be obedient to the command in the name of Jesus Christ to leave.

Deliverance cannot take place against someone's will and can even involve more than just his or her willingness to be free. Often it requires a *desire* to be free.

Demon spirits are very organized and are hierarchy oriented. They are very structured. You might view their kingdom as having a CEO with vice presidents, managers, supervisors, and workers. Or maybe a better description would be a military pecking order. There will be a "boss" who runs everything. They like to be called "princes." The prince may have several princes under him who all have varied functions intent on the believer's demise and destruction. But every one of them will bow at the name of Jesus Christ, so you need not fear.

That Satan has a demonic hierarchy is well documented in Scripture. Ephesians 6:12 tells us that "we wrestle not with flesh and blood, but against principalities, against powers, against the rulers of darkness of this world, against spiritual wickedness in high places."

From Satan's throne or his place of rule, there is a vast kingdom of darkness. I don't know the layers of authority in this kingdom. I can only speculate how many demon powers separate Satan from the attacks on my life. I would guess there are several in the chain of command. I remember an inmate came up to me after a recent service in a Texas prison. He said, "Sir, the Holy Spirit told me to tell you that Satan has assigned a high-ranking spirit to you. Do you know what that means?" Yes, I knew. Before I could even allow fear a place in my heart, the Holy Spirit spoke to me, "Same authority. You have the same authority in Jesus's name. Just keep walking!"

High-ranking spirit? There are many in the heavenlies. I do not believe we have been given authority to challenge these demon powers. Our authority is on this earth, as it has to do with mankind. My authority, I believe, is restricted to what is mine and to where I am, and to whomsoever comes willingly under my authority. To tear down heavenly positions of darkness, I believe, can be very dangerous and foolish. I have seen many come under attack of sickness and family trauma because of unwise ventures into warfare.

Stepping outside our realm of authority is a mistake. Challenging demons is a mistake. Knowing our boundaries and limitations is a must in spiritual warfare. As it has to do with me, my family, and my "stuff," Jesus Christ has given me full authority over all the power of the enemy. As it has to do with "powers in the heavenlies," I believe that battle is won in intercession. That is where the angels fight on our behalf. Repentance and confession of ancestral wrongs lend strength in that battle.

I would guess a spiritual hierarchy would break down similar to the following:

- Satan, the beast, false prophet (Lucifer)
- Beelzebub—"the world is mine," prince of demons
- Abaddon—Apollyon, king of bottomless pit of demons
- Xanthan—claims totality, including universe
- Baphomet
- Samhain
- Ma Ha Bone—prince of all Freemasonry spirits
- Moletha—witchcraft, voodoo, and so on
- Witchcraft—sickness/disease, calamity, distress, poverty, lust, etc.
- Territorial spirits—continents and nations; example: "Adirondack" over North America or "Nemtalia" over Egypt
- District spirits—example: "Elamond" over Colorado, Oklahoma, Kansas, Missouri, New Mexico, and parts of Texas
- Regional spirits—example: "Singfa" over southern Oklahoma
- Counties—example: "Ahmigihad" over Carter County, Oklahoma, and "Oncar" over Estes County, Colorado
- Cities—example: "Cameron" over Fort Worth, TX
- Communities—example: false religion, harassing, hindering, blocking, temptation, blindness (spiritual), floaters, or roaming spirits

- Individual kingdom princes—example: fear and darkness spirits

This is just an opinion of how the kingdom might break down. It is likely much more sophisticated. My guess is that there would be many more levels of authority. My point is that we do not deal directly with Satan but with his underlings. The demon powers that we confront are probably those with the least of demonic power. The demonic kingdom established within an individual is generally on assignment from an outside spirit of higher rank. An example would be that of a person who has demons there by permission of a generational curse from Masonic ancestry. The prince of that kingdom would likely report to Ma Ha Bone. I have found this to be the highest-ranking Masonry spirit.

The assignments can be anything from stealing joy to murder or premature death. Remember, their goal is that of Satan's—to kill, steal, and destroy. I have found the kingdoms established within people to be extremely consistent. There is little variation in the structure of the kingdom. The demons seem not to be very creative or ingenious. The pattern is virtually always the same.

Some of the demons in the internal kingdom are assigned the duty of gatekeeper. It is their function to bring other demons in at every opportunity. In the process of deliverance, I will address these spirits and command that when they leave, every gate is closed and locked!

A typical deliverance session, if there is such a thing, can vary in length from one hour to many hours, but generally it can be accomplished in a couple of hours. The more prepared the individual is, the smoother the process—with some exceptions. I always remind the candidate that the process is not a ritual, and it is permissible to ask questions, pause for a restroom break, or get a drink of water. The deliverance setting is casual; yet, it is holy. We always depend upon the holy presence of God's Spirit to lead us and guide us. Deliverance is a truth encounter; it is not a power encounter!

Demons are all liars, and they will submit to the truth of the Word of God and the powerful name of Jesus Christ. Demons totally understand the battle. They know they are defeated and know they must be obedient to the commands of the Lord Jesus. They will bow their knee, and they will leave when they are commanded to leave!

It is not uncommon for the person seeking deliverance to experience manifestations of the evil spirits prior to the session as well as during the session. They (or the demons in them) may become extremely nervous, because they know their time is short. The demons will attempt to frighten the person or plant lies about the destruction they (the demons) may do. It is also common to have nightmares or to experience sickness. Demons may also confuse or disorient the individual.

A Methodist pastor came to me for ministry. He had been a missionary for a few years in Haiti. He was certain that he had picked up some evil spirits while there. He was right! He told me he became nauseated from the moment he contacted me. He called me on his cell phone as he was driving to my office. The pastor said, "I am on Airport Freeway and I know exactly where your office is, but I have become so disoriented that you are going to have to direct me there."

When the pastor arrived, he even looked sick. He said, "Is it normal for me to be seeing demons at this time?"

I assured him that nothing was normal, but that I had not encountered this before. "What are you seeing?" I asked.

"I see one large demon standing between you and me and I see two on my back." He felt like he was getting very ill.

I immediately bound the spirits and started the deliverance. He was delivered of many evil spirits. Some of them had come to him when he ministered in Haiti. He also had many spirits by permission of Freemasonry in his ancestry. There was a strong occult kingdom established. However, it was crushed in the name of Jesus Christ, and the pastor is now free.

The demons may attack the individual's mind to make them think they must be crazy if they really think demons are the problem. They may tell the individual that the deliverance minister is a jerk and that he doesn't know what he is doing or that the deliverance will not work. All of these things are common, and it is an attempt to keep the person in bondage. The truth is, the demons know how all of this works. They know much better than we do. They become very nervous when they know they are going to be confronted in the name of Jesus.

WHERE DO DEMONS LIVE IN A BELIEVER?

Jesus said, "Out of [your] belly shall flow rivers of living water.... But this spake he of the Spirit" (John 7:38–39). He was talking about the Holy Spirit of God. However, it seems the belly, the midsection, is also the seat of the evil spirits. It is very common for them to manifest in this area with a stirring or discomfort in the stomach. Headaches are also very common occurrences prior to and during deliverance. Demon spirits live in the central nervous system. This is their control center. Numbness, tingling, and dizziness are also very common when the demons are aroused. I always tell those who are candidates for deliverance not be alarmed and that the demons will not harm them! I let them know these are very common symptoms. I have seen literally thousands, and rarely is there not some of these conditions present.

When demons inhabit a believer, they dwell in the body and the soul. I once encountered a spirit and commanded the spirit to reveal where he was (in the person). He responded, "In the mind." I said, "So, you are in the brain?" With a measure of frustration in the response, the spirit, speaking through the individual, said, "No! I'm in the mind." The mind is part of the soul. The brain is part of the body. The mind, will, and emotions make up the soul. The only way a demon could enter the spirit of a man would be if the person was lost. This would clearly be demonic possession.

When the demons are expelled or commanded to leave, they most often come out on the individual's breath, sometimes with a deep sigh, cough, yawn, or burp. Occasionally some gagging takes place, but they will come out and they must be obedient. I have witnessed many types of releases. Some have said the demons have left out of the pores of their skin. Others feel them coming out of the top of their heads. "My fingers got very hot, and then I sensed them leave through the tips of my fingers," some have said. Or, "I see them leave like a flock of birds." The candidate always knows when the demons leave. The demons cannot be disobedient to the command of the Lord Jesus.

When the demons leave, I always command them to into the abyss, never to return. I will discuss this later. I also command that they cannot harm the individual, nor can they leave them and go to someone else. Often the individual may hear the demons in their mind say, "I'll leave, but I'll go to your kids." I remind everyone to not be alarmed by their threats. They will do as they are commanded—period!

Generally, the candidate will hear the demon's response in their mind and report to me what they have heard. Sometimes they may see something when the demons are commanded to obey the Holy Spirit and when the holy angels force them to obedience.

For example: Jesus spoke to the demoniac in Gadera (Mark 5) and said, "What is your name?" The demons in the man responded, "Legion, because we are many." The demons always respond. I command, always in the name of Jesus Christ, the prince demon to reveal his identity either by name or function. The deliverance candidate will immediately get a response in their mind. I ask them to report what they hear or see.

The names will be very unusual, sometimes names that will surprise the individual. What most commonly happens is that the demon will reveal his function—fear, doubt, and hatred. It is really not complicated. Once the demon is identified, there is just one question, "Do you have consent from Jehovah God to stay?" It is over at that point. If the spirit does not have consent, he will be commanded to go to the abyss—and he will!

At this point in the deliverance, we will have canceled all permissions for demons to stay. This is done in the beginning and will be discussed later.

There can be any number of demons present; the number is not significant. Every demon power will bow at the name of Jesus Christ!

Now, I don't know how many deliverance ministers there are. But that's how many varied opinions there are about the correct way to minister deliverance. Some say don't speak to the demons or allow the demons to talk, and they are very successful ministers. Many say to do it all by discernment, calling the spirits out as the Holy Spirit reveals them to you. I do not disagree with this method, but I have found it to be ineffective and thus incomplete in my ministry.

Others say to put the demons under oath before Jehovah God and command them to obey, to reveal how many are present, what their function or assignment is, and then to cancel that in the name of Jesus

Christ and command the spirits to the abyss and to never return in Jesus Name. I have found this to be most successful in my ministry.

Some scoff and say, "Don't interview the demons; just command them to go." My personal experience, first of all, is that it is not an interview; it is breaking their permission to be in one's life. It is not conversation; it is *confrontation*! If a demon has consent to stay from Jehovah God (curse or through the individual's disobedience) or from the individual (unconfessed sin or unwillingness to repent), then the demons do not have to leave no matter who is giving the command or how many times it is given. The permission to be there must be canceled, or the demons will not leave. Perhaps they will leave when commanded, but if doorways are not closed, then other demons can enter.

There is not a "correct" way spelled out in Scripture for how to command demons to leave. Jesus certainly spoke to the demons and demanded a name. That is clear. There was also conversation recorded in the Mark 5 encounter. My first reference when I was faced with deliverance was, what did Jesus do? There certainly are other instances where Jesus commanded demons to not speak; however, this was in the temple and the demon was trying to expose Jesus. (See Mark 1:23–26.)

Just below is a list for how God has shown me to conduct a deliverance session, and with the Holy Spirit's help I have been very successful at seeing folks delivered and healed.

PREPARATION FOR DELIVERANCE

Deliverance candidate

1. Make sure that you are sincere. Be open and honest, and don't hold back.

2. Desire to be free so that you can serve the Lord.

3. Ask the Holy Spirit to reveal areas of demonic bondage or torment.

4. Look over your life (and ancestry) to discover possible doorways.

5. Determine to be free no matter what grip the demons may have (addictions and the like).

6. Don't be intimidated by "what others may think."

7. Associate deliverance with Jesus and freedom rather than demons and bondage.

8. Exercise your faith as much as possible.

9. View this as part of God's gift to us in Jesus Christ.

10. Know this may be the beginning of freedom for your family and offspring.

Deliverance minister

1. Make sure your life is clean and that the Holy Spirit reigns in your life.

2. Gather all the information possible from the individual concerning possible doorways in his or her life. This, of course, includes generational information and possible curses.

3. Make the individual comfortable, and make certain they understand that this is an act of love.

4. Lead them through prayers of renunciation, breaking of soul ties, repentance, confessing that they are born again, that Jesus is Savior, Lord, deliverer, healer, and that He has broken the power of curse. Have them confess that they truly desire to be free.

5. Bind the demon powers according to Scripture in Jesus Christ's name.

6. Command the prince, the boss of the kingdom, to identify himself by name or function.

7. Determine if any spirit present has consent to stay. If yes, command that the consent be revealed, and then lead the individual to pray/confess to cancel that consent.

8. Command the spirits to become one spirit, with no passing on of duties, and as one spirit to leave the individual, go into the abyss, and never return.

9. Go back and check, maybe two or three times, making sure nothing is left.

10. Pray anointing and protection for the individual, and put some literature in their hands to help them to walk in continued freedom.

For the deliverance minister, I believe the most important thing he should remember is John 15:5: "Without me ye can do nothing."

I tell every candidate, "Expect to be free!"

CHAPTER 18

THE DELIVERANCE COURTROOM

ACH TIME I PREPARE FOR A DELIVERANCE SESSION, I VISUALIZE the process. I "see" the scriptural application of what is taking place. Deliverance is a particular course of action that is bound to certain rights of the believer as well as to certain legal rights that demon spirits have according to Scripture.

I preached recently in a Florida prison, and my message was titled, "I'm Taking You to Court." When I told the inmates this title, a voice from the full chapel said, "Oh, no, not again!" I had to chuckle, because his response caught me off guard. I want to share some of that message with you.

Try to imagine this spiritual picture: a courtroom where Jehovah God is seated at the judge's bench. He is the judge of all truth and righteousness. It is His legal system. Law is what He has spoken! Whatever God speaks becomes law. You can't see His face, just His glory. Holy angels encircle the bench and proclaim His holiness. He is the righteous judge.

> Henceforth there is laid up for me a crown of righteousness, which the Lord, *the righteous judge*, shall give me at that day: and not to me only, but unto all them also that love his appearing.
> —2 TIMOTHY 4:8, EMPHASIS ADDED

THIS IS NO ORDINARY COURTROOM

Already we see that this is not an ordinary courtroom; only truth will be recognized here. You see, deliverance is not about power, and it is not just about authority, though we certainly have it in Jesus Christ's name. Demonic oppression causes us to believe a lie. Demons' rights to our lives are obtained through sin and disobedience in our lives. All demons are liars. Their rights to a believer's life are through deception and our ancestors.

What is a typical right that demons have? Unforgiveness and believing that it is OK to hold onto to anger, resentment, and bitterness. This is an example of what gives demons access to believers. These issues must be confessed as sin before the righteous judge, and we must receive forgiveness through the blood of Jesus Christ. Once this is done, demons no longer have rights to our lives. Confessing the sin cancels the demons' rights to one's life, but it does not necessarily mean that the demon leaves. They must be commanded to go in the name of Jesus Christ. They must be cast out.

PROSECUTING DEMONS

Now, in this courtroom, I am part of the firm, Father, Son, and Holy Spirit. I am a legal representative of Jesus Christ. Visualize that I am the defense attorney for the deliverance candidate. I am the prosecuting attorney against demons! I am defending the believing candidate and protecting their rights in the name of Jesus Christ. As His ambassador and by the authority given me in His name, I will be the deliverance candidate's attorney.

I will prosecute demon powers based upon the truth of God's Holy Word. All demons are liars, so what they say must be challenged with the question, Will that stand as truth before Jehovah God? I have found that demons will not lie to Jehovah God!

The line of questioning is simple. Ask the demon to state his name and occupation. Jesus commanded this of the demoniac in Gadera: "What's your name? Who are you?" Demons have names given them by their creator, Jehovah God. They have personalities, rank, and particular functions.

DEMONS HAVE JOB ASSIGNMENTS

Their jobs always will fall into three categories: steal, kill, and destroy. Some are principalities and powers, some are rulers of darkness, and others are demons of spiritual wickedness. Some are serpents, and some are scorpions. Their assignments are against the purposes of God and against believers.

Once their name and job assignment are established, always as "truth before Jehovah God," one main question remains: Do you have any legal rights to remain in this person's life? Permission or rights must be from Jehovah God or from the individual. If their answer is no, then we have absolute authority in Jesus Christ's name to cast these demons from the individual and into the abyss.

Holy angels are the bailiffs in this courtroom. They are there to enforce the commands and minister to the believer. There is always victory in this courtroom when righteous justice is the goal of the believer. What is righteous justice? In this case, it is desiring to be free from any lies of the demons, not having any secret deals with the enemy and not participating with the opposition.

DELIVERANCE PRINCIPLES

Obviously, there are some basic rules or standards that apply to deliverance. At the risk of oversimplifying these principles, I will list them in brief:

1. Either a believer has demons or he does not.
2. If he has them, then it must be that the demons are there by some kind of legal consent.
3. The believer must have a sincere desire to be free from demonic powers. The human will is absolutely recognized in this process: confession, denunciation, renunciation, and repentance.
4. Coming into agreement with God's Word can cancel any legal consent that demons may have.
5. Once the consent, or legal right, has been removed, the demons can be cast out in Jesus Christ's name.

ONLY THROUGH THE NAME OF JESUS CHRIST

The removal of legal rights takes place in the courtroom of God's recognized legal system. Rights can only be removed through the name of Jesus Christ. It is His redemptive work on the cross and miraculous resurrection that makes this possible. Because we are believers, heirs of

God and joint-heirs with Jesus Christ, we can be represented "legally" in Christ's name. I love representing Him. We always win!

> Depart from evil and do good; and dwell for evermore. For the LORD *loveth judgment*, and forsaketh not his saints; they are preserved for ever: but the seed of the wicked shall be cut off.
>
> —PSALM 37:27–28, EMPHASIS ADDED

CHAPTER 19

WHAT IS THE CORRECT TERMINOLOGY?

THE KING JAMES BIBLE, AS WELL AS MOST OTHER TRANSLATIONS, uses the word *possessed* when talking about demons in people. However, that is not the meaning of the Greek word translated *possessed* in the Bible. The Greek word *daimonizomai*, which would be better translated "demonized," means to be under the influence of demons, to be affected by demons, or to have demons. There are very few people who are totally owned or possessed by demons. Obviously a Christian cannot be "possessed" by a demon because Christians belong to God and have been purchased and bought with a price by the shed blood of Jesus. The question is, can Christians have demons? The answer is yes! What does the Bible say?

Ephesians 2:2 says that demons are at work in the children of disobedience. Disobedience certainly grants permission to evil spirits. The truth is, people who are disobeying God are giving evil spirits a right to work not only around them but also in them. Peter declared that Satan had filled the heart of Ananias. "Filled the heart" implies access to the body and soul through disobedience. Doesn't that indicate that anyone who lies (one of the sins we seem to classify as a small one) could have their heart filled by Satan or, more correctly, by one of his demon spirits?

Paul told the believers in Ephesus: "Neither give place to the devil" (Eph. 4:27). This implies that it is possible for a Christian to give a place to the devil or to his demons. The place given in this verse is by not confessing the sin and allowing it to linger. If a person has given space or a place to demons by their own choices, they are in need of deliverance.

Correct terminology for a believer with demons is probably "demonized." However, "oppression" is also scripturally correct. Acts

10:38–43 is a great section of Scripture to describe scriptural deliverance. In Peter's sermon at Caesarea he was talking about the Son of God who had been rejected but had risen from the dead. Peter was preaching about a saving, delivering, and healing Jesus. He is describing the ministry of the Anointed One sent from God and the One whom he served.

> ...God anointed Jesus of Nazareth with the Holy Ghost and with power: who went about doing good, and healing all that were oppressed of the devil; for God was with him....And he commanded us to preach unto the people, and to testify that it is he which was ordained of God to be the Judge of quick and dead. To him give all the prophets witness, that through his name whosoever believeth in him shall receive remission of sins.
>
> —Acts 10:38–43

Jesus "went about doing good, and *healing all that were oppressed of the devil*." Deliverance in its truest sense is oppression healing. It is removing the oppressive source and being released from the consequences of demonic presence.

The word *exorcism* is certainly frightening to folks today because of the misuse and abuse of the word. Obviously the movie *The Exorcist* has left a lasting negative impression on the public. However, the word is correct terminology in that it speaks of expelling demon powers. *Deliverance* is probably the second most frightening term to use when describing the process, but it is the word Jesus used in Luke 4:18: "He hath sent me...to preach deliverance to the captives." The prophetic word from Isaiah 61:1 is "to proclaim liberty..." That is what deliverance is! It is freedom from the presence of demon powers that abide in the soul or flesh, or that are attached to a believer's life.

What About Them Returning in Greater Numbers and Strength?

> When the unclean spirit is gone out of a man, he walketh through dry places, seeking rest, and findeth none. Then he saith, I will return to *my house* from whence I came out; and when he is come, he findeth it *empty*, swept, and garnished. Then goeth he, and taketh with himself seven other spirits more wicked than himself, and they

enter in and dwell there: and the last state of that man is worse than the first.

—MATTHEW 12:43–45, EMPHASIS ADDED

This passage of Scripture has caused great concern for those who contemplate deliverance. It has always been interpreted that when evil spirits have been *cast* out of someone, they have the option to someday return. I don't believe that is what this verse indicates. My personal experience is that I have never seen this happen, and I don't believe this is an option. Demonic invasion by other spirits is certainly possible if the individual opens doorways through disobedience. That is possible whether demon spirits have been cast out or not.

This scripture says that "when the unclean spirit is *gone* out," but it does not say why he has gone out. It seems to me that the spirit here has left on his own volition. Maybe he left because "his house" was spiritually clean and he found it very uncomfortable? In every translation the word *gone* means to leave by one's own volition. He must have had permission to be there, else he could not be there. That is a scriptural given. There is no indication that this permission had been canceled. The doorway by which this demon spirit left would still be open if he chose to return.

Maybe he thought he would find a better house. Whatever the reason for leaving, he decides to return and check out the situation. Now look how he found the house—"empty, swept, and garnished [put in order]." This does not indicate to me that the spirit had permission because of reopened doors. The house was clean and in order. What seems obvious to me is that the demon had permission through a previous doorway that had never been closed. An empty house is not permission for demons to enter a believer. An unclean house is permission. This house was clean and swept—and decorated.

There have been volumes written about filling the house with the Holy Spirit and with the Holy Word to keep the cast-out spirits from returning. That is not suggested here. Obviously, the Holy Spirit should be welcomed. He should be invited to fill every void that was once occupied by demonic spirits. But the Holy Spirit does not keep demon spirits out. We do by obedience and confession of sin, by not believing the lie. The Word of God will not keep demons out if there is an open doorway.

For instance, you can read the Word, memorize it, teach it, quote it, love it, share it, and still, by having unconfessed sin in your life, open a door to demons. You can be bathed in the Holy Spirit and carry unforgiveness in your life and God will turn you over to the tormentors. So the point of the story that Jesus shared in Matthew 12 seems to be that if there is a doorway (portal, gate, or legal right), the demon can leave by his own choice. If the doorway by which he left is not closed, he can return and bring others with him. This is how kingdoms are established anyway, by bringing others in.

I believe Scripture teaches that when demons have been expelled by the authority of the name of Jesus Christ, returning to that person is not an option. In one case Jesus made that clear when He said, "Enter no more" (Mark 9:25). I personally believe they are to go into the abyss and are taken out of circulation until they are released during the Tribulation. I have found that the demons will bring to the mind of the deliverance candidate the possibility that they may return. Often the lie is that they will come back in greater force. Some are frightened to the point that they are not certain they want to go through with deliverance. There has been great misuse of the above scripture.

CHAPTER 20

WHERE DO THE DEMONS GO?

L ET ME REPEAT SOMETHING I SAID EARLIER. I DON'T HAVE ALL the answers, and I certainly can't guarantee that demons must go into the abyss. However, since I have been given authority in Jesus's name to cast them out, I also give them specific instructions on what they can and cannot do. I command that they cannot leave and go to someone else and that they cannot pass their duties on to other demons. If we are just freeing one person so that the demons may go find another person, it seems contradictory to all that Jesus came to do.

Some ministers are very certain that their way of performing the deliverance process is the only way. Some are very dogmatic on where the demons are commanded to go. One will say, "They must go to the feet of Jesus to be judged by Him and then sent where He determines." I say, they have already been to the feet of Jesus. They are now under His feet! I believe the authority He gives us to cast them out includes telling them where to go. Have you ever wanted to tell a demon where to go?

Others will say they should be banished to "dry places." I have never understood this. Scripture clearly says that those in dry places have the option to return. The abyss seemed to be the understood place where demons would go when Jesus cast them out. I command demons to go not just *to* the abyss but *into* the abyss. They are such legalists that I try not to give them any loopholes.

Generally, demons won't stay in anyone who consistently submits to God and resists the devil. (See James 4:7.) The devil and all demons must flee from such a person when they are resisted in the name of Jesus Christ. Submitting to God in this way is to not grieve the Holy Spirit (Eph. 4:30). It is certainly clear that as believers we can "grieve the Holy Spirit," and we can "quench" the Holy Spirit. But as we are submitted to God, it is then that we please the Holy Spirit. Remember, demons *must* have consent to torment believers. When all consent is canceled and demon powers have been commanded to leave in Jesus Christ's name, demons have no choice but to obey.

Can I tell you for certain where demons go? No, but I can with some degree of certainty. After each demon is expelled in the name of Jesus Christ, I always command a remaining spirit to reveal where that spirit is. The command is that the demons go immediately and directly into the abyss. When the remaining spirit is put under oath before Jehovah God, they will confess that the expelled spirit is in the abyss.

There was a time when my command was simply, "Come out immediately and go to the abyss." Again, I learned that the demons are such legalists and masters of deceit that they would go *to* the abyss but not *into* it. It was like telling them to go to the house instead of telling them to go into the house. I found when they would do this, that often they did return. Sometimes they would come back before the deliverance session was over.

My experience has been that once they are in the abyss with the command to never return, they are taken out of circulation. I do not get too caught up in this because there is no genuine way of knowing. Jesus certainly did command spirits to "enter no more." (See Mark 9:25.)

I know of one deliverance ministry that commands spirits to go to dry and barren places. This, of course, is because of the reference in Matthew 12:43, but it is not an accurate interpretation of Scripture. And, even if it was, it is clear that when demons are in "dry places" they are able to return.

Other ministries believe that we do not have authority to command demons into the abyss. Their thinking is that this amounts to judgment upon the demon spirits, and that right belongs to Jesus Christ alone. People in this camp often command the spirits to go to the feet of Jesus so Jesus can judge then and send them where He determines. I respect this viewpoint but believe it is also incorrect. The demons have already been to the feet of Jesus, and they have already been judged by Him. He trampled on them at Calvary and has already put all things under His feet! (See Ephesians 1:22.)

There have been occasions when I have a demon power bound and ready to be cast out that I have given the demon a choice of where he wants to go—to the feet of Jesus or into the abyss. I would say that nine out of ten times he chooses the feet of Jesus. This in itself is not conclusive.

I am aware that all demons are liars, but you do get a measure of truth when the demon power is commanded to speak truth before Jehovah God. Demons do not like to be brought before God's throne and commanded to speak truth. They get very angry. Truth greatly disturbs demon powers.

I suppose there are enough demons that sending a couple of hundred into the abyss does not greatly impact their affect on humanity. One thing we can be certain of is that Satan was only able to recruit a third of the heavenly host. There will always be twice as many holy angels as there are demon powers. The Bible calls demons powers Satan's angels: "Then shall he say also unto them on the left hand, Depart from me, ye cursed, into everlasting fire, prepared for the devil and his angels" (Matt. 25:41).

We do know the final abode for demon spirits will be everlasting fire. They will be cast along with Satan, the beast, and the false prophet into the lake of fire. (See Revelation 20:10.)

We also know that there are demons already in the abyss according to Revelation chapter 9. These demons will not be released until the Tribulation. I believe this is where demon spirits should be sent today. I also believe Jesus gave us the authority to do so. To me, it makes no sense to simply command a spirit to leave. What's the purpose if that spirit can then go to someone else or perhaps return.

I deal with these creatures of evil with a measure of finality! I believe that is what Jesus did, and I believe that demons understand that the abyss is where they are to go. I don't give them any breaks and try not to leave any loopholes.

CHAPTER 21

AUDIENCE OR ARMY?

THERE IS GROSS IGNORANCE OF DEMONS AS IT RELATES TO CHRISTians. Why is there so much ignorance in the body of Christ about spiritual warfare? A pastor and his wife were in my office recently. He had brought a member of his congregation to see me. He could not bring freedom to the man through wise counsel and scriptural encouragement. After the deliverance session was over and the man had been freed of many demonic spirits, the pastor and his wife asked to stay and visit awhile.

They had many questions. The pastor's wife was almost angry that she had not been taught about this. "Why is this not being taught?" she questioned. "Why has this been kept from us?" The pastor who had just finished his seminary training posed much of the same type questioning. "I have not heard one word about deliverance in my three years of schooling. I knew it was real. I knew from experience that demons were active in the lives of believers, but I am ignorant of this process I just witnessed. I want to know how to do this." They had seen firsthand a member of their congregation set free. The man was in deep depression and was suicidal. He had spirits of *rejection* and *doubt*, and *fear* tormented him. But not anymore; he is free. The pastor asked if he could come and sit in on some deliverance sessions so he could teach his people how to be free and so that he could "proclaim liberty to the captives."

Because this message, for the most part, has been omitted from the pulpit, there is an anemic church in bondage to the enemy, and the church is living beneath the oppressing power of the enemy. There will be great accountability for pastors who refuse to preach this truth. The blame for an anemic, powerless, sickly church can be nowhere but at the feet of the pastors. Like it or not, that is the truth!

BUILDING AUDIENCES INSTEAD OF ARMIES

I believe focus is the issue, fear is a consideration, and faith is the missing ingredient. What do I mean by that? The focus of most churches seems to be in building an audience instead of an army. A large audience seems to make everyone happy—pastors, deacons, and finance committees. We all go home and say, "Wow!" But maybe we should look closer. Maybe it should be "whoa" that we are saying. Aren't we supposed to be building soldiers, equipping them for battle? How can we build an army when the church is not aware of the reality of the enemy?

The focus is wrong. The main objective is out of focus. Somewhere along the way we dropped an important part of the gospel message. I will tell you, without blinking or without consideration of backing up, that the average local church has so limited the work of the Holy Spirit that it is virtually impossible for God to bless what we do! This is sad! This must be corrected.

DIDN'T GOD SAY IT?

If what Jesus said about Himself is true, if the job description He gave for Himself is true, then we have fallen short of being like Him and presenting Him in the pulpit. Did He come to seek and to save that which is lost? Absolutely! We do a pretty good job of presenting this Jesus. Did He say, "Go ye therefore, and teach all nations, baptizing them in the name of the Father, and of the Son, and of the Holy Ghost" (Matt. 28:19)? Of course He did, and we do a good job of that. But what about the other things He said that we have virtually ignored?

Didn't He say, "The Spirit of the Lord is upon me, because he hath anointed me to preach the gospel to the poor; he hath sent me to heal the brokenhearted, to preach deliverance to the captives, and recovering of sight to the blind, to set at liberty them that are bruised, to preach the acceptable year of the Lord" (Luke 4:18–19)? Are those not the words of our Lord Jesus when He announced His ministry purpose? Absolutely they are! Did He not also say, "As my Father hath sent me, even so send I you" (John 20:21)?

Let's look and see if we are ministering as Jesus said He had come to minister. Are we preaching the gospel to the poor? Does the prosperity gospel work in the ghetto? Maybe we are doing a fair job of presenting the good news of Jesus Christ to the poor. I'll let you make you own conclusion here. But it seems in our audience-driven churches that the poor are not the focus of our desired audience. We generally want people who are most like us.

Are we healing the brokenhearted?

I'll tell you that this can't be done with an audience. It takes an army. Broken hearts are all about us. The sweet Lord Jesus proclaimed this as part of His mission. Is the broken heart being ministered to in your church? Do messages from your pulpit do anything to mend and bind broken hearts? Doesn't this require an arm around your brother? Doesn't this require compassion from individuals? Does it not include action on our part?

It requires that—and more. It involves an army that will come against the demonic forces with the authority of the name of Jesus Christ and in the power of His shed blood. Pastors must teach every believer and must be an example of the authority and power. We don't back up; we don't back down. We come against the very gates of hell in the mighty name of Jesus Christ. We don't fear the enemy because we know who we are and what Christ has given us. We look demon powers in the eye and command that they retreat!

Are we preaching deliverance to the captives?

I know this will strike a nerve in many a pastor's heart. Are you even mentioning the word *deliverance*? Does that frighten you? Are you fearful of members' reactions? Are you a little fearful that some may leave or become very uncomfortable? What about your seminary connections? Is there some fear here as well? Denominational standing, is that an issue? Is retirement funding an issue? Withdrawing fellowship from your circle of denominational acquaintances? What is keeping you from preaching deliverance to the captives? Pastors, if you are curious who in your church has demons, just preach about them, and you'll find out. They'll be knocking on your door and demanding no more preaching about such nonsense.

Could it be that you have really bought into the lie that demons no longer exist? Where did they go? I heard a foolish pastor say that "demons" were just really mental problems that people had, but because the people in Jesus's time on Earth believed they actually were evil spirits, He spoke to them on their level of understanding. I believe this ignorance is border-line blasphemy.

Could you possibly believe that demonic spirits do not exist? If you do, then you are the most deceived of all, and you have chosen not to believe the Word of God. Plain and simple, you have denied Scripture! I want you to deal with the issue for your sake and for the sake of your people. Demonic bondage for believers is a reality! I believe the day is coming—and I believe it will be very soon—that every pastor in every church will be faced with people in their congregation crying desperately to be free. I believe every pastor should go through deliverance and should prepare himself for the warfare that is going to intensify. Already, pastors, your people are in bondage.

Let me just add that I am a member of a very large Baptist church. I am not on staff. I direct Don Dickerman Ministries to prisons and to healing and deliverance needs. I have ministered deliverance to more than one hundred members of this congregation, including deacons, Sunday school teachers, musicians, singers, moms, dads, and children. This is not the exception; it is the rule! Good people, God's people, are being held captive by Satan's kingdom of darkness, and it is very real! Pastors, you must be obedient to the Holy Spirit regardless of the denominational pressures. You must.

I cannot help but ask, Why is this omitted from the gospel being taught in the seminaries and in the pulpits? My only conclusion is the focus is wrong. We don't need an audience; we need an army. Fear can no longer control the pastors' preaching. And faith must be placed in the holy Word of God. God will honor the pure preaching and teaching of the Word.

There is a great need today for a church with balance, balance in the Word and the Spirit. In one body there is great emphasis on the Word but little dependence upon the Spirit. In another there is focus on the gifts and workings of the Holy Spirit but little emphasis on the Word. God will bless the pastor who sees that there is proper balance, and the people of that church will become an army.

Are we preaching recovering of sight to the blind?

When is the last time you heard your preacher talk to you about the healing mercies of the Lord Jesus? Pastor, why are you not laying hands on the sick and expecting them to be healed? Why are you not teaching your people who are sick to call for the elders of the church to let them pray over them, anointing them with oil in the name of the Lord?

Do you not believe that the prayer of faith will bring healing to the sick? Are you afraid it might not happen? Fearful of being embarrassed? If you are not doing it, you are not preaching the gospel, and you are not being obedient to the call on your life.

I ask you to consider this: What pastor has not opened his Bible to John 14 at a funeral and read the powerful words of Jesus for comfort and hope? This same Jesus who promised that He is preparing a place for us also spoke in the same passage these words: "Verily, verily, I say unto you, He that believeth on me, the works that I do shall he do also; and greater works than these shall he do; because I go unto my Father. And whatsoever ye shall ask in my name, that will I do, that the Father may be glorified in the Son. If ye shall ask any thing in my name, I will do it" (John 14:12–14). I don't hear many pastors talking about this portion of John 14.

Are we preaching Jesus came to set at liberty those who are bruised?

Well, if you're not preaching deliverance to the captives, then you are not preaching this, because they are linked. What powerful gospel words are in this declaration by Jesus—"set at liberty"? Is this not the essence of the gospel? Liberation by the Lord Jesus! Liberation, freedom—for whom? For them who are bruised! Preaching deliverance to the captives allowed me to learn that the captives are in bondage most often because of bruises! Bruises. Wounds from childhood. Unkind words and deeds they were victims of. Deep hurts that keep them bound!

Jesus can set at liberty those who are bruised because He was bruised for our iniquities! A bruise is bleeding beneath the surface! The damage shows up on the outside, but the bleeding is inside; the hurt and the pain are beneath the surface. Oh, the need is great for the church to minister in this area! Jesus was bruised for our iniquities. Our sins? No, our iniquities! Iniquity is evil and wicked. It is often a spirit or the result of someone else's sin. (The mystery of iniquity does now already work.) He was wounded for our transgressions (sin). He was bruised for our iniquities. Generational sins allow access of iniquity spirits to the children of the third and fourth generation.

The abusive sinful acts of someone else allow iniquity spirits to the victim. He was bruised for our iniquities. The chastisement of our peace was upon Him, and with His stripes we are healed. One verse in Isaiah 53 tells us that Jesus paid for our sins, iniquities, peace, and healing! The blood paid for more than what we are claiming!

I can't tell you how many I have seen "set at liberty" from the bruises of the past—evil spirits who gained access through some trauma, who keep the bruises painful, who torment because it is their work, robbing, stealing, destroying, and ultimately killing. The church must deal with this! We must.

Are we preaching the acceptable year of the Lord?

Many are responding to altar calls to receive Jesus as Savior. I know this is what must happen first. But He is more than just Savior! He is Savior first, but He is also Lord, deliverer, healer, and the One who broke the power of the curse. We cannot be truthful in our declaration of the gospel if we do less than what Jesus said He came to do.

Will you take a moment and refresh yourself by reading Luke 3:21–23? Jesus was baptized, and God proclaimed, as the dove of the Spirit descended upon Jesus, "Thou art my beloved Son: in thee I am well pleased" (v. 22). The beginning of His earthly ministry began by the Spirit driving Him into the wilderness for a face-to-face encounter with Satan. No big deal. Jesus defeated Satan with the same Word I have today.

However, after this encounter and after the angels ministered to Him, He came back to His hometown and went to the synagogue where it was His custom to worship. Listening for so many years to the scholars and the scribes, Pharisees, and teachers of the law, Jesus stood and chose a passage from Isaiah to read. He proclaimed that He was the fulfillment of that prophecy in Isaiah 61. Then something interesting happened: the people in Nazareth rejected Him. They actually tried to kill Jesus, but He slipped through the crowd and made His way to Capernaum about fifteen miles away.

The people there graciously received Him, and they were "astonished" at His doctrine for His word was delivered with power! In the synagogue there, worshiping with the others, was a man with a spirit of an unclean devil! This spirit spoke to Jesus saying, "Let us alone; what have we to do with thee, thou Jesus of Nazareth? art thou come to destroy us?" (Luke 4:34). "For this purpose the Son of God was manifested, that he might destroy the works of the devil" (1 John 3:8). Yes, He came to destroy Satan's work! May I put in Texas terms what Jesus said to that spirit? "Shut up and come out of him." And the devil did!

The people in the synagogue in Capernaum were amazed and said, "What a word is this! For with authority and power he commandeth the unclean spirits, and they come out" (Luke 4:36).

He went to Simon's house and rebuked the fever in Peter's mother-in-law! Word must have gotten out about Jesus. I tell you, pastors, word will get out about the healing and delivering Jesus. Everyone in the city who knew of any who were sick brought them to Jesus, and He laid hands on every one of them and healed them. The devils also came out of many, and the people didn't want Jesus to leave town. They wanted Him to stay. He healed them all and cast out demons!

What was the difference between Nazareth and Capernaum? Why does the Scripture say that Jesus could not do many mighty works in Nazareth? Because of their unbelief (Matt. 13:58)! In Capernaum, there was great revival, great change, liberation, deliverance, and healing. In Nazareth, there was anger, self-righteous tradition, doubt, and unbelief. In essence, the people of Nazareth said, "This is not the message we wanted to hear from You." They got what they wanted. Churches today are saying, "This is not the message we want." They get what they want.

The difference in Nazareth and Capernaum is attitude! Capernaum had a faith attitude. They welcomed Jesus with no strings attached. They were impressed with His Word, His power, and His authority. They saw great results. But Nazareth refused to believe and stubbornly decided to stay in bondage of the elders and religious tradition.

Every pastor has a choice. Do you realize that if you don't expect the gifts of the Spirit you will not receive them? We are told to "desire" spiritual gifts. Why would a pastor not desire something from God's Holy Spirit? That is a question I cannot answer.

There is a sleeping giant that must be freed. The body of Christ is sickly and without power. Pulpits are trying more and more gimmicks to bring people in, to build a great audience. What about the army? God's people are sick, and they need healing. Many are demonically oppressed. They are hurting, and many lives and families are broken. A powerless church cannot minister to these needs. From the outside looking in, we are no different from the world. That should not be! We have an untapped source in the Holy Spirit, but great restriction has been placed on His role in the church.

CONSIDER THE CALL ON MOSES'S LIFE

Do you believe the call on your life is less real than the call on the life of Moses? Do you think Moses may have been a little intimidated when he was instructed to go into the physical and spiritual stronghold of Egypt, look Pharaoh in the eye, and say, "Let my people go"? Do you suppose he wondered about the consequences of being a child of God and taking on the empire of Egypt? Did any of that matter?

The only thing that seems important about Moses's call was who called and who promised to go with him.

I believe the call on every preacher's life is virtually the same: to look the devil(s) right in the eye and command, "Let my people go!" That's what deliverance is. It is coming against demon powers, by the authority of the name of Jesus, that keep God's people in bondage and commanding their release. God's people are hurting. The church is full of sick people. The hospital's record has as many Christians as non-Christians as patients, maybe more. The church should be free! Jesus paid for our freedom. Demons have intimidated our preachers and Christian leaders. We must take back what is ours. The blood of Jesus Christ has not lost any power, nor will it. The name of Jesus Christ still causes demons to tremble and retreat. The gates of hell still will *never* prevail against the church of the Lord Jesus.

I look around the churches where I minister and where I attend. There is always a long list of prayer requests for the sick. However, it seems the best most churches do is a courtesy prayer on a weeknight.

We take too much from the kingdom of darkness! We have authority to *bind* evil spirits just as Jesus did and command them to come out of people. Spirits of sickness and disease will retreat in the name of Jesus Christ. We have been given authority to *loose* heaven's blessings, ministering spirits (Heb. 1:14), and holy angels to minister for us. How about let's do it!

I have sat in church many times over the years and felt in my spirit, "Why do we just talk about what Jesus came to do? Let's just do it. Anybody sick? Would you like to have the elders of the church anoint you with oil and lay hands on you for your healing? Come on!" I feel this in my spirit: why don't we get on the offensive? Why don't we fight demon powers in the name of Jesus with the intention of winning?

I am talking about becoming an *army*, not just an audience.

God help us!

CHAPTER 22

KEEPING GATES CLOSED

KEYS ARE FOR LOCKING OR UNLOCKING. JESUS GAVE US KEYS TO the kingdom of heaven in Matthew 16:19 and in Matthew 18:18.

My paraphrase of those verses would read like this: "Whatever you speak to be bound on Earth, I will bind it from heaven. And whatever you speak to release on Earth, I will release it from heaven."

We bind, lock, or restrain on Earth by faith, and that faith is honored in heaven. For instance, when we bind demons in the name of Jesus Christ, we speak it and God honors it. Demons are restrained, bound, and locked by the authority He has given to us in Jesus's name.

Also, when we loose angels to minister for us, we have spoken it by faith, and God honors it in heaven. Keys are also spiritual principles and insight that we have been given to live a liberated life in Christ Jesus.

This section is aimed primarily to those who have been set free from demonic oppression. However, it is also good information for anyone desiring to live in the freedom that is ours through the Lord Jesus. Keeping the enemy out of our lives and keeping the Word of God in us is the focus. Evil spirits must have some kind of legal permission to enter a believer's life. As I mentioned in an earlier chapter, unconfessed sin is a gate for demons to enter. Perhaps the best example of doors or entryways is the example Jesus used in Revelation 3:20: "Behold, I stand at the door, and knock: if any man hear my voice, and open the door, I will come in to him, and will sup with him, and he with me." Obviously, Jesus is saying that we must open the door for Him to enter. He patiently, lovingly knocks but will come in when He is invited. Demon spirits must also have a door or gate that we open to allow them entrance into our lives. Evil spirits must honor our will and abide by guidelines spelled out in Scripture. They cannot enter our life by force. There must be legal permission when we live in disobedience, believe their lie, or when permission is granted by a curse.

Gates serve two purposes: keeping something in and keeping something out. What a person lets in after deliverance is totally up to the individual. If gates are kept closed, the enemy cannot gain access! Perhaps the most important aspect of the warfare that we are engaged in is awareness of it. I have put these together in a simple format so that it will be easy to remember. I call it the three Rs. Like reading, 'riting, and 'rithmatic, these are some basic strategies for walking in the liberty that have been given by the Lord Jesus Christ.

1. Recognize

Recognizing the enemy and their plan of attacks is imperative in this fight. You may have expected me to say *his* plan of attack rather than *theirs*. While it is the kingdom of Satan that we deal with, we encounter his demonic spirits.

Being aware of the strategies and cognizant of how warfare takes place is necessary to keep the victory. It is good to know how doorways are opened to demonic spirits and what doorways were opened to allow them access prior to deliverance.

Make some notes about your deliverance, if you can. What were the strongholds? Do you recall the entryways that gave them access to enter your flesh and soul (not spirit; we are possessed by the Spirit of God)? Being aware of how evil spirits gained legal access to your life before may help you keep that doorway closed!

For instance, if doubt and unbelief granted them consent before, they may well try to stir that in you by giving you thoughts and suggestions from the outside. You must recognize their subtle attempts to get you to believe their lie. That is, when you have granted them permission! Be aware, stay alert, and don't be caught off guard. The sequence of deliverance follows a simple pattern: CAUSE-CURSE-CONSEQUENCES-CONFESSION-CAST OUT-CURE.

> To whom ye forgive any thing, I forgive also: for if I forgave any thing, to whom I forgave it, for your sakes forgave I it in the person

of Christ; *lest Satan should get an advantage of us*: for we are not ignorant of his devices.

—2 Corinthians 2:10–11, emphasis added

As the bird by wandering, as the swallow by flying, so the curse causeless shall not come.

—Proverbs 26:2

Like a flitting sparrow, like a flying swallow, so a *curse without cause* shall not alight. What's the curse? No. What's the cause? Below is a list of causes or doorways that give demons legal rights to indwell believers.

1. Ancestry—"I the Lord thy God am a jealous God, visiting the iniquity [absence of moral or spiritual values; morally objectionable behavior] of the fathers upon the children unto the third and fourth generation of them that hate me" (Deut. 5:9).

2. Lying—Tell a lie, you might get a demon. Live a lie, you have a demon. You cover it, and God will expose it. You confess it, and God will cover it. Believing a lie is the power of the demon. Victory for the believer hinges upon truth.

3. Unforgiveness—". . . delivered him to the tormentors, till he should pay all that was due unto him. So likewise shall my heavenly Father do also unto you, if ye from your hearts forgive not every one his brother their trespasses" (Matt. 18:34–35).

4. Anger, bitterness, hatred, and related sins—"Be ye angry, and sin not: let not the sun go down upon your wrath: neither give place to the devil. . . . And grieve not the holy Spirit of God, whereby ye are sealed unto the day of redemption. Let all bitterness, and wrath, and anger, and clamour, and evil speaking, be put away from you, with all malice" (Eph. 4:26, 30–31).

5. Rejection, perception, and dejection—"He is despised and rejected of men; a man of sorrows, and acquainted with grief: and we hid as it were our faces from him; he was despised,

and we esteemed him not" (Isa. 53:3). Rejection, grief, and having no esteem are the vilest of painful emotions.

6. Trauma—disappointment, fear, betrayal, and emotional wounds; surgery; accidents; sexual, verbal, and physical abuse; unusual fear from horror movies or events

7. Childhood abuse—sexual, mental, verbal, physical, emotional

8. Sexual impurity—promiscuity, homosexuality, and pornography; also rape, incest, and molestation.

9. Dishonoring your body—alcohol, drugs, nicotine, body piercings, tattoos, vanity, surgical cosmetic enhancements, and so on. (See Romans 1:24.)

10. Occult/secret organizations—pledges, oaths, vows, ceremonies. Curiosity or involvement, however innocent, in horoscopes; astrology; fortune-telling; psychics; palm reading; Ouija boards; Magic 8 Ball; witchcraft; levitation games; reading tea leaves; heavy metal music; Dungeons and Dragons and similar video games; Pokémon cards; Harry Potter children's books; and books about the occult, pagan deities, Greek mythology, and so on. The list is long, and I have seen doorways from each of these. This also includes involvement in certain secret or fraternal organizations such as Freemasons, Eastern Star, Rainbow Girls, Oddfellows, Rebecca Lodge, college fraternities or sororities, and the like.

11. Doubt, unbelief, and pride

12. Blasphemy—vulgar, hate-filled language is the ultimate dishonor to a holy God.

13. Certain objects in the home or in one's possession

Permission is granted by disobedience to the Lord. Consent is given by making wrong choices and believing the demons' lie. When we accept the lie rather than believing the truth of God's Word, we have granted permission to demons. The same is true when we choose the curse instead of the promised blessings. Don't accept the subtle lies of the enemy.

Awareness of what allowed demon spirits access to your life before will help you keep that doorway closed. The demon spirits that were there by a generational curse or ancestral permission cannot return by that permission. However, similar spirits can attach to your life by other doorways. The goal is to walk in freedom and live liberated. It is not in the *fighting*, but most of it is in the *abiding*. Abiding in Christ keeps you aware because the focus is on the One who defeated the enemy. However, still be in a position to recognize the enemy. Know that demons are deceptive, and they do not give up territory easily. Be spiritually perceptive. Know that they will wage strategic warfare, and be ready. Keep doorways closed by keeping your spiritual house clean.

2. RESIST

Satan is a thief, and a thief must be resisted! The promise is that if you resist the devil, he will flee from you! (See James 4:7.) However, the promise is twofold: (1) Submit yourself to God. That is, abide, focus on Him, and obey what you know to do. (2) Resist the devil and he will flee from you.

It is your obedience to the Lord Jesus in submission that enriches your authority to resist. Humility and faith open the door of your soul to the power of God and close it to the enemy. Pride and unbelief open it to the enemy and close it to God.

It is not scripturally correct to ask God to resist Satan for you, because it has already been done. The Word tells you to do it, and because Satan is defeated, his demons will flee from you at the name of the Lord Jesus Christ. Jesus spoke these words to the church: "Behold, I give unto *you* power to tread on serpents and scorpions, and over all the power of the enemy: and nothing shall by any means hurt you" (Luke 10:19, emphasis added). Power over the enemy has been given to you, and you must act on it. The kingdom of darkness understands this a whole lot better than we do, and they know they have to flee in Jesus Christ's name.

Some of the first words to the church from Jesus were for us to take authority. He said, "Whatsoever *you* bind on Earth, I'll bind in heaven, and whatsoever *you* loose on Earth, I loose in heaven." (See Matthew 16:19; 18:18.) *You* take authority, and God will honor it.

You must resist the enemy at every turn. He is a coward. Cowards run when they are resisted, and that is exactly what the Word says the enemy will do if believers will resist. Peter says to resist, remaining steadfast in the faith. (See 1 Peter 5:9.) I think that involves an attitude of knowing who you are in Christ! The responsibility lies squarely on your shoulders. If you resist, then you can walk in freedom.

The third of the three Rs is the best of all.

3. REMAIN

As a pastor friend put it, rest in the Lord. (See Hebrews 4.) Abide in Him, and relax in the promises of God. Martin Luther is attributed as the author of this neat little poem:

> Feelings come and feelings go,
> And feelings are deceiving;
> My warrant is the Word of God,
> Naught else is worth believing.

Jesus insists that we abide in Him because, He says, "Without me ye can do nothing" (John 15:5–6). David Berkowitz (who was also known as the Son of Sam), the New York inmate who also shares his story in this book, was deeply involved in satanic worship. He was involved in some horrible crimes. Today he is a believer and a preacher of the gospel in his New York prison. I once asked him if he had experienced a personal deliverance. I found his words interesting and encouraging. "Don, I found the more I filled my life with the Word of God, the freer I became." That is also how he *remains* free from the bondage he once knew.

It is by resting in Christ that wholeness comes and inner healing takes place from all the damage the enemy has done. I often say that if you were to be in my car and me unaware of it, you might think I had lost my mind. Often I speak aloud to the enemy when I *recognize* his attacks. I *resist* immediately with words like, "Don't even try it. I know what this is. I rebuke you, and I resist you in the name of the Lord Jesus Christ. And if you come back tomorrow, I'll be standing on the same Word. I am free, and I'll *remain* free in Jesus Christ's name."

Another picture of *remaining* in freedom is saying what the Scripture says, confessing the Word, coming into agreement with the Word of God, and disagreeing with the adversary. This is bringing your soul (mind, will, and emotions) into agreement with what God's Spirit in you says. (See Galatians 2:20.)

There is power in confession. Your salvation came through confession, and restoration to fellowship comes through confession. When you fall, don't linger. Immediately claim truths, instantly confess sin, and receive God's gracious forgiveness and cleansing. The goal is to *remain* free!

Here is a brief summary of the three Rs that we have just discussed and of how to walk in the liberated life afforded by the Lord Jesus through deliverance.

Recognize

1. *Awaken* to Satan's intentions and purpose for your life.
2. *Alertness*—Be alert to his tactics and schemes that worked before. What gave demons access previously is likely the method they will try again. Don't minimize the enemy, because the warfare is real.
3. *Acknowledge* the Holy Spirit as your daily helper, and He will give you spiritual discernment.

Resist

1. *Arm* yourself. Put on the whole armor God (Eph. 6:11).
2. *Act* immediately. Remember it is *your* responsibility to resist. Jesus already did His part for us. He has given *you* authority in His name.
3. *Attend* to detail. Be specific with *your* commands in Jesus Christ's name. Bind them with authority.
4. *Aggress*—Be the aggressor; having done all to stand, stand in the power of the Lord. Don't back down. Don't back up!

Remain

1. *Abide* in Christ, for this is the key to finding full peace and healing. He *is* life, and He *is* wholeness. Abide in Him and rest in His Word and promises.

2. *Agree* with Him, agree with the Word, and speak faith. Do not allow doubt a place in your life. The power of life and death is in the tongue (Prov. 18:21). Say what the Word says.

3. *Apply* the Word to your life. Seek to do those things that please Him (praise, prayer, and practice). Avoid things that do not bring Him honor.

4. *Associate* with Spirit-filled believers. Fellowship with mature believers who love the Lord and His Word.

5. *Adore* Him with praise and worship. Make a concerted effort to give honor, praise, and glory to the Lord Jesus. Demons hate praise. It is a constant reminder to them of their defeat. It was once their privilege to praise God. They have lost their position in heaven. God deserves our praise, and there are promises that accompany heartfelt praise and worship. The Holy Spirit of God inhabits our praises. Praise and worship music will make the demons uncomfortable and often will cause them to leave. Fill your life with praise. Play praise music in your home, your vehicle, and in your office. Praise is power in spiritual warfare.

The following steps are suggested for daily use to help you as you grow in Christ and continue in your spiritual authority to walk in freedom and exercise power over the enemy.

FREEDOM PRINCIPLES

1. Confess sin immediately. Memorize 1 John 1:9, and keep this verse alive in your spirit.

"If we confess our sins, he is faithful and just to forgive us our sins, and to cleanse us from all unrighteousness." Apply this to your life. Don't allow sin to linger. It must be forgiven, and you must be cleansed immediately. Deliverance is only as good as our obedience!

2. When negative thoughts come, you must rebuke them and replace them with positive thoughts.

Here is a verse for you to apply: "Finally, brethren, whatsoever things are true, whatsoever things are honest, whatsoever things are just, whatsoever things are pure, whatsoever things are lovely, whatsoever things are of good report; if there be any virtue, and if there be any praise, think on these things" (Phil. 4:8).

Make sure the thoughts that enter your mind fall in this category.

3. Premeditated sin will invite demons. Keep your plans holy and pleasing to God.

"For this is the love of God, that we keep his commandments: and his commandments are not grievous" (1 John 5:3). There is an awesome promise that goes with keeping His commandments and doing those things that please Him. "And whatsoever we ask, we receive of him, because we keep his commandments, and do those things that are pleasing in his sight" (1 John 3:22). Focus on pleasing Him.

4. Anticipate increased freedom as you walk in obedience.

You must learn to dismiss immediately painful memories of your past and live in anticipation of life without bondage. "Brethren, I do not count myself to have apprehended; but one thing I do, forgetting those things which are behind and reaching forward to those things which are ahead, I press toward the goal for the prize of the upward call of God in Christ Jesus" (Phil. 3:13–14, NKJV).

5. Never forget that Satan and all of his demons are liars. Learn to recognize the lie

"When he speaks a lie, he speaks from his own resources, for he is a liar and the father of it" (John 8:44, NKJV). One of the favorite ploys of demons is to try to convince you that what took place was only emotional and that you are still in the enemy's grip. "Therefore submit to God. Resist the devil and he will flee from you. Draw near to God and He will draw near to you. Cleanse your hands, you sinners; and purify your hearts, you double-minded" (James 4:7–8, NKJV).

6. Trust God daily to help you make correct choices, and He will!

"Having begun in the Spirit, are you now being made perfect by the flesh?" (Gal. 3:3, NKJV).

7. Use the name of Jesus, the blood of the Lamb, and your confession of faith against all Satan's temptations and condemnation.

All condemnation comes from Satan. Never believe him. You have been cleansed by the blood and through the name of Jesus Christ; you are blood protected! "And they overcame him by the blood of the Lamb and by the word of their testimony, and they did not love their lives to the death" (Rev. 12:11, NKJV). "There is therefore now no condemnation to those who are in Christ Jesus, who do not walk according to the flesh, but according to the Spirit" (Rom. 8:1, NKJV).

8. Allow the Holy Spirit to control your life—all of you, all the time.

Make a conscious choice to make Jesus Lord of every day and every situation. "I beseech you therefore, brethren, by the mercies of God, that you present your bodies a living sacrifice, holy, acceptable to God, which is your reasonable service. And do not be conformed to this world, but be transformed by the renewing of your mind, that you may prove what is that good and acceptable and perfect will of God" (Rom. 12:1–2, NKJV). "And do not be drunk with wine, in which is dissipation; but be filled with the Spirit" (Eph. 5:18, NKJV). "Therefore He who supplies the Spirit to you and works miracles among you, does He do it by the works of the law, or by the hearing of faith?" (Gal. 3:5, NKJV).

9. God's Holy Word must have a predominant place in your life.

This may mean not doing something that would take you away from it. Take time or make time to read, learn, and meditate on God's Word every day. If time is limited, carry Scripture verse cards with you for your free times. Get cassette tapes of the Bible and play it in your car or office. "This Book of the Law shall not depart from your mouth, but you shall meditate in it day and night, that you may observe to do according to all that is written in it. For then you will make your way prosperous, and then you will have good success" (Josh. 1:8, NKJV). "Let the word of Christ dwell in you richly in all wisdom, teaching and admonishing one another in psalms and hymns and spiritual songs, singing with grace in your hearts to the Lord" (Col. 3:16, NKJV).

10. Learn about your battle gear. It has the promise of protection and victory from the Word of God.

> Finally, my brethren, be strong in the Lord and in the power of His might. Put on the whole armor of God, that you may be able to stand against the wiles of the devil. For we do not wrestle against flesh and blood, but against principalities, against powers, against the rulers of the darkness of this age, against spiritual hosts of wickedness in the heavenly places. Therefore take up the whole armor of God, that you may be able to withstand in the evil day, and having done all, to stand. Stand therefore, having girded your waist with truth, having put on the breastplate of righteousness, and having shod your feet with the preparation of the gospel of peace; above all, taking the shield of faith with which you will be able to quench all the fiery darts of the wicked one. And take the helmet of salvation, and the sword of the Spirit, which is the word of God; praying always with all prayer and supplication In the Spirit, being watchful to this end with all perseverance and supplication for all the saints.
>
> —Ephesians 6:10–18, NKJV

Make this so that it soon becomes effortless and is part of your lifestyle.

11. You must severe ties with old unhealthy friendships. This is a must!

"Do you not know that friendship with the world is enmity with God? Whoever therefore wants to be a friend of the world makes himself an enemy of God" (James 4:4, NKJV). You can count on the enemy to try to use whatever worked before to get access to your life again. You must avoid old patterns as well and break former habits that led to sin.

12. Be serious in your efforts to glorify the Lord Jesus.

"If then you were raised with Christ, seek those things which are above, where Christ is, sitting at the right hand of God. Set your mind on things above, not on things on the earth. For you died, and your life is hidden with Christ in God" (Col. 3:1–3, NKJV).

13. This battle is one of dependency. Be careful to not get confident in the flesh.

Admitting you can't do it all by yourself is not weakness; it is strength. Do things with His help. The lie of Satan is to tell you that you can do it without God. "I am the vine, you are the branches. He who abides in Me, and I in him, bears much fruit; for without Me you can do nothing" (John 15:5, NKJV). "Let your conduct be without covetousness; be content with such things as you have. For He Himself has said, 'I will never leave you nor forsake you'" (Heb. 13:5, NKJV).

14. Remember the wiles and the sneaky traps of the devil.

Act in your God-given authority. It will always be honored by the Father, who gave it to Jesus to give to you. "Therefore submit to God. Resist the devil and he will flee from you. Draw near to God and He will draw near to you. Cleanse your hands, you sinners; and purify your hearts, you double-minded" (James 4:7–8, NKJV).

15. Praise invites God's presence and causes the enemy to run.

Praise Him because He deserves it. Give thanks to God for His continuous goodness. Psalm 103:6 says, "The LORD executes righteousness and justice for all who are oppressed" (NKJV).

16. Be ready to receive your inheritance that is given liberally by the Spirit of God.

Your inheritance was given through the glory of Jesus Christ, who is seated at the right hand of *His* Father, who is also *your* Father. Remind the demons that you are an heir of God and a joint-heir with Jesus Christ. You are! "But the fruit of the Spirit is love, joy, peace, longsuffering, kindness, goodness, faithfulness, gentleness, self-control. Against such there is no law" (Gal. 5:22–23, NKJV). "So Jesus said to them again, 'Peace to you! As the Father has sent Me, I also send you'" (John 20:21, NKJV).

17. Remember that there are certain things that require diligent warfare.

Criticism, negativity, grieving over the past, oversensitivity, doubt, selfishness, putting feelings before faith, and lack of genuine prayer are all on the list. Be an outgoing person and help others. Helping others will bring blessings. You cannot allow self-pity a place in your life.

Now the works of the flesh are evident, which are: adultery, fornication, uncleanness, lewdness, idolatry, sorcery, hatred, contentions, jealousies, outbursts of wrath, selfish ambitions, dissensions, heresies, envy, murders, drunkenness, revelries, and the like; of which I tell you beforehand, just as I also told you in time past, that those who practice such things will not inherit the kingdom of God....Let us not become conceited, provoking one another, envying one another.
—GALATIANS 5:19–21, 26, NKJV

THE WARFARE IS REAL

As the body of Christ, we are engaged in spiritual warfare with the powers of darkness. "For our struggle is not against flesh and blood, but against the rulers, against the authorities, against the powers of this dark world and against spiritual forces of evil in the heavenly realms" (Eph. 6:12, NIV). A great portion of Jesus's own earthly ministry was devoted to casting out demon powers, and this authority was passed on to believers in Jesus Christ. (See Mark 16:17.) Walking in the Spirit after deliverance is essential in order to keep a person free. The fact is that Satan is determined to rob us of our freedom and every other good thing we have from God. We must learn to stand our ground by means of the weapons that are at our disposal. (See Ephesians 6:13–18.)

HE ALWAYS FINISHES THE WORK

It may be that the demon powers from which you are now free had been associated with you for a very long time. The demons have been such a part of your personality and thinking habits that the flesh must be put under subjection daily before realizing the fullness of your freedom. The Lord will gradually heal your mind and emotions in some cases. The Holy Spirit is always gentle and does not give us more than we can handle at one point in time. But, no matter how long it takes, He always finishes the work that He has begun in us.

Regardless of what happens, remember that Jesus Christ won victory for you nearly two thousand years ago. Satan can only try to get you to doubt this truth or convince you to give up your freedom voluntarily. Do not be defeated by negative thoughts, emotions, or circumstances. "In all these things we are more than conquerors through Him who loved us" (Rom. 8:37, NKJV).

FOUR TYPICAL METHODS OF ATTACK

In order to avoid the enemy's snares, it helps to recognize some of his strategy. Four typical methods of attack encountered by people after deliverance can be outlined as follows.

1. *Lies.* The Scriptures say that *Satan is the father of lies.* Even though they are now outside of you, demon powers may still talk to you. Do not accept thoughts, ideas, or guidance as coming from the Lord unless it lines up with Scripture and unless it gives you peace and is a part of normal Christian behavior. The Holy Spirit never contradicts the Bible, never creates chaos within, and never tells us to do strange things. Typical lies from the enemy might sound like this: "You haven't been delivered." "It wasn't real." "It wasn't completed." "You can't keep your freedom." "The demons are still inside you." Or, "God demands that you do such a thing or else." Do not believe it. Make your stand on the Word of God. "So if the Son sets you free, you will be free indeed" (John 8:36, NIV).

2. *Accusation.* One meaning for the name *Satan* is "accuser." You may find yourself feeling guilty for having had demon powers from your past sins. Remember that all your sins and failings are under the cleansing of the blood of Jesus Christ, and God has put them out of His memory. On the other hand, you may be told that you are too weak to resist the devil, that you are failing God, and that you are just a lousy person generally. The trick behind these lies, and the ones discussed above, is getting you to focus on yourself instead of Jesus Christ.

    No matter what we are or have been, Jesus Christ is perfect, and He loves us. Remember that your strength comes not from your own faithfulness but rather from your faithful Lord. "But I trust in your unfailing love; my heart rejoices in your salvation" (Ps. 13:5, NIV). Relax in God's full salvation for you. The name *Jesus* means "God saves," not "man must save himself."

3. *Intimidation.* The enemy may try to intimidate you with demonstrations of his power. Do not be frightened if things seem to go wrong for you for a while or if some symptoms from before deliverance seem to reappear. Remember that if Satan was as powerful as he claims to be, he would have swept us all away a long time ago. The reason that we are still here is that his power, in fact, is very limited. There is only one all-powerful Person, and He is the same God, the Father of our Lord Jesus Christ, who sends us the Holy Spirit to dwell within us and in whom we are baptized. We are on the winning side.

4. *Temptation.* You may find yourself tempted with old habits or behavior that do not fit in with the Christian life. The devil has a way of making the old times seem rosy to us, just as he tricked the Israelites in the desert into missing the "leeks and onions" that they had left behind in Egypt. Of course Satan forgot to mention the misery and slavery that went along with those tasty onions. Do not become nostalgic about the past, but keep your eyes on the future as you prepare to enter God's promised land. Jesus Christ did not come to take good things away from you but rather to bring you real life. "I have come that they may have life, and have it to the full" (John 10:10, NIV). Put your trust in Jesus Christ, and you will have the desire of your heart. (See Psalm 37:4.)

POSITIVE PRINCIPLES TO ENABLE YOU

Recognizing the enemy's strategy is helpful, but it does not win the battle for us. It is more important that you learn and practice some positive principles that will enable you to gain ground quickly and hold it. The following five points are easy to remember and will help you tremendously.

1. *Focus your attention on Jesus Christ.* His blood is the most powerful protection in the universe. Moreover, Jesus Christ came and shed His very blood because He loves you. Confess the fact that He loves you, and repeat the following

prayer every morning, both in your heart and aloud: "Lord, I cover my mind, my emotions, my body, my soul, and my spirit with the precious blood of Jesus Christ." Talk to Jesus throughout every day, sharing the good things and the bad with Him. You can be sure He will not leave you. "They overcame him [Satan] by the blood of the Lamb and by the word of their testimony" (Rev. 12:11, NIV).

2. *Allow the Holy Spirit to have His way with you.* Pray throughout the day. Let the Holy Spirit show you negative attitudes, habits, feelings, and behavior that need to be changed. The Holy Spirit is God's power given in order for you to become like Jesus Christ. He will show you things through the Bible, other people, and your experiences. (See Ephesians 6:18; John 16:13.)

3. *Immerse yourself in the Scriptures.* The Bible is the written Word of God. The Word of God is a living thing that works in us even when we may not understand or comprehend fully what we are reading. Read as much as you can, but preferably at least five chapters from the New Testament Gospels each day. If your mental state makes this impossible, then, until the Lord has healed your mind further, concentrate on memorizing a verse from Scripture each day, constantly repeating it to yourself. Select verses that seem to apply to you. You may begin with some verse quoted in this book. (See John 8:31.)

4. *Command the devil and demon powers, in the name of Jesus Christ, to go away and leave you alone.* Make it clear that you intend to follow Jesus Christ no matter what. Above all, do not argue with the enemy and entertain his thoughts because you cannot beat him that way. Instead, clear your mind by gently praising Jesus Christ. (See James 4:7.)

5. *Hang on to other Christians.* The Christian walk is not a solo performance. You will need other people in the Christian fellowship to support you and edify your faith. This is nothing to be ashamed of, but rather it is God's preferred

way. Jesus Christ ministers through His body. "Carry each other's burdens, and in this way you will fulfill the law of Christ" (Gal. 6:2, NIV).

Practice these five faith principles, and your post-deliverance problems will be minimal and your progress steady. Remember that God will not abandon you, and do not be discouraged by any failures. Thank the Father for sending Jesus Christ and anointing Him with the Holy Spirit to bring us out of the kingdom of darkness into the kingdom of light.

> "The Spirit of the Lord is on me, because he has anointed me to preach the good news to the poor. He has sent me to proclaim freedom for the prisoners and recovery of sight for the blind, to release the oppressed, to proclaim the year of the Lord's favor." Then he rolled up the scroll, gave it back to the attendant and sat down. The eyes of everyone in the synagogue were fastened on him, and he began by saying to them, "Today this scripture is fulfilled in your hearing."
>
> —LUKE 4:18–21, NIV

God bless you as you grow and as you lead others into freedom.

CHAPTER 23

PLEDGES AND OATHS

I ALMOST DID NOT INCLUDE THIS INFORMATION IN THIS BOOK. However, because I came under such attack each time I approached it and because it literally disappeared from my computer a couple of times, I decided that was good indication to share what access is given to demon powers by permission of pledges and oaths.

I would guess that 40–50 percent of the people who come to me for deliverance have demons in their life by permission of Freemasonry, secret lodges, and college fraternities and sororities. That may astound you, but it is true. I really don't believe that people get involved in these secret organizations for the purpose of inviting demons into their lives. I have seen many, many healed of various sickness and disease when the curse is broken in their life.

One man who is entangled in Freemasonry told me, "I just joined so I could help crippled children…" Another said, somewhat defensively, "Masons just make good people better." Then there was one Thirty-second Degree Mason who brought his wife to me for deliverance (I didn't know he was a Mason). He said, "I didn't take any vows like what you have mentioned." His wife blurted out, "If they're so good and it is helpful, why do you keep it a secret?"

You see, it's a trap. No believer can take oaths such as you will read below and remain in close fellowship with the Lord Jesus; it is impossible. Now the noose tightens when the believer is asked if he took such blasphemous oaths, and he must either admit that he did, which calls for repentance, or lie. I think you know what most choose to do, and the bondage increases.

I don't condemn people who are Masons. I have many friends who made the choice to join. I do believe they made a choice out of ignorance. Most of them tell me, "Aw, I never go. I just joined because someone asked me to and I thought it was an honor to be considered." Others say, "I thought it might help me in my business ventures and associations."

I would like to see every believer free. I don't think folks who get involved in these occult organizations realize what they are doing, nor do they understand what curses they may have brought on their family and future generations. Selwyn Stevens of Jubilee Ministries in New Zealand has gathered some valuable information to help free people from the curse of Freemasonry. I share this with you and encourage you to prayerfully read through it. Let the Holy Spirit give you direction.

For detailed information about Freemasonry, visit the Web site of Jubilee Ministries: http://www.jubilee-resources.com. The information can also be downloaded. You may write to them at: Jubilee Ministries, Box 36-044, Wellington 6330 New Zealand.

If you were once a member of a Masonic organization or are a descendant of someone who was, I recommend that you pray a prayer similar to the one below. Be sincere in your revocation and denunciation of the vows, pledges, and oaths. Please read it through first so you know what is involved. It would even be helpful to have a Christian witness present.

I have seen many people healed of both physical and spiritual maladies as diverse as long-term headaches, asthma, heart problems, and many other ailments as a result of a conscious choice to denounce the Masonry involvement.

Prayer

> *Father God, Creator of heaven and Earth, I come to You in the name of Jesus Christ, Your Son. I come as a sinner seeking forgiveness and cleansing from all sins committed against You and others made in Your image. I honor my earthly father and mother and all of my ancestors of flesh and blood, those whom I am related to through the spirit by adoption, and godparents, but I utterly turn away from and renounce all their sins. I forgive all my ancestors for the effects of their sins on me and my children. I confess and renounce all of my own sins. I renounce and*

rebuke Satan and every spiritual power of his affecting me and my family.

I renounce and forsake all involvement in Freemasonry or any other lodge or craft by my ancestors and myself. In the name of Jesus Christ, I renounce and cut off witchcraft, the principal spirit behind Freemasonry. I renounce and cut off Baphomet, the spirit of antichrist, and the spirits of death and deception. I renounce the insecurity; the love of position and power; the love of money, avarice, or greed; and the pride that would have led my ancestors into Masonry. I renounce all the fears that held them in Masonry, especially the fears of death, fears of men, and fears of trusting in the name of Jesus Christ.

I renounce every position held in the lodge by any of my ancestors or myself, including "Master," "Worshipful Master," or any other. I renounce the calling of any man "Master," for Jesus Christ is my only master and Lord, and He forbids anyone else having that title. I renounce the entrapping of others into Masonry and observing the helplessness of others during the rituals. I renounce the effects of Masonry passed on to me through any female ancestor who felt distrusted and rejected by her husband as he entered and attended any lodge and refused to tell her of his secret activities. I also renounce all obligations, oaths, and curses enacted by every female member of my family through any direct membership of all women's orders of Freemasonry, the order of the Eastern Star, or any other Masonic or occult organization. I do this, Father, in the name of Your Son, Jesus Christ. Amen.

INFORMATION ABOUT VARIOUS DEGREES AND OATHS TAKEN

Thirty-third and Supreme Degree

The Thirty-third and Supreme Degree of Masonry has secret passwords, and these very words show up as demon powers during a deliverance session. This ungodly oath includes calling Lucifer the great architect of the universe and refers to him as the universal fatherhood of God. This degree includes the cable tow around the neck, the death wish that the wine drunk from a human skull should turn to poison, and the skeleton whose cold arms are invited if the oath of this degree is violated.

This degree also involves greed and witchcraft in the attempt to manipulate and control the rest of mankind. Also introduced in this degree are the three infamous assassins of their grand master: law, property, and religion.

Blue Lodge

Every oath of Masonry invites demons and often brings curse on future generations. The Blue Lodge oath involves the first or entered apprentice degree and especially affects the throat and tongue. Involved is the "hoodwink blindfold" and its effects on spirit, emotions, and eyes, including all confusion, fear of the dark, fear of the light, and fear of sudden noises. Results are often the blinding of spiritual truth, darkness of the soul, false imagination, condescension, and the spirit of poverty that can be caused by the ritual of this degree. There is the "usurping of the marriage" covenant by the removal of the wedding ring; the invoking of the secret word *Boaz*; the serpent clasp on the apron; the spirit of python, which is brought to squeeze out the spiritual life; the ancient pagan teaching from Babylon and Egypt; and the symbolism of the first tracing board. There is the mixing and mingling of truth and error; mythology, fabrications, and lies taught as truth; the dishonesty by leaders as to the true understanding of the ritual; and the blasphemy of this degree of Freemasonry. Also included in Blue Lodge oaths is the presentation of the compass.

I remember a particular encounter with a demonic spirit that claimed to have consent to stay in the individual after being commanded to leave. I commanded the spirit to reveal what the consent was. The demon's response was, "They put on the apron." The reference was to the grandfather who was involved in Freemasonry. The individual confessed the sins of the grandfather and broke the demon's power and permission. It then left immediately when commanded to leave.

There is also the cable tow noose around the neck, resulting often in the fear of choking and possibly causing asthma, hay fever, emphysema, or any other breathing difficulty. There is the ritual dagger, or the compass point, sword, or spear held against the breast, causing the fear of death by stabbing pain, the fear of heart attack from this degree, and the absolute secrecy demanded under a witchcraft oath and sealed by kissing the *Volume of the Sacred Law*. Included also is the kneeling to the false deity known as the Great Architect of the Universe revealed as Lucifer. Results often bring curses of the throat, vocal cords, nasal passages, sinuses, bronchial tubes, and the like.

I have dealt with virtually all of these symptoms in deliverance sessions with folks who have Masonry in their ancestry!

Second or Fellow Craft Degree of Masonry

This includes the curses on the heart and chest, the ancient pagan teaching and symbolism of the second tracing board, and the sign of reverence to the generative principle. Resultant issues are often emotional hardness, apathy, indifference, unbelief, and deep anger. The chest, lung, and heart areas many times are healed when this is denounced.

Third or Master Mason degree

The curses here show up in the stomach and womb area. The ancient pagan teaching and symbols of the third tracing board are used in this ritual. Blows to the head enacted as ritual murder are known to result in the fear of death; false martyrdom; fear of violent gang attack, assault, rape, and helplessness; the falling into the coffin or stretcher involved in the ritual of murder. Hiram Abiff is introduced as the savior of Freemasonry. The stomach, gallbladder, womb, liver, and any other organs of the body can be affected by Masonry.

The demonic spirits of Tubal Cain and Maha Bone have shown up in many deliverance sessions I have directed. They are high-ranking Masonry territorial spirits. In a recent deliverance, demons who were present by permission of Freemasonry in the ancestry began to cry for help. The candidate said, "I am hearing 'Maha, Maha' over and over. I hear this like a cry for help."

There is the pagan ritual of the "Point Within a Circle," with all its bondages and phallus (male reproductive organ) worship, the symbol "G" and its veiled pagan symbolism and bondages, the occult mysticism of the black and white mosaic checkered floor with the tessellated border and five-pointed blazing star. The symbol "G" does not represent God, as some may tell you.

The all-seeing third eye of Freemasonry

This includes Horus in the forehead and its pagan and occult symbolism and the third eye and all occult ability to see into the spiritual realm. Because of the false communions taken and the mockery of the redemptive work of Jesus Christ on the cross of Calvary, unbelief, confusion, and depression are found as a result. This also results in fear of insanity, anguish, death wishes, suicide and death, anger, hatred, murderous thoughts, revenge, retaliation, spiritual apathy, false religion, and all unbelief, especially unbelief in the Holy Bible as God's Word and compromise of God's Word.

York rite

This includes the Mark Lodge and the mark in the form of squares and angles, which marks the person for life. There is the jewel or occult talisman that may have been made from this mark/sign and worn at lodge meetings; the Mark Master Degree, the penalty of having the right ear smote off, the curse of permanent deafness, and the right hand being chopped off for being an imposter.

Why is Masonry so secretive? Read very carefully the penalty of revealing their secrets as taken in the vows: past master penalty—tongue split from tip to root; and of the most excellent master degree penalty—breast torn open and heart and vital organs removed and exposed to rot on a dung hill.

Holy Royal Arch Degree

This includes oaths taken and the curses involved in the Royal Arch Degree, especially the oath regarding the removal of the head from the body and the exposing of the brains to the hot sun. Yes, you are reading correctly. It also includes the false secret name of God and worship of the false pagan gods Bul or Baal and On or Osiris. This degree also includes false communion or Eucharist, mockery, skepticism, and unbelief about the redemptive work of Jesus Christ on the cross of Calvary. Many times healing of the brain and mind come when this is denounced and confessed as sin.

Just look at the curses involved in the Royal Master Degree of the York Rite and the Select Master Degree. The penalty for telling the secrets is to have one's hands chopped off to the stumps, to have their eyes plucked out from their sockets, and to have their body quartered and thrown among the rubbish of the temple.

Super Excellent Master Degree

Its curse is to have one's thumbs cut off, eyes put out, body bound in fetters and brass, and conveyed captive to a strange land.

Knights Order of the Red Cross

Its curse or penalty is having their house torn down and being hanged on the exposed timbers.

Knights Templar and Knights of Malta degrees

The Knights Templar and Knights of Malta degrees include vows taken on a human skull, the crossed swords, the curse and death wish of Judas of having the head cut off and placed on top of a church spire, unholy communion, and especially of drinking from a human skull in many rites.

ANCIENT AND ACCEPTED OR SCOTTISH RITE

Only the Eighteenth, Thirtieth, Thirty-first, Thirty-second, and Thirty-third degrees are operated in British Commonwealth countries.

Eighteenth Degree of Masonry

The Eighteenth Degree of Masonry includes leadership positions such as the Most Wise Sovereign Knight of the Pelican and the Eagle and Sovereign Prince Rose Croix of Heredom. Introduced to the pelican witchcraft spirit, as well as the occult influence of the Rosicrucians and the Kabbala, this degree makes the claim that the death of Jesus Christ was a "dire calamity" and also makes deliberate mockery and twisting of the Christian doctrine of the atonement. Speaking the secret words is a mockery of the communion taken in this degree, including the consumption biscuit, salt, and white wine.

Thirtieth Degree of Masonry

The leaders in this degree are the Grand Knight Kadosh and Knight of the Black and White Eagle. Sublime Princes of the Royal Secret oaths are taken along with the curses involved. Virtually all of the secret passwords are the names of demon powers. To speak their names is to call on that power.

Thirty-First degree of Masonry

The Grand Inspector Inquisitor Commander is the leader in this degree. It also includes the introduction of the *gods and goddesses of Egypt* (which are honored in this degree, including Anubis with the ram's head, Osiris the sun god, Isis the sister and wife of Osiris and the moon goddess), the Soul of Cheres, which is the false symbol of immortality, the Chamber of the Dead, and the false teaching of reincarnation.

Thirty-second Degree of Masonry

The Sublime Prince of the Royal Secret leads this degree, and it includes Masonry's false trinitarian deity Aum and its parts and Brahma the creator, Vishnu the preserver, and Shiva the destroyer. The deity of Ahura-Mazda is the claimed spirit or source of all light. The worship with fire and also the drinking from a human skull is included in many rites. Death and disease are curses passed to virtually all future generations.

All other degrees

This information may prove helpful to you as you seek freedom for yourself and your family. If you are aware of any associations with any of the above, I suggest you renounce it all and make a conscious choice to be free from all its curses in Jesus Christ's name. These include the Allied Degrees, the Red Cross of Constantine, the Order of the Secret Monitor, and the Masonic Royal Order of Scotland. Lodges and secret societies including Prince Hall Freemasonry, Grand Orient Lodges, Mormonism, Order of Amaranth, Royal Order of Jesters, Manchester Unity Order of Oddfellows, Buffalos, Druids, Foresters, Orange and Black Lodges, Elks, Moose and Eagles Lodges, Ku Klux Klan, Grange, Woodmen of the World, Riders of the Red Robe, Knights of Pythias, Mystic Order of the Veiled Prophets of the Enchanted Realm, Eastern Star, Ladies Oriental Shrine, White Shrine of Jerusalem, Daughters of the Eastern Star, Job's Daughters, Rainbow, and Order of DeMolay.

Hippocratic oath

I find many doctors do not take this oath, and many Christian doctors make similar vows to God but not to Apollo or any so-called gods or goddesses.

The number of fraternities and sororities in college life forbid me from mentioning all of their pledges and oaths. But you can be sure that virtually all of them can be openings for demon spirits and should be renounced and confessed as sin. With the confession, the believer must command that the spirit(s) that came by that permission must leave and never return in Jesus Christ's name.

ANOTHER PRAYER FOR FREEDOM

Lord Jesus, because You want me to be totally free from all occult bondage, I will burn all objects in my possession that connect me with all lodges and occult organizations, including Masonry, witchcraft, Mormonism, all regalia, aprons, books of rituals, and rings and other jewelry. I renounce the effects these or other objects of Masonry, including the compass and the square, have had on my family and me in the name of Jesus Christ.

I renounce every evil spirit associated with Masonry and witchcraft and all other sins, and I command in the name of Jesus Christ for Satan and every evil spirit to be bound and to leave me now, touching or harming no one. I command them in the name of Jesus Christ to go to the place appointed for them by the Lord Jesus, never to return to me or my family. I call on the name of the Lord Jesus to be delivered of these spirits in accordance with the many promises of the Bible. I ask to be delivered of every spirit of sickness, infirmity, curse, affliction, addiction, disease, or allergy associated with these sins I have confessed and renounced. I surrender to God's Holy Spirit, and to no other spirit, all the places in my life where these sins have been, in Jesus Christ's name. Amen.

APPENDIX

FAILURE OR REFUSAL TO OBEY GOD'S COMMANDMENTS BRINGS a curse. If we expect to stay free of sin curses, we must walk in obedience to God. Very simply put, disobedience is a door opener, and one of the best biblical evidences is the children of Israel. They came totally and completely out of bondage and went right back into another kind of bondage by disobeying God.

How can you know if you are under a sin curse? First of all, have you despised God or refused to hearken to His voice? God's blessings come to those who are doers of His Word. Curses come upon all who "wilt not hearken unto the voice of the LORD thy God, to observe to do all his commandments and his statutes" (Deut. 28:15). The Bible specifically names many sins that result in curses.

THIRTY-SEVEN BIBLICAL CURSES

1. Idolatry (either making or worshiping an idol) (Exod. 20:5; Deut. 27:15)
2. Incest with one's sister, mother-in law, or father's wife (Deut. 27:22–23)
3. Adultery (Lev. 20:10; Num. 5:27; Deut. 22:22–27; Job 24:15–18)
4. Cruelty to a handicapped person (Deut. 27:18)
5. Oppressing the defenseless (Deut. 27:19)
6. Fornication (Deut. 22:21–29)
7. Dishonoring one's parents (Deut. 27:16)
8. Sexual relationship with any animal (Deut. 27:21)
9. Defrauding one's neighbor (Deut. 27:17)
10. Homosexual relationships (Gen. 19:1–25; Lev. 20:13)

11. Sexual intercourse during menstruation (Lev. 20:18)

12. Marrying a woman and her mother (Lev. 20:14)

13. Rape (Deut. 22:25)

14. Children conceived out of wedlock (Deut. 23:2)

15. Accursed objects in one's possession

16. Any occult practice—divination, sorcery, omens, witch-craft, consulting a medium, and consulting the dead (Lev. 20:6, 27; Deut. 18:9–13)

17. Murder (Deut. 11:28; 27:24)

18. Murder for hire, including those who are paid to perform abortions (Deut. 27:25)

19. Forsaking the Lord (Deut. 28:20)

20. Not serving the Lord joyfully and gladly in the time of prosperity (Deut. 28:47)

21. Not reverencing the name of the Lord God (Deut. 28:1–14, 58)

22. Presumption in thought so that one disregards God's Word and devises his own way (Deut. 29:19)

23. Cursing or mistreating Abraham's seed (Gen. 12:3; Num. 24:9)

24. Refusing to help in the Lord's warfare (Judg. 5:23; Jer. 48:10)

25. Failure to give God the glory (Mal. 2:2)

26. Robbing God of tithes and offerings (Hag. 1:6–9; Mal. 3:9)

27. Neglecting the work of the Lord (Jer. 48:10)

28. Enticing others away from the Lord into a false religion (Deut. 13:6–9)

29. Taking away or adding to the Word of God (Rev. 22:18–19)

30. Teaching rebellion against the Lord (Jer. 28:16–17)

31. Refusing to warn those who sin (Ezek. 3:18–21)

32. Defiling the Sabbath (Exod. 31:14; Num. 15:32–36)

33. Perversion of the gospel of Christ (Gal. 1:8–9)

34. Cursing one's rulers (Exod. 22:28; 1 Kings 2:8–9)

35. Refusal to forgive others after asking God to forgive you (Matt. 18:34–35)

36. Child sacrifice, such as abortion (Lev. 18:21; Deut. 18:10)

37. Disobedience against any of the Lord's commandments (Deut. 11:28; 27:26)

Some people dismiss these truths because they are, for the most part, from the Old Testament. Some pastors teach that they do not apply today, but these are biblical principles or laws set into effect by Jehovah God. Jesus did not come to destroy the law but to fulfill it. He actually broadened it and made it spiritual as well as physical.

Remember what He said about adultery, murder, and anger. (See Matthew 5:17–28.) "The law says...but *I* say." While the law condemned adultery, Jesus included "looking upon a woman with lust in one's heart." The law said not to murder. Jesus said, "Don't be angry," showing that anger is the seed of murder. He did not "destroy the law"; He fulfilled it and widened its scope.

The simplest way to determine whether or not one is under a curse is by comparing his life to the blessings God has promised to those who love Him. If one is not blessed, he is cursed. How does your life measure up to the blessings enumerated in Deuteronomy 28:1–14? Are you "set on high" by God, a lender and not a borrower, the head and not the tail? Is your life characterized by fruitfulness? Do you prosper coming and going? Are you free from the harassment of enemies—both natural and spiritual? Is your life a success? Is your relationship with God gratifying? Are you recognizing and fulfilling His purposes? These are the earmarks of a blessed life. If one is not enjoying the blessing, then he is suffering the curse. There is no in between.

Yet another way to determine if curses are in operation is to look for the effects of curses. Common effects of curses are poverty, barrenness, pestilence, chronic sickness, failure, defeat, humiliation, insanity, torment, perpetual traumas, spiritual hindrances, domination by others, and abandonment by God and others. (See Deuteronomy 28:20–68.)

GROUPING OF VARIOUS EVIL SPIRITS

May I say that while this may be valuable information to some, it is really no more than an identification of the functions of demons. You might even say that any demon could have any of these functions. More important than the curse is the cause. I do not deal with demons by function but rather by their individual names, and then by their assignment in that individual's life. They all have identities. However, here is a listing of many demonic functions.

Abandonment
- Isolation
- Not feeling wanted
- Victim
- Loneliness
- Not belonging

Addictions
- Alcohol
- Dependencies
- Cocaine
- Food
- Marijuana
- Nonprescription drugs
- Pornography
- Street drugs
- Tranquilizers
- Caffeine
- Downers/uppers
- Escape
- Gambling
- Nicotine
- Prescription drugs
- Sports
- Television
- Video games

Anger
- Frustration
- Resentment
- Tantrums
- Hatred rage
- Temper
- Spoiled little boy/girl

Anxiety
- Burden
- Fatigue
- Nervousness
- Weariness
- False responsibility
- Heaviness
- Restlessness

Bitterness
- Blaming
- Critical judging
- Murmuring
- Unforgiveness
- Complaining
- Gossiping
- Ridicule
- Irrational condemnation

Competition
- Driving
- Possessiveness
- Pride
- Jealousy
- Striving

Confusion
- Indecision
- ADD
- OCD
- Memory lapses
- Perception problems
- Unable to grasp simple truth
- Lack of focus
- ADHD
- Disconnected thoughts
- Inability to conclude
- Thought interruption

Deception
- Confusion
- Self-deception
- Lying

Depression
- Despondency
- Discouragement
- Insomnia
- Self-pity
- Suicide fantasies
- Despair
- Hopelessness
- Oversleeping
- Suicide attempt
- Withdrawal

Escape
- Fantasy
- Lethargy
- Procrastination
- Forgetfulness
- Passivity
- Withdrawal

Fears
- Anxiety
- Burdens

- Heaviness
- Superstition
- Phobias
  - of authorities
  - of failure
  - of man
  - of punishment
  - of death
  - of rejection
  - oversensitivity
  - of infirmities
  - of cancer
  - of heart attack
  - of diabetes
  - of being a victim
- Horror movies
- Irrational concerns
- Worry

Financial patterns

- Compulsive shopping
- Inability to plan and save
- Job failures
- Poor financial decisions
- Stinginess
- Greed
- Irresponsible spending
- Job losses
- Poverty

Greed

- Cheating
- Idolatry
- Misrepresentation
- Covetousness
- Stealing
- Fraud

Grief

- Loss
- Sorrow
- Sadness
- Suffering

Infirmities/disease

- Accidents (falls, cars, etc.)
- Asthma
- Cancer
- Family history/disease
- Arthritis
- Barrenness
- Diabetes
- Fatigue

- Fibromyalgia
- Hypertension
- Mental illness
- Physical abnormalities
- Skin diseases/rashes

- Heart disease
- Miscarriage
- Migraines
- Premature death

Mental illness

- Craziness
- Confusion
- Hysteria
- Obsessive-compulsive disorder
- Senility
- Shock treatments

- Compulsions
- Hallucinations
- Insanity
- Paranoid schizophrenia
- Institutionalized
- Mental anguish

Occult

- Astrology
- Black magic
- Casting a spell or hex chanting
- Dispatching demons
- Magic 8 ball
- Fortune-telling
- Freemasonry
- Horoscopes
- Levitation
- Made a blood pact
- Necromancy
- Owned occult jewelry
- Non-Christian exorcism
- Palm reading
- Pendulum
- Read occult/witchcraft books
- Seen any horror movies

- Automatic writing
- Clairvoyance
- Crystal ball
- Divination
- ESP
- Fraternities
- Handwriting analysis
- Hypnosis
- Mental telepathy
- Made a bloody oath or vow
- Owned heavy-metal music
- New Age
- Ouija board
- Past-life readings
- Psychic healing
- Science fantasy
- Seen any science fantasy
- Séances

- Sororities
- Sorcery
- Spiritism
- Tea leaves
- Visited pagan temples
- Voodoo
- White magic

- Spirit guide(s)
- Tarot cards
- Transcendental meditation
- Visited Indian burial grounds
- Water witching
- Witchcraft
- Yoga

Sexual sins

- Demonic sex
- Fornication
- Homosexuality
- Lesbianism
- Lust masturbation
- Premarital sex
- Rape
- Sexual abuse

- Exposure
- Frigidity
- Incest
- Lust/fantasy
- Pornography
- Prostitution/harlotry
- Seduction

Shame

- Condemnation
- Guilt
- Self-disgust/reproach

- Embarrassment
- Self-accusation

Pride

- Arrogance
- Vanity

- Self-importance
- False self-worth

Rebellion

- Insubordination
- Stubbornness

- Lying
- Undermining

Rejection

- Perceived rejection
- Self-rejection

- Perfectionism

Religion
- Antichrist
- Legalism/rules
- Cults
- Tradition

Strife
- Arguing
- Cursing
- Disagreement
- Bickering
- Dissension
- Mocking

Surgeries
- Anesthetized
- Difficult birth
- C-sections
- Epidurals

Trauma
- Accident
- Loss
- Sexual abuse
- Violence
- Emotional abuse
- Physical abuse
- Verbal abuse

Unbelief
- Doubt
- Rationalism
- Unbelief
- Disbelief
- Skepticism

Unworthiness
- Inferiority
- Self-condemnation
- Self-hate
- Self-mutilation

Violence
- Feuding
- Threats
- Retaliation
- Physical harm
- Murder
- Torture

DEMONIC SPIRITS IDENTIFIED IN SCRIPTURE

Old Testament
- Jealous spirit (Num. 5:14)

- Evil spirit (1 Sam. 16:14–23)
- Lying spirit (1 Kings 22:22)
- Spirit of Cyrus, who was the king of Persia (2 Chron. 36:22)
- Broken spirit (Prov. 17:22)
- Wounded spirit (Prov. 18:14)
- Haughty/defiant/rebellious spirit (Eccles. 7:8)
- Spirit of Egypt (Isa. 19:3)
- Spirit of deep sleep (Isa. 29:10)
- Destroying spirit (Jer. 51:1)
- Spirit of the kings of Medes (Jer. 51:11)
- One's own spirit/human spirit (Ezek. 13:3)
- Spirit of harlotry (Hosea 4:12; 5:3)
- Spirit of falsehood (Mic. 2:11)
- Unclean spirit (Zech. 13:2)

New Testament

- Spirit of unclean demon (Luke 4:33)
- Foul spirit/deaf and dumb spirit (Mark 9:25)
- Spirit of infirmity (Luke 13:11)
- Spirit of divination (Acts 16:16)
- Evil spirit (Acts 19:15–16)
- Spirit of lust (Rom. 1:24)
- Spirit of bondage (Rom. 8:15)
- Spirit of slumber (Rom. 11:8)
- Spirit of man (1 Cor. 2:11)
- Spirit of the world (1 Cor. 2:12)
- Demonic spirit (1 Cor. 10:20–21)
- Spirit of the devil (Eph. 6:11–12)
- Spirit in children of disobedience (Eph. 2:2)
- Spirit of fear (2 Tim. 1:7)

- Seducing or deceiving spirit (1 Tim. 4:1)
- Spirit of antichrist (1 John 4:3)
- Spirit of error (1 John 4:6)

SIXTY SYMPTOMS OF DEMONIC ATTACK

1. A compulsive desire to blaspheme God
2. A revulsion against the Bible, including a desire to tear it up or destroy it
3. Compulsive thoughts of suicide or murder
4. Deep feelings of bitterness and hatred toward others without reason—Jews, other races, the church, strong Christian leaders
5. Any compulsive temptations that seek to force thoughts or behavior that the person truly does not want to think or do
6. Compulsive desires to tear other people down, even if it means lying to do so; vicious cutting by the tongue
7. Terrifying feelings of guilt even after honest confession is made to the Lord
8. Certain physical symptoms that may appear suddenly or leave quickly and for which there are no physical or physiological reason; symptoms such as choking sensations, pains that seem to move around and for which there is no medical cause, feelings of tightness about the head or eyes, dizziness, blackouts, or fainting seizures
9. Deep depression and despondency
10. Sudden surges of violent rage, uncontrollable anger, or seething feelings of hostility
11. Terrifying doubt of one's salvation even though they once knew the joy of salvation
12. Seizures of panic or other fear that is terrifying
13. Dreams or nightmares that are of a horrific nature and often recurring; clairvoyant dreams that may even come true are most often demonic

14. Abnormal or perverted sexual desires

15. Questions and challenges to God's Word

16. Sleep or eating disorders without physical cause

17. Most compulsions and obsessions

18. Rebellion and hatred for authority

19. Bizarre terrifying thoughts that seem to come from nowhere and cannot be controlled

20. Fascination with the occult

21. Involvement in criminal activity

22. Extremely low self-image (unworthy, a failure, no good, constant undermining of the self-identity)

23. Constant confusion in thinking (sometimes great difficulty in remembering things)

24. Inability to believe (even when the person wants to)

25. Mocking and blasphemous thoughts against preaching/teaching of the Word of God

26. Perceptual distortions—perceiving anger or hostility in others when it doesn't really exist—seeing only judgment in the Scriptures

27. Horrible nightmares causing fear (often having demonic images)

28. Violent thoughts (suicidal, homicidal, self-abuse)

29. Hatred and bitterness toward others for no justifiable reason

30. Tremendous hostility or fear when encountering someone involved in deliverance work

31. Deep depression and despondency (frequently and at significant times)

32. Irrational fears, panic attacks, and phobias

33. Irrational anger or rage

34. Irrational guilt or self-condemnation to the extreme

35. Desire to do what is right, but an inability to carry it out

36. Sudden personality and attitude changes—severe contrasts, schizophrenia, bipolar disorder

37. A strong aversion toward Scripture reading and prayer (especially one on one)

38. A dark countenance—steely or hollow look in eyes, contraction of the pupils; sometimes facial features contort or change; often an inability to make eye contact

39. Lying, exaggerating, or stealing compulsively, often wondering why

40. Drug abuse, especially when there are demonic hallucinations

41. Eating obsessions—bulimia, anorexia nervosa

42. Compulsive sexual sins, especially perversions

43. Irrational laughter or crying

44. Irrational violence, compulsion to hurt self and/or someone else

45. Sudden speaking of a language not previously known (often an ethnic language of ancestors)

46. Reactions to the name and blood of Jesus Christ (verbally or through body language)

47. Extreme restlessness, especially in a spiritual environment

48. Uncontrollable cutting and mocking tongue

49. Vulgar language and actions

50. Loss of time, from minutes to hours; ending up someplace and not knowing how they got there; regularly doing things of which there is no memory

51. Extreme sleepiness around spiritual things

52. Demonstration of extraordinary abilities (either ESP or telekinesis)

53. Voices are heard in the mind that mock, intimidate, accuse, threaten, or attempt to bargain

54. Voice that refers to him/her in the third person

55. Supernatural experiences—hauntings, movement or disappearance of objects, and other strange manifestations

56. Seizures (too long and/or too regular)

57. Pain without justifiable explanation, especially in head and/or stomach

58. Blackouts

59. Physical ailments such as epileptic seizures, asthma attacks, and various pains

60. Sudden temporary interference with bodily functions—buzzing in ears, inability to speak or hear, severe headache, hypersensitivity in hearing or touch, chills or overwhelming heat in body, numbness in arms or legs, temporary paralysis

Note: A few symptoms may not indicate demonic oppression, but these are very common symptoms for those under demonic attack.

BIBLICAL PROOF THAT A BELIEVER SHOULD ENLIST IN SPIRITUAL WARFARE

- The disciples were told to heal the sick, cleanse the lepers, cast out demons, and raise the dead (Matt. 10:1–8).

- The seventy disciples (representative of all Christians) were sent out with authority and marveled that even the spirits were subject to them (Luke 10:1–9, 17–19).

- Believers were given anointing for discerning the spirits (1 John 2:20, 27).

- The Bible teaches how to identify spirits that are not of God (1 John 4:1–3).

- The Bible talks about tearing down strongholds built in the mind by the enemy and that the believer's weapons are spiritual and mighty through God (2 Cor. 10:3–5).

- The Bible teaches that it is faith's shield that resists the demons' fiery darts (Eph. 6:16).

- The Bible warns against rejoicing in the power that has been given; rather, we are to rejoice in our identity in Christ (Luke 10:20–24).

- The Bible teaches that the Holy Spirit has been sent to lead us and guide us into all truth (John 16:13).

- The Bible says that holy presence and power are revealed when the enemy is shattered (Ps. 18:37–42).

- Jesus commissioned believers to cast out devils in His name (Mark 16:17).

- Evil spirits are most often responsible for sickness and disease (Luke 8:2; 13:11).

- Demon oppression is demons in the soul, flesh, or attached to a life (Ps. 116; Acts 10:38).

- The One who abides in the believer is greater than the "strongman" (1 John 4:4), and the believer is commissioned to bind Satan (Matt. 12:29; Luke 11:22).

- The Bible teaches believers to resist the devil and stand firm in their faith (1 Pet. 5:9).